Diffusion and Sorption in Fibers and Films

Diffusion and Sorption in Fibers and Films

Volume 1 An Introduction with particular reference to dyes

R. McGregor

Department of Textile Chemistry,
North Carolina State University at Raleigh,
North Carolina, U.S.A.

1974

Academic Press . London and New York

A Subsidiary of Harcourt Brace Jovanovich, Publishers

ACADEMIC PRESS INC. (LONDON) LTD.
24/28 Oval Road,
London NW1

United States Edition published by
ACADEMIC PRESS INC.
111 Fifth Avenue
New York, New York 10003

Library of Congress Catalog Card Number: 73-9470
ISBN: 0-12-484101-5

Filmset by the Universities Press, Belfast

Printed in Great Britain by
J. W. Arrowsmith Ltd., Bristol

Preface

Simplicity is desirable in a theoretical approach to any industrial process. Unfortunately, most industrial processes are so complex that no truly simple theory is able to describe the real physical nature of the process. For this reason a distinction is often made between the *mathematical model* which can be used to describe a limited aspect of the behaviour of a system, and the complex *physical theory* which reveals the true nature of the processes.

The mathematics of diffusion has been used extensively in the past in discussions of dyeing kinetics, and has proved useful. The complexity of the mathematics of diffusion has perhaps tended to obscure the real physical significance of the assumptions inherent in the mathematical analyses, and in the interpretation of the measured diffusion coefficients.

This monograph has been written with two distinct objects in view. The first object was to present an account of the relevant physical theory, at a reasonably simple level, and to illustrate the significance of the theory by examining selected data from the extensive literature on the sorption and diffusion of dyes in fibres and films. The second object was to introduce the physical theory in such a way that the reader would be able to distinguish the thermodynamic assumptions from the mechanical ones, and be introduced to concepts that facilitate access to the more difficult, but very relevant, literature of physics, physical chemistry and chemical engineering. In this way, it is hoped that theoretical studies of dyeing will be clearly recognised as but one specialised application of very general physical principles, which are equally relevant to studies in chemical engineering, or in biophysics.

A substantial intellectual effort is required to assimilate these physical principles, but they are necessary for an intelligent appreciation of the complexities of dyeing processes, and for an awareness of which simplifications are justified in a given situation, and which are not. The theoretical perfectionist will probably find parts of this book too facile, and the practical man will find parts of it too difficult. Both will, I hope, find the presentation coherent and apposite. Volume 1 contains the basic theory. Volume 2 will contain a review of the literature on the basis of the theory.

Ralph McGregor

Raleigh, North Carolina
July 1973

Acknowledgements

This book is intended to serve as a bridge between very elementary discussions of the subject matter and the more advanced treatments to be found in standard texts and in the original literature. The material covers a wide range of topics, and in many places I have relied extensively on the work of other authors. Every effort has been made to acknowledge these sources, and the standard texts in this area figure frequently in the lists of references. I have made frequent use of the books by Bird, Stewart and Lightfoot; by De Groot and Mazur; by Fitts; by Hirschfelder, Curtiss and Bird; and by Prigogine.

My interest in this type of approach stems originally from work with Dr. B. Milicevic of Ciba-Geigy, and I am indebted to him for this and for permission to use material from our joint publications. My former colleague, Professor R. H. Peters, introduced me to this area of study and I wish to acknowledge his help and support over the past decade. My wife has been both patient and helpful.

The following specific acknowledgements are made here for permission granted by authors and publishers to use published material:

1. Permission to quote from, and to base Chapter 6 on, the paper by C. Truesdell "Mechanical Basis of Diffusion" in *J. Chem. Phys.* **37,** 2336 (1962).
2. Permission to quote from, and to base Chapter 11 on, the paper "Flow Equations and Frames of Reference for Isothermal Diffusion in Liquids" by J. G. Kirkwood, R. L. Baldwin, P. J. Dunlop, L. J. Gosting and G. Kegeles in *J. Chem. Phys.* **33,** 1505 (1960).
3. Permission to use equations 3.36–3.52 of this text, which follow the presentation given by R. B. Bird, W. E. Stewart and E. N. Lightfoot on pp. 719–726 of "Transport Phenomena", John Wiley and Sons, Inc. (1960).

4. Permission to follow, in equations 8.65–8.102 of this text, a presentation similar to that given by B. Milicevic in "Über die Auswahl von Bezugszuständen bei der Berechnung von Standardaffinitäten fur Verteilungsgleichgewichte," *Helv. Chim. Acta.* **46,** (1963), and in lectures in 1965 at the Eidgenössische Technische Hochschule, Zurich.

Contents

List of Symbols

Mathematical and other conventions

δ	a small increment
δ_{ij}	Kronecker delta
da	total differential
∂a	partial differential
d/dt	substantial time derivative
$\partial/\partial t$	partial time derivative
∇	vector differential operator
∇^2	Laplacian operator
grad T	gradient vector of the
∇T	scalar field $T(r)$
div	divergence
$\exp\{\ \}$	exponential function
$\langle\ \rangle$	denotes an averaging process
[ ]	usually denotes a concentration
1, 2, 3	Cartesian coordinates
x, y, z	Cartesian coordinates
$\mathbf{1}$	unit tensor
$\boldsymbol{i}, \boldsymbol{j}, \boldsymbol{k}$	unit vectors in Cartesian coordinates
$\boldsymbol{\delta}_1, \boldsymbol{\delta}_2, \boldsymbol{\delta}_3$	unit vectors
$[M]$	dimension of mass
$[L]$	dimension of length
$[T]$	dimension of time

Superscripts

ϕ	sub-system index (film or fiber)
σ	sub-system index (solution)
^{o}	characteristic variable, standard variable.
*	isotopically labelled molecules or ions.
$\bar{}$	partial molar quantity i.e. *per mole*; or an apparent value of a quantity (extended bar)
$\hat{}$	partial specific quantity i.e. *per unit mass*
$\tilde{}$	an electrochemical quantity i.e. including electrical terms not explicitly stated.

Subscripts

A	an anion
C	a cation

C	cell-fixed reference frame
i	index for reaction i, component index
j	component index
k	generally a component index
l	component index
M	mass-fixed reference frame
M	denotes a quantity associated with mass flow
n	reference frame fixed on component n
o	solvent-fixed reference frame
Q	denotes a quantity associated with heat flow
R	arbitrary reference frame R
R	denotes chemical reaction
V	volume-fixed reference frame
V	denotes a quantity associated with volume flow
i, j, k	cartesian components
A	area
A	Helmholtz function
A	a thermodynamic driving-force, or affinity
A_i	a local state variable
A_j	concentration of jth type of acidic group
A_{kj}	a friction coefficient
$\boldsymbol{dA}$	area vector
a	characteristic jump distance
a	radius
a	relative activity
a_i	mass of products per unit of reaction i
$\boldsymbol{a}$	acceleration vector
B_i	concentration of ith type of basic group
C	a membrane concentration
C_k	molar concentration of component k
C_p	heat capacity at constant pressure
$C_{jk}^{\pm}$	mean ionic molarity
c	a solution concentration
c	relative concentration
D	diffusion coefficient
D_{app}	apparent diffusion coefficient
D_{exp}	experimental or observed diffusion coefficient
D_f	'steady-state' diffusion coefficient
D_p	diffusion coefficient in film or fiber phase
D_k	self diffusion coefficient
D_l	'time-lag' diffusion coefficient
$(D^+)_V$	intradiffusion coefficient

$(D)_V$	mutual diffusion coefficient
$(D_{11})_V$	mutual diffusion coefficient
$(D_1)_p$	polymer-fixed diffusion coefficient
$(D_{kj})_R$	generalised, practical diffusion coefficients in a reference frame R (mass basis)
$(\mathscr{D}_{kj})_R$	generalised, practical diffusion coefficients in a reference frame R (molar basis)
$\boldsymbol{d}$	displacement vector
E	energy
E_D	experimental activation energy for diffusion
E_p	exhaustion parameter
Eu	Euler number
ΔE_{vap}	energy of vaporisation (per mole)
$\boldsymbol{E}$	electric field vector
e	electronic charge, base of natural logarithms
e_k	electrical charge per unit mass of component k
e_o	activation energy per molecule
e_D	activation energy for diffusion per molecule
e_V	activation energy per molecule for viscous flow
$(\mathrm{exh})_\infty$	equilibrium exhaustion
F	force
F	the Faraday
$F, F^{\neq}$	Partition functions
Fr	Froude number
F_i	a generalised intensive quantitv
F_{kj}	a friction coefficient
$\boldsymbol{F}$	force vector
$\mathscr{F}$	a thermodynamic force, or affinity
$\mathscr{F}o_M$	Fourier number (diffusive mass transfer)
f	correlation factor in diffusion
f	degrees of freedom in activated diffusion
f	fractional free volume
f	mole-fraction activity coefficient, rational activity coefficient
$f_{jk}^{\pm}$	mean ionic activity coefficient (mole fraction basis)
G	Gibbs function, Gibbs free energy
$\Delta G^{\neq}$	free energy of activation
$\boldsymbol{g}$	gravitational force vector
H	enthalpy
$\Delta H^{\neq}$	enthalpy of activation
$\boldsymbol{h}$	Planck's constant
h^0	boundary resistance parameter
I	flow of electricity

$\boldsymbol{I}$	electric current vector
J_R	scalar chemical reaction rate
$\boldsymbol{J}$	total flux vector (cell-fixed reference frame)
$\boldsymbol{J}_k$	total mass flux vector of component k (cell-fixed reference frame)
$(\boldsymbol{J}_k)_R$	diffusion or mass flux of component k in a reference-frame R (mass basis)
$\boldsymbol{J}_X$	total flux vector for an extensive property X
$\boldsymbol{j}$	diffusion flux vector (mass-fixed reference frame)
$\boldsymbol{j}_k$	diffusion flux vector of component k in mass-fixed reference frame
$\boldsymbol{j}_X$	diffusion flux vector for an extensive property X
$\mathscr{J}$	a thermodynamic flow
$(\mathscr{J}_A)_0$	diffusion flux of an anion (solvent-fixed)
$(\mathscr{J}_C)_0$	diffusion flux of a cation (solvent-fixed)
$(\mathscr{J})_0$	solvent-fixed diffusion flux of a neutral salt
$\mathscr{J}_V$	flow of volume
$\mathscr{J}_{Q_2}$	second-law heat flow
$(\mathscr{J}_k)_R$	diffusion flux of component k in a reference frame R (molar basis)
K	an equilibrium distribution coefficient
K_{CA}	a distribution coefficient for a neutral salt CA
K_B^A	a selectivity coefficient
K_{A_j}	dissociation coefficient of jth type of acidic group
K_{B_i}	dissociation coefficient of ith type of basic group
K_V	Kozeny constant
$\boldsymbol{k}$	Boltzmann constant
k	a velocity constant
k_V	shape factor
L	boundary resistance parameter
L	characteristic length
L	dimensionless boundary resistance variable
L	membrane thickness
L	phenomenological coefficient
$(L_{kj})_R$	phenomenological coefficient for diffusion in a reference frame R (mass basis)
$\mathscr{L}$	phenomenological coefficient
$(\mathscr{L}_{kj})_R$	phenomenological coefficient for diffusion in reference-frame R (molar basis)
l	length
l	membrane thickness
l_k	mobility of ion k

Λ	equivalent conductance
M	mass of solute sorbed
M_t	mass of solute sorbed at time t
M_∞	mass of solute sorbed at equilibrium
M_k	molar mass of component k
m	mass
m	molecular mass
m	mean hydraulic radius
m_k	molal concentration of component k
$m_{jk}^{\pm}$	mean ionic molality
N	Avogadro's number
N_k	number of moles of component k
Nu	Nusselt number
P	nonequilibrium pressure
P_f	probability of cooperation of f degrees of freedom in a diffusion step
$P(v^{\neq})$	probability of occurrence of a 'hole' greater than $v^{\neq}$ in volume
P_{ij}	component of pressure tensor
Pe_M	Peclet number (mass transfer)
$\boldsymbol{P}$	pressure tensor
p	equilibrium hydrostatic pressure
$p(x, t)$	probability density function
Q	heat flow
Q^*	heat of transfer
Q_t	quantity of solute diffused through membrane at time t
q	electrical charge per ion
q_x, q_y, q_z	heat flux components
$\boldsymbol{q}$	heat flux vector
R	Gas constant
R_p	rate parameter
Re	Reynolds number
r	rank of a matrix
$\boldsymbol{r}$	position vector
S	entropy
$\Delta S^{\neq}$	entropy of activation
S_0	specific surface area
Sc	Schmidt number
T	temperature (usually absolute temperature)
T_g	glass transition temperature
t	time
t_i	transference number of ion i

U	internal energy
u	velocity
u_x, u_y, u_z	velocity components
μ_k	generalised mobility of an ion k
u_l	velocity of sound in liquid
u_v	velocity of sound in vapour
$\boldsymbol{u}$	velocity vector
$\boldsymbol{u}_{MC}$	velocity of local centre of mass in cell-fixed reference frame
$\boldsymbol{u}_{RC}$	velocity of local reference frame R in cell-fixed reference frame
$(\boldsymbol{u}_k)_R$	average velocity of motion of component k in a reference-frame R
$(\boldsymbol{u}_k)_M$	diffusion velocity of k in mass-fixed reference frame
$\boldsymbol{uv}$	dyadic product
V	volume
V	molar volume
V	velocity
$\Delta V^{\neq}$	activation volume for diffusion
v	molecular volume
Δv	excess volume
$\bar{v}_k$	partial molar volume of component k
v_f	free volume
v_f	free volume per molecule
$\bar{v}_m$	average molecular volume
$\boldsymbol{v}$	vector
$\boldsymbol{v}$	velocity vector
W	work
$W(\ \ )$	a probability
w_k	mass fraction of component k
X	an extensive property
x	mole fraction
x	distance
x_1, x_2, x_3	Cartesian coordinates of position vector
$x_{jk}^{\pm}$	mean ionic mole fraction
$\boldsymbol{X}$	a generalised volume force vector
y_k	molar activity coefficient
$y_{jk}^{\pm}$	mean ionic activity coefficient (molar basis)
z	ionic charge, molar units
z_k	ionic charge, including sign, on component k

Greek Symbols

α	thermal diffusivity

α	isothermal compressibility
α	liquor ratio
α_i	Onsager coordinate
α_i	fractional dissociation of acidic groups
β	isobaric coefficient of volume expansion
β_i	fractional degree of dissociation of basic groups
γ_k	molal activity coefficient, practical activity coefficient
$\gamma_{jk}^{\pm}$	mean ionic activity coefficient (molal basis)
δ_D	apparent or effective thickness of diffusional boundary layer
$\delta_D{}^*$	thickness of diffusional boundary layer
$\delta_H{}^*$	thickness of hydrodynamic boundary layer
ε	dielectric constant
ε	porosity
ζ	friction coefficient
ζ	zeta-potential
η	viscosity
θ	angle
θ	energy flow for combined heat and mass transfer
θ	time lag in establishing steady-state of diffusion
ϑ	coefficient of bulk viscosity
κ	thermal conductivity
κ_s	surface conductivity
κ_l	specific conductivity of a liquid
λ	absolute activity
λ	generalised Donnan distribution coefficient
λ	jump distance
λ	scale factor
λ	specific conductance
λ_i	extent of reaction (mass basis) for the *i*th reaction
λ_R	characteristic diffusion-reaction length
μ	chemical potential
$\tilde{\mu}$	electrochemical potential
$\hat{\mu}'_k$	specific electrochemical potential of component *k*
$-\overline{\Delta\mu^0{}_k}$	apparent standard affinity for mass transfer of component *k*
ν	frequency of diffusional jumps
ν	kinematic viscosity
ν	number of ions
ν	vibrational frequency
ν_{ki}	stoichiometric coefficient
ξ	extent of reaction
π	a dimensionless product
ρ	mass density

ρ_k	partial mass density of component k
σ	reflection coefficient
σ_s	surface charge density
σ_{ij}	component of stress tensor
$\sigma_{xx}, \sigma_{yy}, \sigma_{zz}$	normal stress components
$\sigma_{xy}, \sigma_{xz}, \sigma_{yx}, \sigma_{yz}, \sigma_{zx}, \sigma_{zy}$	shear stress components
$\boldsymbol{\sigma}$	stress tensor
τ	tortuosity factor
τ	a characteristic time
τ_{ij}	viscous component of pressure tensor
$\boldsymbol{\tau}$	viscous contribution to the pressure tensor $\boldsymbol{P}$
ϕ_X	local rate of production of an extensive property X, per unit volume
φ_V	volume fraction
χ_k	structure factor
ψ	electrostatic potential

To my mother and father

Part I Mass Transport in Continuous Media

Chapter 1 The Simple Transport Laws

Consider a homogeneous fluid mixture in thermodynamic equilibrium; there are no external forces, the temperature, pressure and composition are uniform throughout the interior of the fluid and there is no relative motion of different regions of the fluid. Suppose a temperature gradient, a gradient of composition or a stress gradient appears in the mixture. We know from experience that transport processes will eliminate these gradients: the mixture strives to re-attain an equilibrium distribution of temperature, composition and pressure.

The temperature gradient gives rise to a flow of heat from regions of high temperature to those of lower temperature. This heat transport eliminates the temperature gradients.

A concentration gradient causes the diffusion of components from volume elements in which their concentration is high to regions of lower concentration. This diffusive mass transport equalises the composition of the mixture. Velocity gradients in a non-uniform mixture can give rise to convective mass transport; the hydrodynamic flow redistributes the components of the mixture. The composition of a mixture may, for example, be equalised by mechanical stirring. Shear stresses cause a relative motion of different parts of the fluid. This relative motion is opposed by viscous forces, which are frictional in nature. They retard the faster-moving regions and accelerate the slower-moving regions: they tend to eliminate the velocity gradients. The action of the viscous forces between two volume elements of fluid is equivalent to a transport of momentum between the elements. Momentum is transported from the faster-moving element to the slower-moving element and this process equalises the motions of the elements. The shear stresses disappear as the momentum is redistributed throughout the fluid.

A study of transport processes is a study of the approach to thermodynamic equilibrium. It is a study of nonequilibrium processes. We shall return to this theme when the conceptual and mathematical tools necessary for an understanding of nonequilibrium thermodynamics have been developed.

This development can usefully begin with an examination of the simple classical transport laws of Newton, Fourier and Fick. These laws give the simplest possible description of the transport processes and serve to introduce some important concepts.

I. NEWTON'S LAW OF VISCOSITY

Two large flat plates of area A are held parallel, a very small distance l apart. The space between the plates is filled with a fluid of constant temperature and density as shown in Fig. 1; the lower plate is stationary but the upper plate moves parallel to it at a steady velocity V in the x-direction. After a time, a steady state is reached in which the force F needed to keep the upper plate moving at velocity V remains constant.

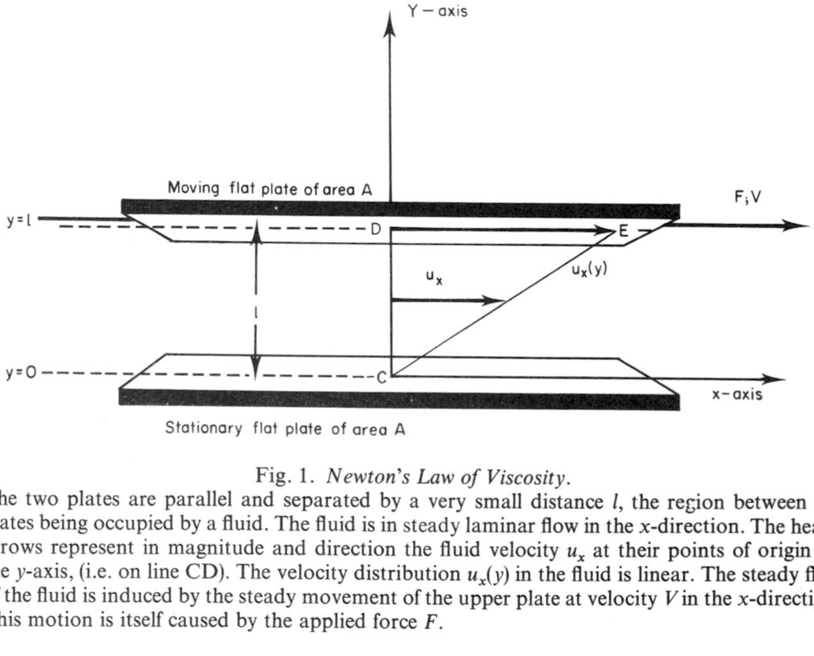

Fig. 1. *Newton's Law of Viscosity.*
The two plates are parallel and separated by a very small distance l, the region between the plates being occupied by a fluid. The fluid is in steady laminar flow in the x-direction. The heavy arrows represent in magnitude and direction the fluid velocity u_x at their points of origin on the y-axis, (i.e. on line CD). The velocity distribution $u_x(y)$ in the fluid is linear. The steady flow of the fluid is induced by the steady movement of the upper plate at velocity V in the x-direction. This motion is itself caused by the applied force F.

For certain fluids known as Newtonian fluids the applied force F is directly proportional to V and a linear velocity gradient is developed in the fluid, which is in steady laminar flow as shown in Fig. 1. The velocity gradient in the fluid is numerically equal to V/l. The force that must be exerted on the upper plate is directly proportional to the area of the plates and to the velocity gradient

$$\frac{F}{A} = \eta \cdot \frac{V}{l} \tag{1.1}$$

The coefficient of proportionality η is called the viscosity or, more precisely, the coefficient of shear viscosity of the fluid.

The fluid layer in contact with the upper plate at $y = l$ in Fig. 1 is stationary with respect to the plate and exerts a tangential shear force on the lower fluid layers, in the direction of increasing x. The shear force per unit area exerted by the layer is known as a shear stress and is equal in magnitude to F/A in the steady state.

The symbol σ_{yx} is used to denote such a shear stress. The second subscript states that the shear force acts in the direction of increasing x, the first subscript y states that the shear stress is exerted on a fluid layer normal to the y-axis. The shear stress σ_{yx} is from Eqn (1.1) directly proportional to the velocity gradient in the fluid. The linear velocity gradient V/l may be written as $\partial u_x/\partial y$ where u_x is the x-component of the fluid velocity so that Eqn (1.1) becomes

$$\sigma_{yx} = \eta \frac{\partial u_x}{\partial y} \tag{1.2}$$

This is *Newton's Law of Viscosity*. It applies only to an isothermal Newtonian fluid of constant density.

According to Newton's second law of motion, the force acting on a body is equal to the time rate of change of momentum of the body. If the body has mass m and the x-component of the force is F_x then

$$F_x = m \cdot \frac{du_x}{dt} = \frac{d(mu_x)}{dt} \tag{1.3}$$

in which the product mu_x is the x-component of the momentum of the body.

The product ρu_x would be the x-momentum of a unit volume of fluid of density ρ moving with a uniform x-velocity u_x. ρu_x has the dimensions of a momentum density. We may regard ρu_x as the local density of x-momentum in a fluid of density ρ, at a point where the local x-component of the fluid velocity is u_x. It is now possible to write Eqn (1.2) in the form

$$\sigma_{yx} = \nu \cdot \frac{\partial(\rho u_x)}{\partial y} \tag{1.4}$$

in which $\nu = \eta/\rho$ is the kinematic viscosity of the fluid.

The shear stress σ_{yx} now appears as a function of the gradient of momentum density in the fluid. A rate of flow per unit area is known as a *flux*. σ_{yx} is not only to be regarded as a shear force per unit area, it can also be interpreted as a viscous momentum flux. (Bird *et al.*, 1964.) σ_{yx} is then the rate of flow of x-momentum per unit area of a reference plane normal to the y-axis, the flow being in the direction of decreasing y: there is from this point of view a steady transport of x-momentum in the fluid from the upper layers to the lower layers. The gradient of momentum density may be regarded as the "driving force" behind the momentum transport. Newton's law of viscosity is also a law of momentum transport.

II. FOURIER'S LAW OF HEAT TRANSPORT

Suppose that both plates in Fig. 1 are stationary and the upper plate is maintained at a temperature $(T + \Delta T)$ which is slightly higher than the temperature T of the lower plate. The fluid between the plates is stationary and no diffusion or convection occurs. The fluid has at all times a constant and uniform density and composition. Under these conditions, which can be satisfied experimentally to a given degree of approximation, it is found that heat flows from the upper plate to the lower plate at a constant rate Q. In addition, the temperature distribution is linear in the fluid between the plates when the steady state is attained. For values of ΔT that are small enough we have

$$\frac{Q}{A} = K\frac{\Delta T}{l} \tag{1.5}$$

the coefficient of proportionality K is the thermal conductivity of the fluid. We can replace Eqn (1.5) by

$$q_y = -K\frac{\partial T}{\partial y} \tag{1.6}$$

in which q_y is the y-component of the heat flux and $\partial T/\partial y$ is the temperature gradient. Equation (1.6) is *Fourier's law of heat conduction* in one dimension: the heat flow here occurs only in the y-direction. The heat flux is directly proportional to the temperature gradient and is directed down this gradient. Hence the minus sign in Eqn (1.6).

It is instructive to replace the temperature gradient in Eqn (1.6) by the corresponding energy gradient. The quantity $\partial(\rho\hat{C}pT)/\partial y$ in which $\hat{C}p$ is the heat capacity per unit mass of fluid at constant pressure, may be regarded as the energy density gradient in the fluid (Cf. Chapter 4). Introducing this quantity into Eqn (1.6), we find the result (Bird *et al.*, 1964)

$$q_y = -\alpha\cdot\frac{\partial(\rho\hat{C}pT)}{\partial y} \tag{1.7}$$

When $\rho\hat{C}p$ is constant, Eqn (1.7) is another form of Fourier's law of heat conduction. The thermal diffusivity α is defined by $\alpha = K/\rho\hat{C}p$ and has the dimensions $[L]^2[T]^{-1}$. $[L]$ is the dimension of length and $[T]$ is the dimension of time.

Equation (1.7) states that the energy flux q_y is directly proportional to an energy density gradient and that the flux is down the gradient. Fourier's law of heat conduction is also a law of energy transport.

III. FICK'S LAWS OF DIFFUSION

A. Fick's First Law

Newton's law of viscosity [Eqn (1.4)] and Fourier's law of heat conduction [Eqn (1.7)] take similar forms for unidimensional processes. Both the kinematic viscosity ν and the thermal diffusivity α have the same dimensions $[L]^2[T]^{-1}$.

Fick's first law of diffusion is based on an analogy with Fourier's law of heat conduction. For unidimensional diffusion in the y-direction the law takes the form

$$j_{iy} = -D \cdot \frac{\partial \rho_i}{\partial y} \tag{1.8}$$

j_{iy} is the diffusion flux of an arbitrary component i; ρ_i is the local mass density (e.g. concentration in $g \cdot cm^{-3}$) of this component. D is a diffusion coefficient and has the same dimensions $[L]^2[T]^{-1}$ as have α and ν.

Equation (1.8) is strictly valid only under especially simple circumstances such as the interdiffusion of the two components of a binary fluid mixture of constant total density ρ. There is a striking formal analogy between the flux equations for these three unidimensional transport processes (Bird *et al.*, 1964)

$$\left.\begin{aligned} \text{i.e.}\ -\delta_{yx} = \tau_{yx} &= -\nu \cdot \frac{\partial(\rho u_x)}{\partial y} \\ q_y &= -\alpha \cdot \frac{\partial(\rho \hat{C}p T)}{\partial y} \\ j_{iy} &= -D \cdot \frac{\partial \rho_i}{\partial y} \end{aligned}\right\} \rho,\ \hat{C}p\ \text{constant} \tag{1.9}$$

Neither the diffusion flux j_{iy} nor the diffusion coefficient D has yet been properly defined. This problem is taken up again in detail later. For the present we shall accept Fick's law, with a constant diffusion coefficient, as it stands in order to derive from it an equation of conservation for component i.

B. Fick's Second Law

If Eqn (1.8) is a complete description of the mass transport of component i within the fluid it is not difficult to derive an equation for the local rate of change of concentration of this component as a consequence of diffusion.

Consider the rectangular element of volume of thickness $2\delta x$ in the x-direction, in Fig. 2. The volume element has surface area A normal to the diffusion flux and is centred about the point P, which is a distance x from the origin of the x-coordinate. δx is very small compared with x and the diffusion flux j_{ix} varies only slightly over the distance $2\delta x$. If j_{ix} is the diffusion flux through the plane BCDE at x, then under these conditions the inward flux through the plane JKLM at $x - \delta x$ is

$$j_{ix} - \left(\frac{\partial j_{ix}}{\partial x}\right)\delta x$$

Similarly, the outward diffusion flux through the plane FGHI at $x + \delta x$ is

$$j_{ix} + \left(\frac{\partial j_{ix}}{\partial x}\right)\delta x$$

The total rate of accumulation of the diffusing species within the volume element, in units of $[M][T]^{-1}$ is clearly

$$\left[\left(j_{ix} - \left(\frac{\partial j_{ix}}{\partial x}\right)\delta x\right) - \left(j_{ix} + \left(\frac{\partial j_{ix}}{\partial x}\right)\delta x\right)\right]A$$

or

$$\text{rate of accumulation} = -2\cdot\left(\frac{\partial j_{ix}}{\partial x}\right)\delta x\cdot A \tag{1.10}$$

But $2\delta xA$ is the volume of the element, so that the time rate of change of concentration, or of mass density ρ_i within the volume element is simply

$$\frac{\partial \rho_i}{\partial t} = -\frac{\partial j_{ix}}{\partial x} \tag{1.11}$$

By Fick's first law, Eqn (1.8), we have finally the result

$$\frac{\partial \rho_i}{\partial t} = D\frac{\partial^2 \rho_i}{\partial x^2} \quad (\rho \text{ constant}) \tag{1.12}$$

which is the equation of conservation of component i in unidimensional diffusion along the x-axis. Equation (1.12) is often referred to as *Fick's second law* of diffusion. This equation is again valid only under very restrictive conditions. Although monographs have been devoted to the mathematical solutions of Eqn (1.12) for a wide variety of initial and boundary conditions

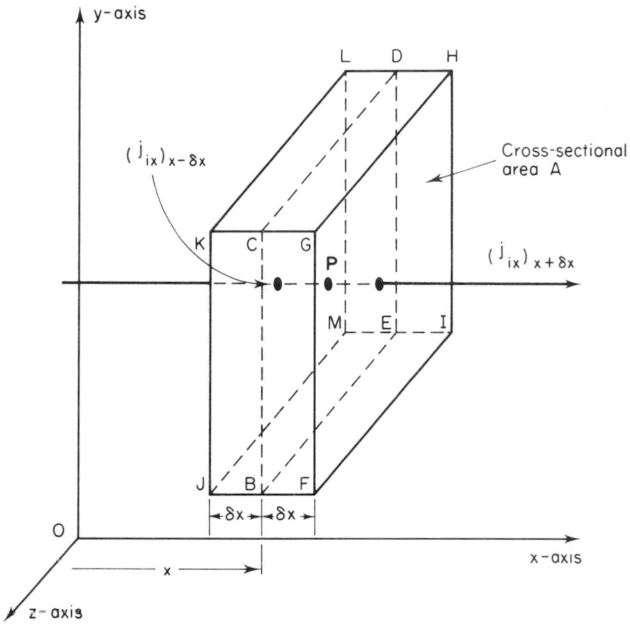

Fig. 2. *The Derivation of Fick's Second Law of Diffusion.*
The rectangular volume element JKLMFGHI is centred about the point P at which the diffusion flux is j_{ix}. The volume element has thickness $2\delta x$ and cross-sectional area A normal to j_{ix}. Fick's second law is derived by considering the rate of accumulation of the diffusing species within the volume element.

(Carslaw and Jaeger, 1959; Crank, 1956), the applicability of these mathematical solutions as a description of the behaviour of real systems can be determined only by careful experiment.

IV. MACROSCOPIC IRREVERSIBILITY

Fick's second law has exactly the same form as the equation of conservation of energy that may be derived in a similar fashion from Fourier's law. For this reason many of the mathematical solutions for problems in heat conduction (Carslaw and Jaeger, 1959) are applied to problems of diffusive mass transport. Situations do exist in which this procedure is justified, but there are situations in which such a procedure can lead to misconceptions, if not to error.

Equation (1.12) is nevertheless very interesting because it reveals a characteristic feature of transport processes, namely their *irreversibility* at the macroscopic level. The Eqn (1.12) is not invariant towards the substitution of $-t$ for $+t$, where t is time. The mathematical solutions of Eqn (1.12) generally exhibit an irreversible progression or development in time. This reflects the irreversible approach to thermodynamic equilibrium which is characteristic of transport processes at the macroscopic level, i.e. at the level of sensitivity of measurement of mass, length and time that is characteristic of "normal" laboratory apparatus.

V. LIMITATIONS OF THE SIMPLE TRANSPORT LAWS

Newton's law, Fourier's law and Fick's law are purely descriptive or *phenomenological*, laws. They take no account of molecular details and provide no basis for the prediction of the magnitude of the transport coefficients (η, ν, K, α, D) in a given situation. When they are applicable, they have the same form for transport processes in solids, liquids and gases.†

The simple laws are subject to many exceptions: non-Newtonian fluids are of frequent occurrence; Fick's law is more often departed from than observed; Fourier's law is not universally obeyed. This situation tends to be obscured by the complex and imposing mathematical superstructures that may be erected on the basis of these simple laws.

The reverence that is often given to Fick's law, and to the mathematical solutions based on this law, stands in marked contrast to the following comment by Truesdell (1962)

> "... the purely kinematical presumptions leading to Fick's law are unsupported by any principle or method of mechanics or physics and cannot be expected to explain or predict motions except in especially simple circumstances."

According to the molecular hypothesis, the key to the macroscopic properties and behaviour of matter is to be sought in the laws that govern the behaviour of the molecules of which matter is composed. It is to be found at the molecular level that is the concern of statistical mechanics.

The statistical mechanics of transport processes in fluids is still in intensive development and presents formidable mathematical difficulties (Hirschfelder *et al.*, 1964; Rice and Gray, 1965; Pryde, 1966).

The statistical, or stochastic, theories of diffusion in solids are in a similar state of intensive development (Shewmon, 1963; Reiss, 1964; Allnatt, 1965; Manning, 1965).

The statistical mechanics of transport processes in gases is rather well-developed and the values of the transport coefficients can often be predicted with some degree of accuracy (Hirschfelder *et al.*, 1964).

We shall refer to molecular theories whenever they appear to offer a

† Transport processes in anisotropic solids require a more complex description.

physical insight into the nature of the transport processes. In this context it is interesting that the Chapman–Enskog theory of transport processes in gases predicts that mass transport may occur as a result of a temperature gradient (thermal diffusion) and that energy transport may arise from a concentration gradient (Dufour effect).

This is in marked contrast to the predictions of the simple kinetic theory of gases and to the simple transport laws (Hirschfelder *et al.*, 1964). These coupling effects between transport processes tend to be small but significant, so that they should be included in any general theory.

REFERENCES

Allnatt, A. R. (1965). *J. Chem. Phys.*, **43,** 1855.

Barrer, R. M. (1941). "Diffusion in and Through Solids." Cambridge University Press.

Bird, R. B., Stewart, W. E. and Lightfoot, E. N. (1964). "Transport Phenomena." John Wiley and Sons, New York; (Reprinted with corrections, Toppan Company Ltd., Tokyo).

Carslaw, H. S. and Jaeger, J. C. (1959). "Condition of Heat in Solids." 2nd. Edn. Oxford University Press.

Crank, J. (1956). "The Mathematics of Diffusion." Clarendon Press, Oxford.

Hirschfelder, J. O., Curtiss, C. F. and Bird, R. B. (1964). "Molecular Theory of Gases and Liquids." (Corrected version, with notes added). John Wiley and Sons Inc., New York.

Jost, W. (1952). "Diffusion in Solids, Liquids, Gases." Academic Press, New York and London.

Manning, J. R. (1965). *Phys. Rev.*, **139,** No. 1A, A 126.

Pryde, J. A. (1966). "The Liquid State." (Hutchinson University Library.) Hutchinson, London.

Reiss, H. (1964). *J. Chem. Phys.*, **40,** 1783.

Rice, S. A. and Gray, P. (1965). "The Statistical Mechanics of Simple Liquids." Interscience, New York.

Shewmon, B. P. G. (1963). "Diffusion in Solids." McGraw-Hill, New York.

Truesdell, C. (1962). *J. Chem. Phys.*, **37,** 2336.

Chapter 2 The Brownian Motion and the Continuum Approximation

I. THE BROWNIAN MOTION

Loschmidt's Reversibility Paradox points out that the basic laws of conservation of energy and momentum, when used to derive equations of motion for assemblies of molecules, lead to equations which are reversible in time. There is in the equations themselves no preferred direction in time in which a molecular process might develop. The paradox lies in the observation that these molecular motions must nevertheless give rise to irreversible macroscopic transport processes.

One attempt to resolve this paradox is based on the recognition of an element of chance in the molecular motions.

Kirkwood (1946) suggested that the instantaneous force acting on a molecule in a fluid might not be completely determined by its value at previous times. He postulated the existence of a characteristic time τ after which the force acting on an individual molecule is statistically independent of its previous values. If measurements are made on a time-scale much longer than the characteristic time τ, the molecular motions can no longer be described in deterministic terms.

The total force exerted on a molecule by its neighbours is a fluctuating force $\boldsymbol{F}(t)$ which, if the molecule were at rest in a fluid at equilibrium, would be completely random in direction. Any transitory displacement of a molecule under the influence of a fluctuating force will, however, be opposed by "frictional" interactions with the surrounding molecules, which retard the motion. As a molecular analogue of Newton's law of viscosity we may suppose that this frictional force is directly proportional to the instantaneous velocity $\boldsymbol{u}$ of the molecule and acts in the opposite direction, i.e. it may be written as $-\xi\boldsymbol{u}$, where ξ is a molecular friction coefficient. The total force acting on a moving molecule is the sum of the directional retarding force $-\xi\boldsymbol{u}$ and a random fluctuating force $\boldsymbol{G}(t)$.

$$\boldsymbol{F}(t) = -\xi\boldsymbol{u} + \boldsymbol{G}(t) \tag{2.1}$$

By Newton's second law of motion [Eqn (1.3)]

$$\boldsymbol{F}(t) = m\frac{d\boldsymbol{u}}{dt} \tag{2.2}$$

where m is now the molecular mass, and the equation of motion of a molecule is

$$m\frac{d\boldsymbol{u}}{dt} + \xi\boldsymbol{u} = \boldsymbol{G}(t) \tag{2.3}$$

Equation (2.3) includes a random or stochastic element $\boldsymbol{G}(t)$: it is not a deterministic equation. A rigorous development of Eqn (2.3) as a description of molecular motion is difficult (Rice and Gray, 1965). It is sufficient for our purposes to note that if the time scale of observation t is long by comparison with the characteristic time τ, and with the time-scale of the fluctuations in $\boldsymbol{G}(t)$, the movement of a molecule will show the essential characteristics of Brownian motion. Langevin (1908) first proposed Eqn (2.3) as a description of Brownian motion, so that this equation is known as Langevin's equation.

The motion of a Brownian particle appears as a succession of discrete random jumps in three dimensions. Observation in the ultramicroscope (Perrin, 1923) gives a projection of this motion in two dimensions. We consider only the idealised motion in one dimension of a particle which is constrained to carry out a "random walk" along a series of equally-spaced positions on the x-axis (Rice and Gray, 1965; Smoluchowski, 1906).

The probability of movement up or down the x-axis is equal and has the value $\frac{1}{2}$. After N steps from the origin the particle may be at any of the positions

$$-N, -N+1, -N+2, \ldots, -2, -1, 0, +1, +2, \ldots, N-2, N-1, N$$

The probability of any given sequence of N steps is $(\frac{1}{2})^N$. The probability of arrival at position m after N steps is (Chandrasekhar, 1943)

$$W(m, N) = (\tfrac{1}{2})^N \times \begin{pmatrix}\text{The number of distinct sequences} \\ \text{that lead to } m \text{ in } N \text{ steps}\end{pmatrix} \tag{2.4}$$

A particle that is at position m after N steps has made, say, n backward steps and $(m + n)$ forward steps: since, however, the total number of steps is

$$N = (m + n) + n \tag{2.5}$$

there must have been $n = \frac{1}{2}(N - m)$ backward steps and $(m + n) = \frac{1}{2}(N + m)$ forward steps. The number of ways in which N steps can be divided up into two groups, one containing $\frac{1}{2}(N + m)$ forward steps and the other $\frac{1}{2}(N - m)$ backward steps, is

$$\frac{N!}{[\frac{1}{2}(N + m)]!\,[\frac{1}{2}(N - m)]!} \tag{2.6}$$

But this is the number of distinct sequences of steps that lead to m in N steps, so that Eqn (2.4) becomes

$$W(m, N) = (\tfrac{1}{2})^N \frac{N!}{[\frac{1}{2}(N + m)]!\,[\frac{1}{2}(N - m)]!} \tag{2.7}$$

$W(m, N)$ is a binomial distribution for the probability of observing $\frac{1}{2}(N + m)$ forward steps in N steps. This distribution has a mean value $\frac{1}{2}\langle N + m\rangle = \frac{1}{2}N$ and variance $\langle[\frac{1}{2}(N + m) - \frac{1}{2}N]^2\rangle = \frac{1}{4}N$. This means that the distribution of possible positions of the particle after N steps has the most probable value, or expected value

$$\langle m\rangle = 0 \tag{2.8}$$

and variance

$$\langle m^2\rangle = N \tag{2.9}$$

$N^{\frac{1}{2}}$ is therefore the root mean square displacement of the particle. A molecule carries out a large number of "jumps" during any macroscopic time interval, so that we are really interested in the limiting form of $W(m, N)$ for very large values of the number of jumps N. The displacement m after N jumps is also much smaller than N, i.e. a molecule travels an enormous distance along its three-dimensional flight-path in order to achieve a comparatively modest resultant displacement. This limiting form of $W(m, N)$ is *Gaussian*

$$\lim_{\substack{N \to \infty \\ m/N \to 0}} W(m, N) = \left(\frac{2}{\pi N}\right)^{\frac{1}{2}} \exp\left(-\frac{m}{2N}\right) \tag{2.10}$$

Suppose each step is a jump of distance λ so that position m is a distance

$$x = m\lambda \tag{2.11}$$

from the origin and suppose we view the x-axis from such a distance that we can no longer distinguish any of the discrete positions that the particle may occupy: this is analogous to the adoption of a macroscopic viewpoint. The series of distinct points on the x-axis merges into an apparently continuous line and we must adopt a different procedure for specifying the probability of finding a particle in a given position.

We introduce a continuous probability density function $p(x, N)$, (Arthurs, 1965), such that the product $p(x, N)\,\delta x$ is the probability of finding the particle within the range δx of x after N jumps.

If both N and m are large enough, we may so choose δx that it is small compared with x and yet contains many possible sites for the particle. This is analogous to the adoption of a continuum approximation. Since δx is small compared with x, $W(m, N)$ is substantially constant over the interval δx and

$$p(x, N)\,\delta x = W(m, N)\frac{\delta x}{2\lambda} \tag{2.12}$$

Since N must be either even or odd $\delta x/2\lambda$ is the number of "sites" that can be occupied within δx for any *given* value of N. Substitution of Eqn (2.12) into Eqn (2.10) gives

$$p(x, N) = \left(\frac{1}{2\pi N\lambda^2}\right)^{\frac{1}{2}} \exp\left(-\frac{x^2}{2N\lambda^2}\right) \tag{2.13}$$

The time t can be introduced as a variable if the particle is supposed to undergo n steps in unit time: this leads to the result

$$p(x, t) = \left(\frac{1}{4\pi Dt}\right)^{\frac{1}{2}} \exp\left(-\frac{x^2}{4Dt}\right) \tag{2.14}$$

in which the parameter D gives a measure of the rate of spread of the probability density function $p(x, t)$ about the origin: D is defined by

$$D \equiv \frac{n\lambda^2}{2} \tag{2.15}$$

Since N steps are completed in time t we may compare Eqn (2.13) with Eqn (2.14) to find the result

$$D = \frac{N\lambda^2}{2t} \tag{2.16}$$

in which $N\lambda^2$ is the mean square displacement of the particle in N steps or in time t. Representing this quantity by $\langle x^2 \rangle$ we have

$$D = \frac{\langle x^2 \rangle}{2t} \tag{2.17}$$

For problems in three dimensions $D = \langle r^2 \rangle/6t$

The probability density function $p(x, t)$ may be interpreted in a different way: if we consider the behaviour of a very large number of particles concentrated initially in a very small volume element at the origin, then $p(x, t)$ also represents the local *number density* of particles at point x at time t. The product $p(x, t)\,\delta x$ now represents the number of particles to be found within a range δx of x at time t. Only in this second instance is the parameter D to be regarded as a diffusion coefficient. In fact Eqn (2.14) is a mathematical solution to the simple diffusion equation

$$\frac{\partial p(x, t)}{\partial t} = D\frac{\partial^2 p(x, t)}{\partial x^2} \tag{2.18}$$

for the initial and boundary conditions appropriate to the present problem. Although the basic motion of the particle is random, the probability density function for a single particle and the number density in an assembly of a large number of particles show an irreversible development in time Fig. 3. From this point of view it is the statistical nature of the macroscopic measurements that leads to the observation of a directional diffusion flux and to an irreversible development of the number density or concentration in time.

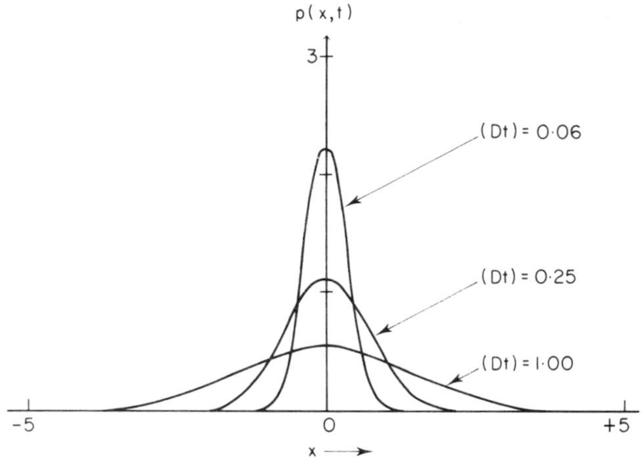

Fig. 3. *The Probability Density Function* $p(x, t)$ *for an Idealised One-dimensional Brownian Movement.*
$p(x, t)$ evolves irreversibly with time t: the probability of finding the particle at the origin progressively decreases and the probability of finding it some distance from the origin increases. Information about the probable position of the particle is lost as time progresses: the *entropy* of the system increases.

II. THE STOKES–EINSTEIN EQUATION

If a Brownian particle is very large by comparison with the molecules of the fluid in which it is immersed it "sees" the fluid as a continuous medium and we may use a hydrodynamic definition of the friction coefficient on the basis of Stokes' law: the viscous retarding force on a spherical particle of radius a moving with a steady velocity $\boldsymbol{u}$ in a fluid of viscosity η is $-6\pi\eta a\boldsymbol{u}$ so that

$$\xi = 6\pi\eta a \tag{2.19}$$

The assumption of motion with a steady velocity $\boldsymbol{u}$ is equivalent to the customary neglect of accelerations in theories of diffusion.

This interpretation of ξ is not generally applicable to the diffusion of molecules of arbitrary size. The diffusion coefficient D is related to the friction coefficient ξ by the equation

$$D = \frac{kT}{\xi} \tag{2.20}$$

The combination of Eqn (2.19) with Eqn (2.20) gives the *Stokes–Einstein equation* for the diffusion coefficient

$$D = \frac{kT}{6\pi\eta a} \tag{2.21}$$

k is the Boltzmann constant and T is the absolute temperature.

III. ASSUMPTIONS INHERENT IN THE DERIVATION OF FICK'S LAW

It may be useful to emphasize some of the assumptions that are necessary to derive Fick's law on the basis of the Brownian motion:

(1) The motion of each particle is random and is unaffected by the presence of other particles.
(2) Each successive jump is independent of the previous jumps—there are no "memory effects" in the movement of the particles and no correlations between jumps.
(3) The mean "jump length" for a particle and the frequency of displacement do not vary with position or time.
(4) There is no hydrodynamic flow of the system.
(5) There are no forces that can give rise to a preferred direction of motion of the individual particles.

The above assumptions may provide clues to possible molecular origins of deviations from Fick's laws, and they also indicate why a more general phenomenological description of diffusion processes is desirable.

We now turn to an examination of the description of diffusion processes in macroscopic terms. As necessary preliminaries we discuss the nature of the variables used, the conservation equations for continuous systems and the behaviour of single-component systems.

REFERENCES

Arthurs, A. M. (1965). *In* "Probability Theory." (Library of Mathematics) (Ed., W. Ledermann), Routledge and Kegan Paul, London.

Chandrasekhar, S. (1943). *Rev. mod. Phys.*, **15,** No. 1, 1; reprinted with other papers (1954) in "Selected Papers on Noise anh Stochastic Processes." (Ed. N. Wax), Dover Publications Inc., New York.

Crank, J. (1956). "The Mathematics of Diffusion." Clarendon Press, Oxford.

Einstein, A. (1905). *Annln Phys.*, **17,** 549; reprinted with other papers (1956) in "Investigations on the Theory of the Brownian Movement." (English translation by A. D. Cowper, Ed. R. Furth), Dover Publications Inc., New York.

Kirkwood, J. G. (1946). *J. Chem. Phys.*, **14,** 180.
Langevin, P. (1908). *C.r. hebd. Seanc. Acad. Sci., Paris*, **146,** 530.
Moelwyn-Hughes, E. A. (1965). "Physical Chemistry." (2nd Revised Edn.), Pergamon Press Ltd., London.
Perrin, J. (1923). "Atoms." (2nd Revised Engl. Edn.), Transl. D. Ll. Hammick, Constable, London.
Pryde, J. A. (1966). "The Liquid State." (Hutchinson University Library), Hutchinson and Co. Ltd., London.
Rice, S. A. and Gray, P. (1965). "The Statistical Mechanics of Simple Liquids." Interscience, New York.
Shewmon, B. P. G. (1963). "Diffusion in Solids." McGraw-Hill, New York.
Smoluchowski, M. von. (1906). *Annln. Phys.*, **21,** 756.

Chapter 3 The Field Quantities

In a continuum approximation the physical variables are treated as continuous and differentiable functions of the space and time coordinates. A region of matter within which this approximation is valid is known as a continuum, or as a continuous medium. Each physical quantity may be allocated a definite value at every point in such a region and, viewed as a whole, this set of values forms a field. An electrostatic field, for example, is characterised by the distribution in space of the values of the electrostatic potential Ψ.

To take a specific example, the mass density ρ at a given point P in a fluid is defined in the following way. The point P is enclosed by the bounding surface of a finite volume element δV. The mass of the fluid within δV is δm, so that the mean mass density of δV is $\delta m/\delta V$. The mass density ρ at the point P is defined by a limiting process in which δV is allowed to contract to zero around P, at constant temperature T and pressure p

$$\rho = \operatorname*{Lim}_{\delta V \to 0} \left(\frac{\delta m}{\delta V} \right)_{T,p} = \left(\frac{\partial m}{\partial V} \right)_{T,p} \tag{3.1}$$

The differential notation always implies such a limiting process, but this is physically unrealistic. The mass density ρ is continuous in a similar sense to the probability density function $p(x, t)$ of Chapter 2: it is so defined that the product $\rho\, \delta V$ gives the mass of a "very small" volume element δV. δV must be so small by comparison with a measurable volume V that ρ is substantially constant within δV, but δV must be so large by comparison with molecular volumes that the equilibrium properties of δV are representative of the equilibrium properties of the bulk fluid. In this sense ρ is some kind of average over an infinitesimal region δV and over some infinitesimal time interval δt. δt must be very short by comparison with the duration of the measurements on the fluid but it must be very long on the time scale of the molecular processes within δV.

The total mass m of a macroscopic volume V of fluid may be written as the summation

$$m = \sum_V \rho\, \delta V \tag{3.2}$$

The corresponding integration over V again involves a limiting process

$$m = \lim_{\delta V \to 0} \sum_V \rho\, \delta V = \int_V \rho \cdot dV \tag{3.3}$$

We shall suppose that δV may be chosen sufficiently small for the summation to be a good approximation to the integral and we shall then use the symbol dV to represent this infinitesimal volume element. A similar convention will be used for the other field quantities.

I. SCALARS AND SCALAR FIELDS

A scalar quantity has magnitude only; it has no intrinsic directional properties and can be specified by a number which remains unchanged in all coordinate systems. Temperature, length, volume, concentration, mass density, electrical potential and energy are all scalars.

A scalar field is characterised by a distribution in space of the values taken by a scalar quantity. We therefore require a notation in which we can express the position of a volume element dV in space. This leads us to a consideration of the position vector $\boldsymbol{r}$ and of the vector notation itself.

II. VECTORS AND VECTOR FIELDS

A vector $\boldsymbol{v}$ has both magnitude and direction. The corresponding italic symbol v is used to denote the magnitude of a vector $\boldsymbol{v}$. The equality of two vectors implies only that they have the same magnitude and point in the same direction; it is not necessary for them to have the same point of origin and they do not have to be collinear. The product $k\boldsymbol{v}$ in which k is a positive number denotes a new vector with the same direction as $\boldsymbol{v}$ but of magnitude kv. When $k = -1$ we obtain the vector $-\boldsymbol{v}$; this has the same magnitude as $\boldsymbol{v}$ but is of opposite sense. The velocity of a particle is a vector quantity; so are a force, a flow of energy, a flow of mass and a displacement of a particle. The rules for the addition, subtraction and multiplication of vectors are chosen so that they correspond to the way in which physical quantities such as forces or displacements may be combined (Kynch, 1955). Some of the more important properties of vectors can be illustrated by a brief discussion of the position vector $\boldsymbol{r}$.

A. The Position Vector

The position of a point P in space can be determined only by reference to some other point O. The position of the volume element dV in Fig. 4 is defined by the straight line OP which joins dV to the origin O of the Cartesian coordinates OX, OY, OZ. This line has magnitude $r = OP$, where OP is the length of the line, and it has direction in the sense from O to P; it represents the position vector $\overrightarrow{OP}$ of P with respect to O. In a more general notation the symbol $\boldsymbol{r}$ is used for the position vector.

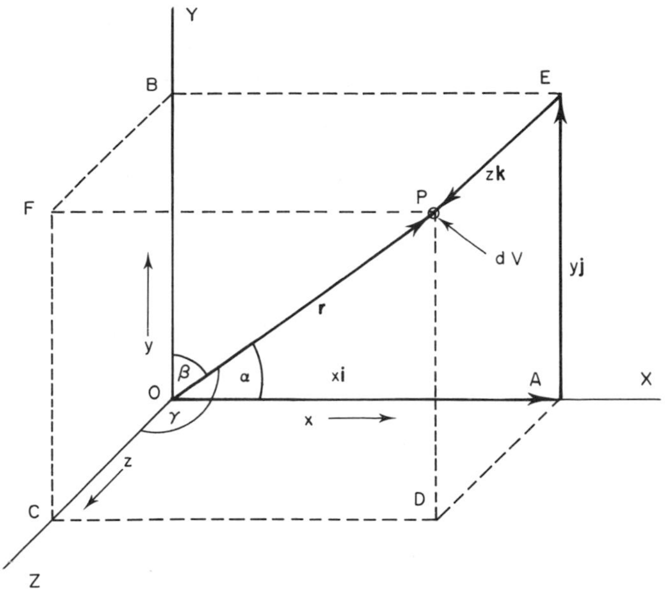

Fig. 4. *The Position Vector* ***r*** *and the Component Vectors* **zk**; **yj**; **xi**.

The projections OA, OB, OC of $\overrightarrow{OP} = \boldsymbol{r}$ on the coordinate axes have lengths x, y, z, respectively. The three numbers x, y, z are the *Cartesian coordinates* of dV; they may also be regarded as the *Cartesian components* of the vector $\boldsymbol{r}$. The magnitude of the component of the vector $\boldsymbol{r}$ along any axis with which it makes an angle θ is, for $\theta < 180°$, equal to $r \cos \theta$. In Fig. 4 for example, we have

$$x = r \cos \alpha; \qquad y = r \cos \beta; \qquad z = r \cos \gamma$$

The three numbers $\cos \alpha$; $\cos \beta$; $\cos \gamma$ are the *direction cosines* of the vector $\boldsymbol{r}$: they play an important part in the transformation laws for vectors. These are the laws that determine the components of a vector in an arbitrary set of Cartesian coordinates.

The magnitude r of the position vector $\boldsymbol{r}$ is related to the magnitude of its components by the equation

$$r^2 = x^2 + y^2 + z^2 \tag{3.4}$$

To specify $\boldsymbol{r}$ more completely we must give the orientation in space of the coordinate axes OX, OZ, OY. If we suppose that some "ultimate" coordinate system exists, with respect to which all orientations in space may be expressed, then we can describe the orientation of the x-axis OX through a characteristic unit vector $\boldsymbol{i}$: this is a vector having the same direction as OX

but of unit magnitude. Any other vector parallel to OX and pointing in the same direction OX can be expressed as a multiple $k\boldsymbol{i}$ of the unit vector $\boldsymbol{i}$. The x-component of the position vector $\boldsymbol{r}$ then serves to define a *component vector* $x\boldsymbol{i}$ of $\boldsymbol{r}$. We can obtain the other component vectors $y\boldsymbol{j}$ and $z\boldsymbol{k}$ in the same manner. The three unit vectors $\boldsymbol{i}, \boldsymbol{j}, \boldsymbol{k}$ characterise the orientation in space of the Cartesian coordinate system and are mutually perpendicular. The three unit vectors, together with the three components x, y, z make it possible to write an equation for $\boldsymbol{r}$ of the form

$$\boldsymbol{r} = x\boldsymbol{i} + y\boldsymbol{j} + z\boldsymbol{k} \tag{3.5}$$

This equation is obtained by applying the parallelogram rule for the addition of vectors.

In general the volume element dV will not be stationary at $\boldsymbol{r}$ and we may wish to state its instantaneous velocity and acceleration. Both these quantities are represented by vectors.

B. Displacement, Velocity and Acceleration Vectors

Suppose a particle undergoes a displacement from a point P to a point Q as in Fig. 5. This displacement is a vector $\boldsymbol{d} = \overrightarrow{PQ}$. The position vector changes

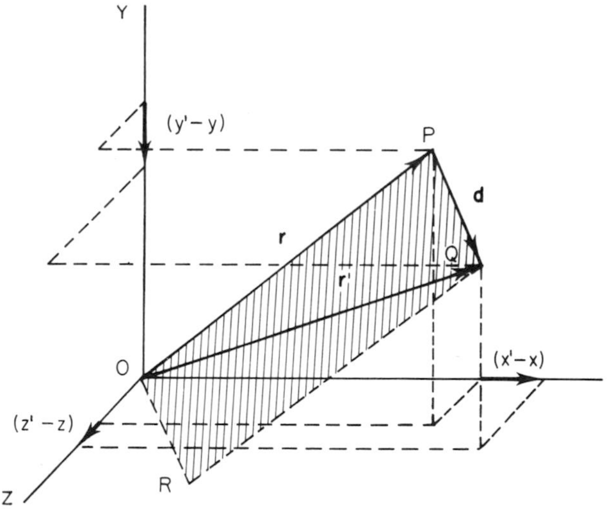

Fig. 5. *The Displacement Vector* **d** *and its Relationship to the Position Vectors* **r** *and* **r**′.

from $\boldsymbol{r}(x, y, z)$ to $\boldsymbol{r}'(x', y', z')$ as a result of the displacement $\boldsymbol{d}$. The displacement vector $\boldsymbol{d}$ has components $(x' - x, y' - y, z' - z)$ and is obtained by vector subtraction of $\boldsymbol{r}$ from $\boldsymbol{r}'$

$$\boldsymbol{d} = \boldsymbol{r}' - \boldsymbol{r} \tag{3.6}$$

Expressed differently, the new position vector $\boldsymbol{r}' = \overrightarrow{OQ}$ is obtained by vector addition of $\boldsymbol{r} = \overrightarrow{OP}$ and $\boldsymbol{d} = \overrightarrow{PQ}$

$$\overrightarrow{OQ} = \overrightarrow{OP} + \overrightarrow{PQ} \quad \text{or} \quad \boldsymbol{r}' = \boldsymbol{r} + \boldsymbol{d} \tag{3.7}$$

This is again the parallelogram rule for the addition of vectors: OQ is the diagonal of the parallelogram $OPQR$ in Fig. 5. An infinitesimal displacement from point P would have the components dx, dy, dz and could be represented in magnitude and direction by an infinitesimal change $d\boldsymbol{r}$ in the position vector $\boldsymbol{r}$. The velocity vector $\boldsymbol{u}$ of the particle is

$$\boldsymbol{u} = \frac{d\boldsymbol{r}}{dt} \tag{3.8}$$

and has components dx/dt, dy/dt, dz/dt or u_x, u_y, u_z. The acceleration vector $\boldsymbol{a}$ is

$$\boldsymbol{a} = \frac{d\boldsymbol{u}}{dt} = \frac{d^2\boldsymbol{r}}{dt^2} \tag{3.9}$$

and has components d^2x/dt^2; d^2y/dt^2; d^2z/dt^2 or a_x, a_y, a_z.

The velocity $\boldsymbol{u}$ within a fluid may change from point to point and we are often interested in the rate at which the fluid flows through some reference plane in the fluid. The rate of flow of fluid through an infinitesimal area element dA of the reference plane will depend on the magnitude of dA and on its orientation. This leads to a consideration of the *area vector* $d\boldsymbol{A}$.

C. Area Vectors

An infinitesimal surface element dA, small enough to be regarded as a plane area, can be represented by a vector: the area vector $d\boldsymbol{A}$ has magnitude dA and is oriented perpendicular to the surface. We adopt the convention that a positive area vector $d\boldsymbol{A}$ is directed along the *outward* normal to the surface enclosing an element of volume. The component of $d\boldsymbol{A}$ in any direction is equal in magnitude to the area occupied by the projection of dA on a plane normal to the direction.

We can now discuss the *flux vectors* that are used to calculate the rates of flow of quantities within a continuum.

D. Flux Vectors

The velocity $\boldsymbol{u}$ with which a fluid moves determines the rate at which the fluid passes through a reference plane in the fluid. It also determines the rate of convective transport across this reference plane of certain extensive properties of the fluid such as mass and volume.

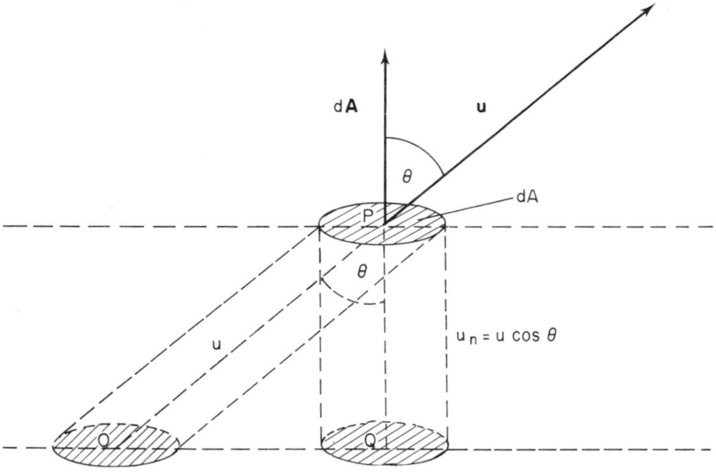

Fig. 6. *The Calculation of the Volume Flux through an Area Element or Surface Element dA.*

Figure 6 shows an infinitesimal area element dA surrounding a point P at which the velocity of the fluid is $\boldsymbol{u}$; dA is so small that $\boldsymbol{u}$ remains constant over dA. The orientation and magnitude of the area element is given by the area vector $d\boldsymbol{A}$. The velocity vector $\boldsymbol{u}$ makes an angle θ with the area vector. The volume of fluid that passes through dA in unit time is contained within the cylinder OP in Fig. 6; this cylinder has axial length $OP = u$, where u is the magnitude of $\boldsymbol{u}$, and base area dA. Its volume is the product (base area × height) and is equal to ($u\,dA \cos\theta$). The *scalar product* $\boldsymbol{u} \cdot d\boldsymbol{A}$ of the vectors $\boldsymbol{u}$ and $d\boldsymbol{A}$ is by definition

$$\boldsymbol{u} \cdot d\boldsymbol{A} = u\,dA \cos\theta \tag{3.10}$$

in which θ is the angle between the two vectors. This particular scalar product gives the volume of fluid that passes through dA in unit time. The corresponding rate of volume flow per unit area at point P is simply $u \cos\theta$: this is the *volume flux* of fluid at point P. Since the velocity vector $\boldsymbol{u}$ can be used in this way to calculate the local volume flux through a reference plane at an angle θ to the vector $\boldsymbol{u}$, it is also known as the convective *volume flux vector*.

If the fluid has mass density ρ, the cylinder in Fig. 5 contains a total mass $\rho u\,dA \cos\theta$ of fluid. The mass of fluid passing through dA in unit time is given by the scalar product

$$\rho\boldsymbol{u} \cdot d\boldsymbol{A} = \rho u\,dA \cos\theta \tag{3.11}$$

The local *mass flux* is then $\rho u \cos\theta$ and we may regard the new vector $\rho\boldsymbol{u}$ as the convective *mass flux vector*. If the symbol $\hat{X}$ represents a scalar property per unit mass of fluid (a specific scalar property) then the vector $\rho\hat{X}\boldsymbol{u}$ is the *convective flux vector* for the transport of this scalar property with the fluid flow. As an example, $\hat{X}$ could be the specific internal energy $\hat{U}$ of the fluid.

The scalar product of two vectors can have a different significance: when a force $\boldsymbol{F}$ acts on a body and displaces it an infinitesimal distance $d\boldsymbol{r}$ the *work done* by the force is defined as the scalar product

$$\boldsymbol{F} \cdot d\boldsymbol{r} = F\, dr \cos\theta = F \cos\theta \cdot dr \tag{3.12}$$

This is the product of the component of the force $\boldsymbol{F}$ in the direction of displacement and the magnitude dr of the displacement.

A charged particle in a nonuniform scalar field of electric potential $\psi(\boldsymbol{r})$ behaves as if it were under the influence of an electrostatic field of force $E(\boldsymbol{r})$: work must be done to move the particle against the electrostatic field. The relationships between vectorial forces and nonuniform scalar fields will become clearer if we now discuss the *gradient vector* of a scalar field.

E. Gradient Vectors

A scalar field such as a temperature field is not often completely uniform. At any given point in space there will normally be one unique direction in which the value of the field quantity changes most rapidly with distance. The magnitude of this maximum rate of change of the field quantity with distance, together with the direction, defines a new vector: this is the gradient vector of the scalar field and, for a temperature field $T(\boldsymbol{r})$, can be written as grad T. The components of this vector are $\partial T/\partial x$, $\partial T/\partial y$, $\partial T/\partial z$

$$\text{grad } T = \boldsymbol{i}\frac{\partial T}{\partial x} + \boldsymbol{j}\frac{\partial T}{\partial y} + \boldsymbol{k}\frac{\partial T}{\partial z} \tag{3.13}$$

An alternative notation regards the right-hand side of Eqn (3.13) as the result of the action of the *vector differential operator* ∇ (del)

$$\nabla \equiv \boldsymbol{i}\frac{\partial}{\partial x} + \boldsymbol{j}\frac{\partial}{\partial y} + \boldsymbol{k}\frac{\partial}{\partial z} \tag{3.14}$$

on the scalar field quantity $T(\boldsymbol{r})$.

$$\text{grad } T = \nabla T \tag{3.15}$$

The heat flux vector $\boldsymbol{q}$ has components q_x, q_y, q_z and we have seen in Chapter 1 that Fourier's law has the form

$$\left.\begin{aligned} q_x &= -K\frac{\partial T}{\partial x} \\ q_y &= -K\frac{\partial T}{\partial y} \\ q_z &= -K\frac{\partial T}{\partial z} \end{aligned}\right\} \tag{3.16}$$

or, in vector form

$$\mathbf{q} = -K \text{ grad } T = -K\nabla T \tag{3.17}$$

The vector form (3.17) of Fourier's law for heat conduction in an isotropic continuous medium provides a compact summary of Eqns (3.16).

Equation (3.17) is independent of the choice of coordinate system, in contrast to Eqns (3.16) which hold only for Cartesian coordinates. There are certain conditions under which the gradient vector defines a force and the scalar field quantity is the *potential* for the force. The gravitational potential energy of a solid body, for example, is determined by the amount of work that has been done in raising the body against the force of gravity. The electric potential ψ at a point in space is determined by the amount of work that is done in bringing a unit positive charge to that point against the electrostatic field of force $E(\mathbf{r})$. These examples can be generalised by discussing in more detail the work done against a force.

The work done by the force when a mechanical force $\mathbf{F}$ displaces a body an infinitesimal distance $d\mathbf{r}$, can be expressed as the sum of the scalar products of the components of $\mathbf{F}$ and $d\mathbf{r}$

$$\mathbf{F} \cdot d\mathbf{r} = F_x\, dx + F_y\, dy + F_z\, dz \tag{3.18}$$

The total work done during a sequence of infinitesimal displacements leading from a point P to a point Q is

$$W = \int_P^Q \mathbf{F} \cdot d\mathbf{r} \tag{3.19}$$

The integral in Eqn (3.19) is a *line integral* following the path from P to Q and its value generally depends on the path taken; if the path is reversed in detail each $d\mathbf{r}$ changes sign and so does the integral. When the work done in moving the particle from P to Q is *independent* of the detailed nature of the path followed, then $\mathbf{F}$ is described as a *conservative force;* no net work is done in taking the particle around a closed path which returns it to its starting point, i.e.

$$\oint \mathbf{F} \cdot d\mathbf{r} = 0 \tag{3.20}$$

In this situation it is possible to introduce a potential ψ for the force $\mathbf{F}$: ψ has the property that

$$\int_P^Q \mathbf{F} \cdot d\mathbf{r} = -\int_P^Q d\psi = \psi_P - \psi_Q \tag{3.21}$$

which is equivalent to saying that both $\mathbf{F} \cdot d\mathbf{r}$ and $d\psi$ must be exact differentials, or total differentials. The total differential $d\psi$ of the potential $\psi(\mathbf{r})$

is (Kynch, 1955)

$$d\psi = \frac{\partial \psi}{\partial x} dx + \frac{\partial \psi}{\partial y} dy + \frac{\partial \psi}{\partial z} dz \tag{3.22}$$

A comparison of Eqns (3.18) and (3.22) implies that the components of $\boldsymbol{F}$ are in this instance

$$F_x = -\frac{\partial \psi}{\partial x}; \qquad F_y = -\frac{\partial \psi}{\partial y}; \qquad F_z = -\frac{\partial \psi}{\partial z} \tag{3.23}$$

but these are the components of the gradient vector grad ψ and so

$$\boldsymbol{F} = -\text{grad}\ \psi = -\nabla\psi \tag{3.24}$$

Equation (3.24) is generally applicable to conservative fields of force. The minus sign in Eqns (3.21), (3.23), and (3.24) is a convention which ensures that a positive force is directed *down* the potential gradient. A movement *up* the potential gradient means that work must be done *against* the force $\boldsymbol{F}$ which is associated with the potential gradient grad ψ.

The transport processes induced by the gradient vectors lead to local variations of the field quantities with time. It is necessary to consider the different time derivatives that may be used.

III. THE TIME DERIVATIVES

A. The Total Time Derivative

The local concentration c, for example, may depend both on position $\boldsymbol{r}$ and on time t, i.e.

$$c = c(\boldsymbol{r}, t) = c(x, y, z, t) \tag{3.25}$$

The total differential dc is (Kynch, 1955)

$$dc = \left(\frac{\partial c}{\partial t}\right)_{x,y,z} dt + \left(\frac{\partial c}{\partial x}\right)_{y,z,t} dx + \left(\frac{\partial c}{\partial y}\right)_{x,z,t} dy + \left(\frac{\partial c}{\partial z}\right)_{x,y,t} dz \tag{3.26}$$

in which the subscripts indicate the variables held constant during the partial differentiations: from now on these subscripts will be dropped. The *total time derivative* dc/dt is

$$\frac{dc}{dt} = \frac{\partial c}{\partial t} + \left(\frac{\partial c}{\partial x}\right)\frac{dx}{dt} + \left(\frac{\partial c}{\partial y}\right)\frac{dy}{dt} + \left(\frac{\partial c}{\partial z}\right)\frac{dz}{dt} \tag{3.27}$$

dc/dt is the time rate of change of concentration within a reference volume element dV that is moving or "scanning" the fluid with a velocity $\boldsymbol{v}$, the components of which are dx/dt, dy/dt, dz/dt.

B. The Convected Time Derivative

When the "scanning velocity" $\boldsymbol{v}$ is the local fluid velocity $\boldsymbol{u}$ we obtain the time derivative "following the motion"; the volume element dV is a moving element of the fluid. This time derivative is also known as the *substantial time derivative* and will be written as d/dt. If the components of $\boldsymbol{u}$ are u_x, u_y, u_z then

$$\frac{dc}{dt} = \frac{\partial c}{\partial t} + \left(\frac{\partial c}{\partial x}\right)u_x + \left(\frac{\partial c}{\partial y}\right)u_y + \left(\frac{\partial c}{\partial z}\right)u_z \tag{3.28}$$

The term "convected time derivative" is preferable because of the implication that the time derivative is taken "following the motion" or convection of a volume element. However, the term "barycentric time derivative" is also used.

C. The Partial Time Derivative

If the "scanning-region" dV is stationary, the time rate of change within dV is given by the *partial time derivative*

$$\frac{\partial c}{\partial t} = \left(\frac{\partial c}{\partial t}\right)_{x,y,z} \tag{3.29}$$

This is the rate of change at a given point in the system.

D. The Relation Between the Time Derivatives

In Eqn (3.28) the components u_x, u_y, u_z of the velocity vector $\boldsymbol{u}$ are multiplied by the corresponding components $\partial c/\partial x$, $\partial c/\partial y$, $\partial c/\partial z$ of the gradient vector ∇c. A comparison with Eqn (3.18) shows that we can write Eqn (3.28) in terms of the scalar product $\boldsymbol{u} \cdot \nabla c$

$$\frac{dc}{dt} = \frac{\partial c}{\partial t} + \boldsymbol{u} \cdot \text{grad } c = \frac{\partial c}{\partial t} + \boldsymbol{u} \cdot \nabla c \tag{3.30}$$

This is a specific example of the very general relationship

$$\frac{d}{dt} = \frac{\partial}{\partial t} + \boldsymbol{u} \cdot \text{grad} = \frac{\partial}{\partial t} + \boldsymbol{u} \cdot \nabla \tag{3.31}$$

between the two time derivatives d/dt and $\partial/\partial t$. This relationship is important in the development of the phenomenological theories. Before we proceed to a discussion of the equations of conservation for continuous systems, it will be useful to present a brief discussion of tensors and an alternative tensor notation for the field variables.

IV. TENSORS

In a given set of rectangular Cartesian coordinates, a tensor quantity is defined by an ordered array of scalar components or numbers. For each type of tensor quantity a definite transformation law exists whereby the values of the scalar components may be calculated for any other system of Cartesian coordinates. The definition of a tensor in general implies the existence of a set of coordinates and of a transformation law. The higher the order of a tensor the greater is the number of scalar components necessary to define it and the more complex is the transformation law (Jeffreys, 1965).

The simplest tensor quantity, which is uniquely determined in all coordinate systems by the magnitude of a single scalar "component" and which has as its transformation law the law of invariance in transformation, is a *scalar*. The temperature T in a fluid is determined by the magnitude of the single scalar component in the array

$$T = (T_i) \cdots i = 1 \tag{3.32}$$

This is a tensor of *zero order*.

A *first order* tensor is defined in rectangular Cartesian coordinates by an ordered array of *three* scalar components which obey the transformation laws for the components of a *vector*. The velocity vector

$$\boldsymbol{u} = (u_1 \quad u_2 \quad u_3) = (u_i) \cdots i = 1, 2, 3 \tag{3.33}$$

is a first order tensor.

It is possible to construct a tensor quantity known as the *dyadic product* $\boldsymbol{uv}$ of two vectors $\boldsymbol{u}$ and $\boldsymbol{v}$. This product is defined in a given set of rectangular Cartesian coordinates by the square array of *nine* scalar components

$$\boldsymbol{uv} = \begin{pmatrix} u_1v_1 & u_1v_2 & u_1v_3 \\ u_2v_1 & u_2v_2 & u_2v_3 \\ u_3v_1 & u_3v_2 & u_3v_3 \end{pmatrix} \tag{3.34}$$

or

$$\boldsymbol{uv} = (u_iv_j) \qquad i, j = 1, 2, 3 \tag{3.35}$$

This dyadic product is a *second order* tensor.

In Chapter 5 we meet the *stress tensor* $\boldsymbol{\sigma}$ and the convective "momentum flux" $\rho\boldsymbol{uu}$, both of which are second order tensors. In anisotropic systems diffusion processes can no longer be described by a single scalar diffusion coefficient D: it is necessary to use a diffusivity tensor $\boldsymbol{D} = (D_{ij})\ i, j = 1, 2, 3$ to account for differences in the ease of diffusion in different directions.

V. AN ALTERNATIVE TENSOR NOTATION

The three coordinate axes X, Y, and Z are represented in that order by the three numbers 1, 2, and 3. The scalar components $(x; y; z)$ of the position vector $\boldsymbol{r}$ are written as $(x_1; x_2; x_3)$. The scalar components $(u_x; u_y; u_z)$ of the velocity vector $\boldsymbol{u}$ are written as $(u_1; u_2; u_3)$ i.e. the subscripts 1, 2, and 3 replace the subscripts x, y, and z. The three unit vectors $\boldsymbol{i}, \boldsymbol{j}$, and $\boldsymbol{k}$ are written, in that order, as $\boldsymbol{\delta}_1, \boldsymbol{\delta}_2$, and $\boldsymbol{\delta}_3$. Since $\boldsymbol{\delta}_1, \boldsymbol{\delta}_2$, and $\boldsymbol{\delta}_3$ are mutually orthogonal or mutually perpendicular vectors of unit magnitude their scalar products are

$$\boldsymbol{\delta}_1\boldsymbol{\delta}_1 = \boldsymbol{\delta}_2\boldsymbol{\delta}_2 = \boldsymbol{\delta}_3\boldsymbol{\delta}_3 = 1 \tag{3.36}$$

$$\boldsymbol{\delta}_1\boldsymbol{\delta}_2 = \boldsymbol{\delta}_2\boldsymbol{\delta}_3 = \boldsymbol{\delta}_3\boldsymbol{\delta}_1 = 0 \tag{3.37}$$

These relations may be summarised concisely as

$$\boldsymbol{\delta}_i\boldsymbol{\delta}_j = \delta_{ij} \tag{3.38}$$

in which the Kronecker delta δ_{ij} satisfies the conditions

$$\begin{aligned} \delta_{ij} &= 1 \quad \text{if} \quad i = j \\ \delta_{ij} &= 0 \quad \text{if} \quad i \neq j \end{aligned} \tag{3.39}$$

We may now write the following explicit expressions for the more important field quantities (Bird *et al.*, 1964), which will be needed in later chapters.

(1) *A vector* $\boldsymbol{u}$

$$\boldsymbol{u} = \sum_{i=1}^{i=3} \boldsymbol{\delta}_i u_i \tag{3.40}$$

(2) *The sum of two vectors*

$$\boldsymbol{u} + \boldsymbol{v} = \sum_{i=1}^{3} \boldsymbol{\delta}_i(u_i + v_i) \tag{3.41}$$

(3) *Multiplication of a vector by a scalar*

$$k\boldsymbol{u} = k\sum_{i=1}^{3} \boldsymbol{\delta}_i u_i = \sum_{i=1}^{3} \boldsymbol{\delta}_i(ku_i) \tag{3.42}$$

(4) *Scalar product of two vectors*

$$\begin{aligned} \boldsymbol{u} \cdot \boldsymbol{v} &= \left(\sum_i \boldsymbol{\delta}_i u_i\right) \cdot \left(\sum_j \boldsymbol{\delta}_j v_j\right) \\ &= \sum_i \sum_j (\boldsymbol{\delta}_i \cdot \boldsymbol{\delta}_j) u_i v_j \\ &= \sum_i \sum_j \delta_{ij} u_i v_j \\ &= \sum_i u_i v_i \end{aligned} \tag{3.43}$$

(5) *The vector differential operator* ∇

$$\nabla = \sum_i \boldsymbol{\delta}_i \frac{\partial}{\partial x_i} \tag{3.44}$$

(6) *The gradient of a scalar field*

$$\text{grad } T = \nabla T = \sum_i \boldsymbol{\delta}_i \frac{\partial T}{\partial x_i} \tag{3.45}$$

(7) *The divergence of a vector field*

$$\begin{aligned}
\text{div } \boldsymbol{u} = \nabla \cdot \boldsymbol{u} &= \left(\sum_i \boldsymbol{\delta}_i \frac{\partial}{\partial x_i}\right) \cdot \left(\sum_j \boldsymbol{\delta}_j u_j\right) \\
&= \sum_i \sum_j (\boldsymbol{\delta}_i \cdot \boldsymbol{\delta}_j) \frac{\partial}{\partial x_i} u_j \\
&= \sum_i \sum_j \delta_{ij} \frac{\partial}{\partial x_i} u_j \\
&= \sum_i \frac{\partial u_i}{\partial x_i}
\end{aligned} \tag{3.46}$$

(8) *The Laplacian of a scalar field*

If we take the divergence of the gradient of a scalar field we obtain the *Laplacian* of that field, i.e.

$$\begin{aligned}
\text{div } (\textit{grad } T) &= \nabla \cdot \nabla T \\
&= \left(\sum_i \boldsymbol{\delta}_i \frac{\partial}{\partial x_i}\right) \cdot \left(\sum_j \boldsymbol{\delta}_j \frac{\partial T}{\partial x_j}\right) \\
&= \sum_i \sum_j \delta_{ij} \frac{\partial}{\partial x_i}\left(\frac{\partial T}{\partial x_j}\right) \\
&= \sum_i \frac{\partial^2 T}{\partial x_i^2}
\end{aligned} \tag{3.47}$$

Equation (3.47) can be regarded as arising from the action of the *Laplacian operator* ∇^2

$$\nabla^2 = \frac{\partial^2}{\partial x_1^2} + \frac{\partial^2}{\partial x_2^2} + \frac{\partial^2}{\partial x_3^2} \tag{3.48}$$

on the scalar T, i.e.

$$\text{div (grad } T) = \nabla \cdot \nabla T = \nabla^2 T = \sum_i \frac{\partial^2 T}{\partial x_i^2} \tag{3.49}$$

(9) *The Laplacian of a vector field*

In rectangular Cartesian coordinates but not in curvilinear coordinates

$$\nabla^2 \boldsymbol{u} = \nabla^2\left(\sum_i \boldsymbol{\delta}_i u_i\right) = \sum_i \boldsymbol{\delta}_i \nabla^2 u_i$$

$$= \boldsymbol{\delta}_1 \nabla^2 u_1 + \boldsymbol{\delta}_2 \nabla^2 u_2 + \boldsymbol{\delta}_3 \nabla^2 u_3 \qquad (3.50)$$

(10) *The convected time derivative of a scalar field*

$$\frac{dT}{dt} = \frac{\partial T}{\partial t} + (\boldsymbol{u} \cdot \nabla)T = \frac{\partial T}{\partial t} + \boldsymbol{u} \cdot \nabla T$$

$$= \frac{\partial T}{\partial t} + \sum_i u_i \frac{\partial T}{\partial x_i} \qquad (3.51)$$

(11) *The convected time derivative of a vector field*

$$\frac{d\boldsymbol{u}}{dt} = \frac{\partial \boldsymbol{u}}{\partial t} + (\boldsymbol{u} \cdot \nabla)\boldsymbol{u}$$

$$= \sum_i \boldsymbol{\delta}_i\left(\frac{\partial u_i}{\partial t} + (\boldsymbol{u} \cdot \nabla)u_i\right)$$

$$= \sum_i \boldsymbol{\delta}_i\left(\frac{\partial u_i}{\partial t} + \boldsymbol{u} \cdot \nabla u_i\right) \qquad (3.52)$$

The tensor notation shows explicitly the structure of the more complex field variables. Equation (3.52) is not valid in curvilinear coordinates.

REFERENCES

Bird, R. B., Stewart, W. E. and Lightfoot, E. N. (1964). "Transport Phenomena." John Wiley and Sons, London; Toppan Company Ltd., Tokyo.

Glauert, M. B. (1960). "Principles of Dynamics." (Library of Mathematics) Routledge and Kegan Paul, London.

Hilton, P. J. (1958). "Differential Calculus." (Library of Mathematics) Routledge and Kegan Paul, London.

Hilton, P. J. (1960). "Partial Derivatives." (Library of Mathematics) Routledge and Kegan Paul, London.

Jeffreys, H. (1965). "Cartesian Tensors." Cambridge University Press.

Kynch, G. J. (1955). "Mathematics for the Chemist." Butterworths, London.

Ledermann, W. (1964). "Integral Calculus." (Library of Mathematics) Routledge and Kegan Paul, London.

Ledermann, W. (1966). "Multiple Integrals." (Library of Mathematics) Routledge and Kegan Paul, London.

Margenau, H. and Murphy, G. M. (1956). "Mathematics of Physics and Chemistry." (2nd. Edn.) Van Nostrand, New York.

Chapter 4 Conservation Equations for Continuous Systems

I. THE BEHAVIOUR OF A FINITE VOLUME V

The mathematical solution of many problems requires the statement of the appropriate equations of conservation.

For continuous systems it is necessary to derive local equations of conservation that are applicable at any point in the system.

Such an equation relates the local rate of change (per unit volume) of the property of interest to the contributions made by the local transport processes and by the local generation or by the local removal of the property of interest.

One begins by considering the behaviour of a finite, arbitrary reference volume V of the system. The local equation of conservation is obtained by examining the behaviour in the limit as the reference volume V shrinks around the point of interest.

The mathematical formalism is rather complex, but the basic ideas are quite simple.

A. The Rate of Change of an Extensive Property X

Let X be an arbitrary extensive property of the system and let $\hat{X}$ be the amount of X per unit mass. Both X and $\hat{X}$ are scalars.

An infinitesimal volume element dV, if it has density ρ, will have mass $\rho\, dV$ and be associated with an amount $\rho\hat{X}\, dV$ of X. $\rho\hat{X}$ is the average density of X within dV.

A macroscopic volume V of the system will contain a total amount

$$X = \int_V \rho\hat{X}\, dV \tag{4.1}$$

of X. *If* the system is *homogeneous* the mass density ρ is everywhere uniform and

$$X = (\rho\hat{X})V \tag{4.2}$$

The total amount of X is now proportional to the total volume V of the system, as is required for any extensive property of the volume V.

If the system is not homogeneous, the total amount of X associated with the volume V need no longer be proportional to V.

If the volume V is stationary in an external coordinate system, the rate of change of X may be written as

$$\frac{dX}{dt} = \int_V \frac{\partial(\rho\hat{X})}{\partial t}\, dV \tag{4.3}$$

B. The Transport of an Extensive Property X

Let $\boldsymbol{J}_X$ be the total flux of X at any point, with respect to a stationary external coordinate system.

If $d\boldsymbol{A}$ is the area vector for an arbitrary surface element of the volume V, the scalar product $\boldsymbol{J}_X \cdot d\boldsymbol{A}$ is the rate of *loss* of X from the volume V, through the surface element dA because of the transport processes.

The total rate of loss of X by transport processes is

$$-\left(\frac{dX}{dt}\right)_{\mathrm{tr}} = \int_A \boldsymbol{J}_X \cdot d\boldsymbol{A} \tag{4.4}$$

The local rate of loss of X per unit volume at any point, through transport processes, is given by a limiting process in which V shrinks around the point in question

$$\lim_{V\to 0} \left\{\frac{1}{V}\int_A \boldsymbol{J}_X \cdot d\boldsymbol{A}\right\} \equiv \mathrm{div}\,(\boldsymbol{J}_X) \tag{4.5}$$

Equation (4.5) defines a new function div $\boldsymbol{J}_X$, the divergence of the flux vector $\boldsymbol{J}_X$.

The divergence of the flux vector (div $\boldsymbol{J}_X$) gives the scalar rate of *loss* of X per unit volume at any point as a consequence of the flux $\boldsymbol{J}_X$. The simple derivation in Chapter 1 of Fick's second law of diffusion introduced the conservation equation

$$\frac{\partial \rho_i}{\partial t} = -\frac{\partial j_{ix}}{\partial x} \tag{4.6}$$

in which $\partial\rho_i/\partial t$ is the local rate of increase of the mass of species i per unit volume as a consequence of the diffusion flux of this component along the x-axis; $\partial j_{ix}/\partial x$ is in fact the divergence of the diffusion flux vector j_{ix} for this unidimensional diffusion process. In a more general three-dimensional case the divergence takes the form

$$\mathrm{div}\,\boldsymbol{j}_i = \frac{\partial j_{ix}}{\partial x} + \frac{\partial j_{iy}}{\partial y} + \frac{\partial j_{iz}}{\partial z} \tag{4.7}$$

where j_{ix}; j_{iy}; j_{iz} are the scalar components of the diffusion flux vector $\boldsymbol{j}_i$.

Equation (4.7) has the form of a scalar product $\nabla \cdot \boldsymbol{j}_i$ of the vector differential operator ∇ with the flux vector $\boldsymbol{j}_i$

$$\operatorname{div} \boldsymbol{j}_i = \nabla \cdot j_i \tag{4.8}$$

The use of the point function $\operatorname{div} \boldsymbol{j}_i$ or $\operatorname{div} \boldsymbol{J}_X$ is a part of the continuum approximation. Within this approximation the rate of loss of X from an infinitesimal volume dV is $(\operatorname{div} \boldsymbol{J}_X)\, dV$.

For the volume V it can be shown that

$$-\left(\frac{dX}{dt}\right)_{\text{tr}} = \int_A \boldsymbol{J}_X \cdot d\boldsymbol{A} = \int_V (\operatorname{div} \boldsymbol{J}_X)\, dV \tag{4.9}$$

Equation (4.9) expresses a relationship between a *surface integral* and a *volume integral* and is a statement of Gauss's divergence theorem. This theorem is often used to replace a surface integral by a volume integral in a mathematical expression.

C. The Local Production of an Extensive Quantity

If ϕ_X is the local rate of production of X per unit volume, then $\phi_X\, dV$ is the rate of production of X within dV.

For the volume V

$$\left(\frac{dX}{dt}\right)_{\text{pr}} = \int_V \phi_X\, dV \tag{4.10}$$

D. The Equation of Conservation for the Volume V

If the quantity of X for the volume V may change only by the two processes transport and "production," then

$$\int_V \frac{\partial(\rho \hat{X})}{\partial t}\, dV = \int_V \phi_x\, dV - \int_V \operatorname{div} \boldsymbol{J}_x\, dV \tag{4.11}$$

so that

$$\int_V \left[\frac{\partial(\rho \hat{X})}{\partial t} + \operatorname{div} \boldsymbol{J}_X - \phi_X\right] dV = 0 \tag{4.12}$$

II. THE LOCAL EQUATION OF CONSERVATION

Equation (4.12) is to be valid for an arbitrary volume V and so the integrand itself must vanish

$$\frac{\partial(\rho \hat{X})}{\partial t} + \operatorname{div} \boldsymbol{J}_X - \phi_X = 0 \tag{4.13}$$

Equation (4.13) is a balance equation for the local rate of change of the density of X in the system. It is the general equation of conservation for an arbitrary scalar extensive property X of a continuous system.

The *total flux vector* $\boldsymbol{J}_X$ may include a contribution from the bulk flow of the system. The convective flux vector for this convective transport of X is the vector $(\rho\hat{X})\boldsymbol{u}$.

A new flux vector $\boldsymbol{j}_X$ may be defined by

$$\boldsymbol{j}_X \equiv \boldsymbol{J}_X - (\rho\hat{X})\boldsymbol{u} \tag{4.14}$$

$\boldsymbol{j}_X$ is a vector which expresses the rate of transport of X with respect to the local centre of mass of a volume element, i.e. after correction for transport by convection.

From Eqn (4.14)

$$\text{div}\,\boldsymbol{J}_X = \text{div}\,\boldsymbol{j}_X + \text{div}\,(\rho\hat{X})\boldsymbol{u} \tag{4.15}$$

From the properties of the divergence

$$\text{div}\,\boldsymbol{J}_X = \text{div}\,\boldsymbol{j}_X + \rho\hat{X}\,\text{div}\,\boldsymbol{u} + \boldsymbol{u}\cdot \mathit{grad}(\rho\hat{X}) \tag{4.16}$$

Substituting for div $\boldsymbol{J}_X$ in Eqn (4.13), and using Eqn (3.31) we obtain the result.

$$\frac{d(\rho\hat{X})}{dt} + \text{div}\,\boldsymbol{j}_X + (\rho\hat{X})\,\text{div}\,\boldsymbol{u} - \phi_X = 0 \tag{4.17}$$

This is an alternative form of the general equation of conservation (4.13) in terms of the substantial time derivative. $\boldsymbol{j}_X$ can be regarded as a "*diffusion flux*" of the property X, defined with respect to the local centre of mass.

REFERENCES

Bird, R. B., Stewart, W. E. and Lightfoot, E. N. (1964). "Transport Phenomena." John Wiley, London; Toppan Company Ltd., Tokyo.

Fitts, D. D. (1962). "Nonequilibrium Thermodynamics." McGraw-Hill, New York.

Landau, L. and Lifshitz, E. M. (1959). "Fluid Mechanics." Addison–Wesley, Reading.

Love, A. E. H. (1944). "The Mathematical Theory of Elasticity." Dover Publications, New York.

Chapter 5 Systems of a Single Component

We examine briefly the equations of conservation of mass and of linear momentum for a single component system (Bird *et al.*, 1964; Fitts, 1962; Love, 1944; Landau and Lifshitz, 1959), and we do this, without any claim to rigor, in an attempt to bring out some basic principles.

I. CONSERVATION OF MASS

The equation of conservation of mass, also known as the *equation of continuity*, follows readily from the general equation of conservation in the form of Eqn (4.13) or (4.17). We have $\hat{X} = 1, \phi_X = 0, \boldsymbol{J}_X = \rho\boldsymbol{u}$ and $\boldsymbol{j}_X = 0$ so that

$$\frac{\partial\rho}{\partial t} = -\text{div}\,(\rho\boldsymbol{u}) \tag{5.1}$$

and

$$\frac{d\rho}{dt} = -\rho\,\text{div}\,\boldsymbol{u} \tag{5.2}$$

For an incompressible fluid of constant density ρ

$$\text{div}\,\boldsymbol{u} = \frac{\partial u_x}{\partial x} + \frac{\partial u_y}{\partial y} + \frac{\partial u_z}{\partial z} = 0 \tag{5.3}$$

II. CONSERVATION OF LINEAR MOMENTUM

Newton's second law of motion in the form

$$\boldsymbol{F} = m\boldsymbol{a} \tag{5.4}$$

where $\boldsymbol{a}$ is the acceleration of a point mass m under the action of a force $\boldsymbol{F}$, can be put into the form of an equation of conservation of linear momentum $(m\boldsymbol{u})$. For a constant mass m we have

$$\frac{d(m\boldsymbol{u})}{dt} - \boldsymbol{F} = m\frac{d\boldsymbol{u}}{dt} - \boldsymbol{F} = 0 \tag{5.5}$$

The force $\boldsymbol{F}$ plays the role of a "momentum source" for the point mass m. The application of Newton's second law of motion to the flow of continuous media requires a more complex mathematical formalism because the forces which act on a volume element of a fluid are not so simply described.

A rigorous derivation of the equation of conservation of linear momentum in a fluid can be found in many texts (Fitts, 1962; Love, 1944; Landau and Lifshitz, 1959). For our purposes the following qualitative discussion will suffice.

The linear momentum of a volume element dV (of constant mass density ρ), which is moving with linear velocity $\boldsymbol{u}$ is $(\rho\boldsymbol{u})\, dV$. This volume element is subject to two kinds of forces, *surface forces* and long-range *volume forces*.

A typical long-range volume force is the gravitational force. If the vector X represents a generalised volume force and $\hat{\boldsymbol{X}}$ is the corresponding force per unit mass, the volume force acting on dV may be represented by the vector $(\rho\hat{\boldsymbol{X}})\, dV$.

The surface forces result from the short-range interactions between the molecules of the volume element dV and the molecules of the surrounding fluid. They may be viewed as stresses acting on or across the bounding surfaces of the volume element, and their proper description requires the introduction of the *stress tensor* $\boldsymbol{\sigma}$. The surface force per unit volume acting on a volume element dV is given by the divergence div $\boldsymbol{\sigma}$ of the stress tensor, and is a *vector* quantity. The resultant surface force acting on dV is (div $\boldsymbol{\sigma}$) dV and the total force is $(\text{div}\, \boldsymbol{\sigma} + \rho\hat{\boldsymbol{X}})\, dV$.

This result may be compared with the definition of the divergence div $\boldsymbol{J}_X$ of the flux vector $\boldsymbol{J}_X$ in Eqn (4.5). There div $\boldsymbol{J}_X$ represented the local (*scalar*) rate of loss of the extensive property X per unit volume. Here div $\boldsymbol{\sigma}$ represents the local (*vectorial*) rate of change of linear momentum per unit volume, arising from the stress field in the liquid. Within the continuum approximation used here, the quantity (div $\boldsymbol{\sigma}$) dV represents the vectorial rate of change of linear momentum of the volume element dV as a consequence of the stress field acting on the surfaces of the volume element.

The conservation of linear momentum for the volume element dV is expressed by the equation

$$\left[\rho \frac{d\boldsymbol{u}}{dt} - (\text{div}\, \boldsymbol{\sigma} + \rho\hat{\boldsymbol{X}})\right] dV = 0 \tag{5.6}$$

Since dV is to be arbitrary, we obtain the result

$$\rho \frac{d\boldsymbol{u}}{dt} - (\text{div}\, \boldsymbol{\sigma} + \rho\hat{\boldsymbol{X}}) = 0 \tag{5.7}$$

which is related in form to Eqn (5.5).

If we introduce the acceleration vector $\boldsymbol{a}$ into Eqn (5.7) we obtain the *equation of motion*

$$\rho \boldsymbol{a} - (\operatorname{div} \boldsymbol{\sigma} + \rho \hat{\boldsymbol{X}}) = 0 \tag{5.8}$$

This equation still contains quantities such as div $\boldsymbol{\sigma}$ which remain to be specified in terms of more directly accessible variables such as the velocity gradients in the system.

III. NEWTON'S LAW OF VISCOSITY

The simple presentation of this law in Chapter 1 referred to the unidimensional flow of an isothermal and incompressible fluid of constant shear viscosity η. This *Newtonian fluid* was in steady laminar flow in the x-direction; the x-velocity of the fluid changed as one moved in the y-direction. In this simple situation Newton's law of viscosity took the form (1.2) where σ_{yx} is the shear stress acting in the x-direction on a plane in the fluid which is oriented normal to the y-axis. If the shear stress at a point P on this plane does not act exclusively in the x-direction it may generally be resolved into the three components σ_{yx}, σ_{yy}, σ_{yz}. Consider a volume element in the form of an infinitesimal cube centred on a point P, with surfaces parallel to the x, y, z axes Fig. 7. The combined effect of the surface forces which act on the volume element can be described in terms of the nine stress components σ_{xy}, σ_{yy}, σ_{zy}; σ_{xx}, σ_{yx}, σ_{zx}; σ_{xz}, σ_{yz}, σ_{zz}, which together define the stress tensor $\boldsymbol{\sigma}$. The absence of a torque on the volume element requires $\boldsymbol{\sigma}$ to be a *symmetric tensor*

$$\boldsymbol{\sigma} = \begin{pmatrix} \sigma_{xx} & \sigma_{xy} & \sigma_{xz} \\ \sigma_{yx} & \sigma_{yy} & \sigma_{yz} \\ \sigma_{zx} & \sigma_{zy} & \sigma_{zz} \end{pmatrix} \tag{5.9}$$

in which $\sigma_{xy} = \sigma_{yx}$; $\sigma_{zx} = \sigma_{xz}$; $\sigma_{yz} = \sigma_{zy}$. If $\boldsymbol{\sigma}$ is known at any point P in the fluid then the force acting at a point P on a surface of arbitrary orientation in the fluid may be calculated. The diagonal components σ_{xx}, σ_{yy}, σ_{zz} are known as the *normal stress* components. The remaining components are the *shear stress components*. In a nonequilibrium situation the pressure P in the fluid is defined as (Kay, 1963)

$$P = -\tfrac{1}{3}(\sigma_{xx} + \sigma_{yy} + \sigma_{zz}) \tag{5.10}$$

The negative sign appears because a positive pressure P is regarded as exerting a compressive force on a volume element, but the normal stress components are defined in an opposite sense. They have a positive sign when directed outward from a volume element. Instead of the stress tensor $\boldsymbol{\sigma}$ the

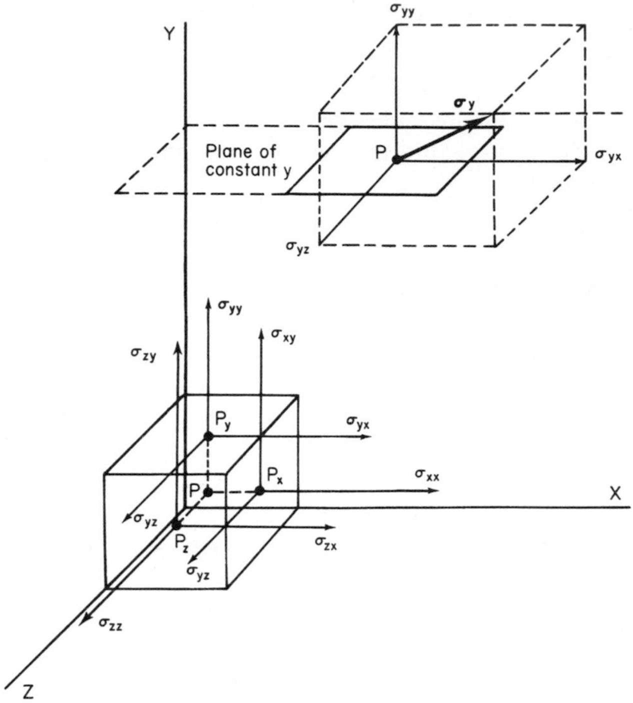

Fig. 7. *The Components* σ_{ij} $(i, j = x, y, z)$ *of the Stress Tensor* $\boldsymbol{\sigma}$.
The stress $\boldsymbol{\sigma}_y$ at a point P on a plane of constant y has stress components σ_{yx}; σ_{yy}; σ_{yz}. The total surface force acting at a point P on a plane of arbitrary orientation in the fluid may be defined in terms of the nine scalar stress components σ_{ij} $(i, j = x, y, z)$ of the stress tensor $\boldsymbol{\sigma}$. These component stresses may be visualised as acting on the surface of an infinitesimal cube surrounding the point P.

pressure tensor **P** may be used (De Groot and Mazur, 1962)

$$\mathbf{P} = \begin{pmatrix} P_{xx} & P_{xy} & P_{xz} \\ P_{yx} & P_{yy} & P_{yz} \\ P_{zx} & P_{zy} & P_{zz} \end{pmatrix} = \begin{pmatrix} -\sigma_{xx} & -\sigma_{xy} & -\sigma_{xz} \\ -\sigma_{yx} & -\sigma_{yy} & -\sigma_{yz} \\ -\sigma_{zx} & -\sigma_{zy} & -\sigma_{zz} \end{pmatrix} \tag{5.11}$$

The shear stresses disappear at equilibrium in a nonelastic fluid and we have also

$$-\sigma_{xx} = -\sigma_{yy} = -\sigma_{zz} = P_{xx} = P_{yy} = P_{zz} = p \tag{5.12}$$

in which p is the equilibrium *hydrostatic pressure*. The equilibrium component of the pressure tensor **P** may be separated out by introducing a viscous component $\boldsymbol{\tau}$ such that

$$\mathbf{P} = \begin{pmatrix} (\tau_{xx} + p) & \tau_{xy} & \tau_{xz} \\ \tau_{yx} & (\tau_{yy} + p) & \tau_{yz} \\ \tau_{zx} & \tau_{zy} & (\tau_{zz} + p) \end{pmatrix} \tag{5.13}$$

The relationships of Eqns. (5.11) and (5.13) are conveniently summarised in tensor notation as

$$\mathbf{P} = -\boldsymbol{\sigma} = (p\mathbf{1} + \boldsymbol{\tau}) \tag{5.14}$$

where $\mathbf{1}$ represents the unit tensor. We may also write Eqn (5.14) in the form

$$P_{ij} = -\sigma_{ij} = (p\delta_{ij} + \tau_{ij}); \qquad i, j = 1, 2, 3 \tag{5.15}$$

in which δ_{ij} is the Kronecker Delta.

The form (5.15) is a more obvious statement of the relationships between the different stresses than is Eqn (5.15) and this particular notation is often helpful.

Newton's Law remains linear in the three-dimensional case but has a much more complex form, i.e. (Condon and Odishaw, 1958)

$$\tau_{ij} = [(\tfrac{2}{3}\eta - \vartheta)\,\mathrm{div}\,\boldsymbol{u}]\delta_{ij} - \eta\left(\frac{\partial u_j}{\partial x_i} + \frac{\partial u_i}{\partial x_j}\right) \qquad i, j = 1, 2, 3 \tag{5.16}$$

η is the coefficient of *shear viscosity* and ϑ is the coefficient of *bulk viscosity*. For an incompressible fluid $\mathrm{div}\,\boldsymbol{u} = 0$ and so Eqn (5.16) becomes simpler. If the shear viscosity η is constant Eqn (5.16) and Eqn (5.15) can then be used to show that

$$\mathrm{div}\,\boldsymbol{\sigma} = \eta\,\nabla^2\boldsymbol{u} - \mathrm{grad}\,p \tag{5.17}$$

(cf. Chapter 4).

The equation of motion (5.8) for a system subject to the gravitational force vector $\boldsymbol{g}$ now becomes

$$\rho\boldsymbol{a} - \eta\,\nabla^2\boldsymbol{u} + \mathrm{grad}\,p - \rho\boldsymbol{g} = 0 \tag{5.18}$$

which is the *Navier-Stokes Equation* for the motion of an isothermal incompressible fluid of constant shear viscosity η.

If there are no viscous forces ($\eta = 0$) then we have

$$\rho\boldsymbol{a} + \mathrm{grad}\,p - \rho\boldsymbol{g} = 0 \tag{5.19}$$

This is the equation of motion (*Euler's equation*) for a so-called "perfect fluid": a perfect fluid has constant mass density and zero viscosity. For such a fluid

$$\mathrm{div}\,\boldsymbol{\sigma} = -\mathrm{grad}\,p \tag{5.20}$$

Although no real fluid is perfect, some aspects of the behaviour of real fluids are well described by Euler's equation. The Navier–Stokes equation and Euler's equation define the motion of particular types of fluid. The conservation equations alone do not suffice to determine the pattern of behaviour, they must invariably be supplemented by appropriate flux equations. Before we consider the flux equations for diffusion in multicomponent systems, it is useful to emphasize the role played by the equations of state.

IV. EQUATIONS OF STATE

When the preceding ideas are extended to nonisothermal systems a serious complication arises. It is necessary to take into account, for example, the variation of the mass density ρ with the local temperature and pressure. The volume $\hat{V}$ of a unit mass of fluid at equilibrium is determined by the thermodynamic temperature T and pressure p through the *thermal equation of state:*

$$\hat{V} = \hat{V}(p, T) \tag{5.21}$$

Only if it may be assumed that the local mass density ρ is the same function of the local temperature and pressure in a nonequilibrium situation as at equilibrium, is it correct to use the thermal equation of state in hydrodynamics. There is also the further complication of the definition and measurement of temperature and pressure in equilibrium and in nonequilibrium situations. These difficulties will be examined in more detail later in the context of nonequilibrium thermodynamics. For the moment it will suffice to point out that thermodynamic assumptions are commonly used in continuum mechanics and in hydrodynamics and have proved their worth.

Before one can discuss the conservation of energy in continuum theories, it is necessary to assume that the thermodynamic internal energy $\hat{U}$ per unit mass of fluid in a nonequilibrium situation is the same function of the local mass density ρ and temperature T as given at equilibrium by the *caloric equation of state*

$$\hat{U} = \hat{U}(\rho, T) \tag{5.22}$$

To show the usefulness of these assumptions we may anticipate future arguments and simply state the equation of conservation of energy for a stationary fluid of constant density

$$\frac{d(\rho\hat{U})}{dt} = -\operatorname{div} \boldsymbol{q} \tag{5.23}$$

in which $\boldsymbol{q}$ is the heat flux vector.

The specific enthalpy $\hat{H}$ of the fluid is defined as

$$\hat{H} = \hat{U} + p\hat{V} \tag{5.24}$$

and the heat capacity at constant pressure $\hat{C}p$, per unit mass of fluid, is

$$\hat{C}p = \left(\frac{\partial \hat{H}}{\partial T}\right)_p = \left(\frac{\partial \hat{U}}{\partial T}\right)_p + p\left(\frac{\partial \hat{V}}{\partial T}\right)_p \quad (5.25)$$

We may write the caloric equation of state in the form $\hat{U} = \hat{U}(p, T)$ so that for a single-component fluid at constant pressure

$$d\hat{U} = \left(\frac{\partial \hat{U}}{\partial T}\right)_p dT \quad (5.26)$$

and

$$d\hat{V} = \left(\frac{\partial \hat{V}}{\partial T}\right)_p dT \quad (5.27)$$

Equation (5.25) rearranges to

$$d\hat{U} = \hat{C}p\, dT - p\, d\hat{V} \quad (5.28)$$

For a fluid of constant density in which the product $\rho\hat{C}p$ is also constant

$$d(\rho\hat{U}) = d(\rho\hat{C}pT) \quad (5.29)$$

and Eqn (5.23) now takes the form

$$\frac{d(\rho\hat{C}pT)}{dT} = -\operatorname{div} \boldsymbol{q} \quad (5.30)$$

If we now introduce Fourier's law of heat conduction

$$\boldsymbol{q} = -\alpha \operatorname{grad} (\rho\hat{C}pT) \quad (5.31)$$

the conservation of energy requires that (cf. Chapter 4)

$$\frac{dT}{dt} = \alpha \nabla^2 T \cdots (\rho, \rho\hat{C}p, \alpha \text{ const}) \quad (5.32)$$

Equation (5.32) is the starting point for the mathematical solution of many problems in heat conduction and is based on thermodynamic assumptions.

REFERENCES

Bird, R. B., Stewart, W. E. and Lightfoot, E. N. (1964). "Transport Phenomena." John Wiley, London; Toppan Company Ltd., Tokyo.

Condon, E. U. and Odishaw, H. (1958). "Handbook of Physics." McGraw-Hill, New York.

De Groot, S. R. and Mazur, P. (1962). "Nonequilibrium Thermodynamics." North-Holland Publishing Co., Amsterdam.

Fitts, D. D. (1962). "Nonequilibrium Thermodynamics." McGraw-Hill, New York.

Kay, J. M. (1963). "An introduction to Fluid Mechanics and Heat Transfer," 2nd Edn., Cambridge University Press.

Landau, L. and Lifshitz, E. M. (1959). "Fluid Mechanics." Addison–Wesley, Reading.

Love, A. E. H. (1944). "The Mathematical Theory of Elasticity." Dover Publications, New York.

Chapter 6 Multicomponent Systems

In this chapter we concentrate attention on the equations of motion for multicomponent systems. We follow Truesdell's approach (1962) to a discussion of the mechanical basis of diffusion in an arbitrary continuous medium and begin by defining the variables to be used.

I. DIFFUSION AND MASS FLOWS

The continuous medium contains the n components $k = 1, 2, \ldots, n$. The mass of component k in a volume element dV is $\rho_k \, dV$, where ρ_k is the partial mass density (or concentration in g/cm^3) of component k within dV. ρ_k is an average value over dV. The average velocity of motion of the molecules of k within dV, with respect to an externally-fixed set of coordinates, is $\boldsymbol{u}_k$. The mass flux vector $\boldsymbol{J}_k$ represents the *total* mass flux of k in this coordinate system

$$\boldsymbol{J}_k = \rho_k \boldsymbol{u}_k \qquad k = 1, 2, \ldots, n \tag{6.1}$$

The total mass flux $\boldsymbol{J}$ of the continuum is the sum of the component mass flows

$$\boldsymbol{J} = \sum_{k=1}^{n} \boldsymbol{J}_k = \sum_{k=1}^{n} \rho_k \boldsymbol{u}_k \tag{6.2}$$

The total mass density ρ of the continuum is the sum of the partial mass densities

$$\rho = \sum_{k=1}^{n} \rho_k \tag{6.3}$$

We may define an average velocity $\boldsymbol{u}$ for the mean motion of the continuum by the equation

$$\rho \boldsymbol{u} = \sum_{k=1}^{n} \rho_k \boldsymbol{u}_k \quad \text{or} \quad \boldsymbol{u} = \frac{1}{\rho} \sum_{k=1}^{n} \rho_k \boldsymbol{u}_k \tag{6.4}$$

Other definitions are possible for the velocity of the mean motion. Eqn (6.4) defines $\boldsymbol{u}$ as the velocity of the centre of mass of a volume element dV in the externally-fixed coordinates. This particular mean velocity $\boldsymbol{u}$ is known by various names: as the barycentric velocity (De Groot and Mazur, 1962); as the mass velocity (Truesdell, 1962); as the velocity of the local centre of mass (Fitts, 1962) and as the local mass average velocity (Bird *et al.*, 1964). It is necessary to define a velocity of mean motion in order to be able to discuss the diffusion flows.

When $\boldsymbol{u}$ is not zero, the bulk flow of the mixture will transport with it each of the components of the mixture. This is *convective mass transport*. The flux vector for the convective mass transport of component k is $\rho_k \boldsymbol{u}$.

There may in addition be a *diffusive mass transport* of component k to which we allot the *diffusion flux vector* $\boldsymbol{j}_k$. The total mass flux $\boldsymbol{J}_k$ is the sum of the diffusive and convective fluxes

$$\boldsymbol{J}_k = \boldsymbol{j}_k + \rho_k \boldsymbol{u} \tag{6.5}$$

It follows from Eqn (6.1) that

$$\boldsymbol{j}_k = \rho_k(\boldsymbol{u}_k - \boldsymbol{u}) = \rho_k(\boldsymbol{u}_k)_M \tag{6.6}$$

where $(\boldsymbol{u}_k)_M = \boldsymbol{u}_k - \boldsymbol{u}$ is the *diffusion velocity* of component k with respect to the local centre of mass, i.e. in the *mass-fixed reference frame*. $\boldsymbol{j}_k$ is the diffusion flux vector in this reference frame. Other reference frames are possible and will be discussed later: there is a reference frame for each of the possible choices of the definition of the velocity of the mean motion. The $\boldsymbol{j}_k$ are not independent since

$$\sum_{k=1}^{m} \boldsymbol{j}_k = \sum_{k=1}^{m} \rho_k \boldsymbol{u}_k - \boldsymbol{u} \sum_{k=1}^{m} \rho_k = 0, \tag{6.7}$$

i.e. there is no net flux of mass across a reference plane that is stationary with respect to the local centre of mass. For some purposes the preceding relationships are more usefully expressed in terms of the *mass fractions* W_k

$$W_k = \rho_k/\rho; \qquad \sum_{k=1}^{n} W_k = 1 \tag{6.8}$$

II. CONSERVATION OF MASS

If chemical reaction is excluded from consideration, the conservation of mass for species k requires

$$\frac{\partial \rho_k}{\partial t} = -\operatorname{div} \boldsymbol{J}_k \qquad k = 1, 2, \ldots, n \tag{6.9}$$

If Eqn (6.9) is summed over all components k and Eqns (6.1) to (6.4) are used, we recover the equation of continuity (Eqn 5.1) in which $\boldsymbol{u}$ is now the mass average velocity.

When Eqn (6.9) is written using the convected time derivative

$$\frac{d\rho_k}{dt} = -\rho_k \operatorname{div} \boldsymbol{u} - \operatorname{div} \boldsymbol{j}_k \tag{6.10}$$

a further simplification can be made by introducing the mass fractions W_k and substituting for div $\boldsymbol{u}$ from the equation of continuity (5.2)

$$\rho \frac{dW_k}{dt} = -\text{div}\, \boldsymbol{j}_k \tag{6.11}$$

If the mixture has a constant density ρ the equation of continuity for component k takes the simple form

$$\frac{d\rho_k}{dt} = -\text{div}\, \boldsymbol{j}_k \tag{6.12}$$

which has the same form as Eqn (5.30) for the conservation of energy and leads to Fick's Second Law of diffusion [Eqn (1.12)].

III. FICK'S LAWS

On the basis of an intuitive analogy with Fourier's equations for the flow of heat, Fick (1855) suggested that the diffusion of a simple salt in water could be described by the equations

$$(J_k)_x = -D \frac{\partial \rho_k}{\partial x} \qquad \textit{Fick's First Law} \tag{6.13}$$

and

$$\frac{\partial \rho_k}{\partial t} = D \frac{\partial^2 \rho_k}{\partial x^2} \qquad \textit{Fick's Second Law} \tag{6.14}$$

According to the original formulation of these laws (Fick, 1855) the diffusion coefficient D is to be "*eine von der Natur der Substanzen abhängige Constante*." Strictly speaking then, Fick's laws in their original form implied the *constancy* of D in Eqns (6.13) and (6.14). It was expressly stated by Fick that these equations would be valid only if there was no significant convective transport of the salt. This implies the use of a very dilute salt solution having a virtually constant mass density.

A more modern formulation of the essential content of Fick's Laws (Truesdell, 1962) no longer implies the constancy of the diffusion coefficient D. For a binary mixture of uniform and constant total density ρ Fick's First Law is written as

$$\boldsymbol{j}_k = -D \,\text{grad}\, \rho_k \qquad (D > 0;\, k = 1, 2) \tag{6.15}$$

where D may be a function of the mass densities ρ_k and of the temperature of experiment, but shows no explicit dependence on time, on position, or on grad ρ_k.

Fick's Second law is an equation of conservation of mass for the diffusing species and for the present assumptions it is equivalent to Eqn (6.12) with $\boldsymbol{j}_k$ given by Eqn (6.15) (it is implied that the fluid is stationary with $\boldsymbol{u} = 0$).

IV. THE MECHANICAL BASIS OF DIFFUSION

We now examine the mechanical basis of diffusion to see if it is possible to derive Fick's laws on a sound mechanical basis. The discussion is based on a more detailed article by Truesdell (1962).

A. The Conservation of Linear Momentum in Mixtures

The conservation of linear momentum in a single component fluid is expressed by Eqn (5.8) which we may write as

$$\rho(\boldsymbol{a} - \hat{\boldsymbol{X}}) - \operatorname{div} \boldsymbol{\sigma} = 0 \tag{6.16}$$

One may ask if it is possible to write an equation of motion for each constituent of a multicomponent mixture and to derive from these an equation of motion for the mixture itself. Noll (1955) and Bearman and Kirkwood (1958) have shown on the basis of statistical mechanics that this is possible. Truesdell (1957) has given a purely phenomenological analysis which shows that, if the diffusion processes are properly accounted for, equations of motion may be written for the individual components and then combined to give an equation of the form of Eqn (6.16) for the mean motion of the mixture.

The equation of motion for an arbitrary component k which moves as if it were *isolated* from the other components would be written

$$\rho_k(\boldsymbol{a}_k - \hat{\boldsymbol{X}}_k) - \operatorname{div} \boldsymbol{\sigma}_k = 0 \tag{6.17}$$

$\hat{\boldsymbol{X}}_k$ is the volume force per unit mass acting on k as the result of external forces; $\boldsymbol{\sigma}_k$ is a partial stress tensor that defines the "surface forces" acting on component k.

When component k is not isolated it experiences additional forces ("diffusive drags" or "diffusive frictions"), which arise from the transfer of linear momentum between the diffusing components. The diffusive drags supply linear momentum to component k. The momentum supply $\boldsymbol{p}_k$ of that component is defined by

$$\rho_k(\boldsymbol{a}_k - \hat{\boldsymbol{X}}_k) - \operatorname{div} \boldsymbol{\sigma}_k = \rho \hat{\boldsymbol{p}}_k \qquad k = 1, 2, \ldots, m \tag{6.18}$$

In a single-component fluid the momentum supply $\hat{\boldsymbol{p}}_k$ is zero. In a multicomponent mixture the total volume force $\hat{\boldsymbol{X}}$ is

$$\hat{\boldsymbol{X}} = \sum_{k=1}^{m} W_k \hat{\boldsymbol{X}}_k \tag{6.19}$$

The total stress tensor $\boldsymbol{\sigma}$ is (Truesdell, 1957)

$$\boldsymbol{\sigma} = \sum_{k=1}^{n} [\boldsymbol{\sigma}_k - \rho_k(\boldsymbol{u}_k)_M(\boldsymbol{u}_k)_M] \tag{6.20}$$

in which the dyadic product of the diffusion velocity $(\boldsymbol{u}_k)_M$ appears (Fitts, 1962). The condition

$$\sum_{k=1}^{n} \hat{\boldsymbol{p}}_k = 0 \tag{6.21}$$

expresses the conservation of linear momentum in the mixture since it leads to Eqn (6.16) for the mean motion (Truesdell, 1957).

The *constitutive equations for diffusion* define the relationships between the diffusive motions and the momentum supplies of the components. A simple but general linear theory of this effect may be given in terms of the diffusion velocities $(\boldsymbol{u}_k)_M$. The diffusion of component j with respect to component k occurs with a relative velocity

$$(\boldsymbol{u}_j)_M - (\boldsymbol{u}_k)_M = \boldsymbol{u}_j - \boldsymbol{u}_k \tag{6.22}$$

which is *independent of the choice of reference-frame for the diffusive motions*. This relative motion is assumed to contribute to the linear momentum of k via the diffusive drags, i.e.

$$(\rho\hat{\boldsymbol{p}}_k)_j = F_{kj}[\boldsymbol{u}_j - \boldsymbol{u}_k] \tag{6.23}$$

F_{kj} is a coefficient of proportionality which describes the efficiency of transfer of momentum from component j to component k in the direction of $\boldsymbol{u}_j - \boldsymbol{u}_k$: it also provides a measure of the extent to which component k exerts a diffusive drag on component j. For diffusion in an isotropic medium we have the constitutive equations for diffusion

$$\rho\hat{\boldsymbol{p}}_k = \sum_{j=1}^{n} (\rho\hat{\boldsymbol{p}}_k)_j = \sum_{j=1}^{n} F_{kj}(\boldsymbol{u}_j - \boldsymbol{u}_k) \tag{6.24}$$

which are independent of the choice of reference frame for the diffusion flows.

Any term in which a coefficient of the form F_{kk} appears is to be taken as zero. The remaining coefficients F_{kj} are uniquely defined, and are independent of the choice of reference frame for the diffusion flows. The condition

$$\sum_{k=1}^{n} (F_{kj} - F_{jk}) = 0 \tag{6.25}$$

is necessary and sufficient to ensure that Eqns (6.24) are consistent with the balance of linear momentum in the mixture. The n^2 coefficients of Eqns 6.24) are reduced to $n^2 - n = n(n - 1)$ by the elimination of the n coefficients of the form F_{kk}. The condition (6.25) reduces the number of independent non-vanishing coefficients F_{kj} to a maximum of $n(n - 1) - (n - 1) = (n - 1)^2$.

In a *binary mixture* ($n = 2$) the symmetry relationship

$$F_{12} = F_{21} \tag{6.26}$$

is a necessary consequence of the conservation of linear momentum in the mixture (Truesdell, 1962).

The more general symmetry relations

$$F_{kj} = F_{jk} \qquad k, j = 1, 2, \ldots, n \tag{6.27}$$

have been suggested as a generalisation of Maxwell's analysis (1860) of diffusion in a binary mixture, and may be referred to as *Stefan's relations*.

Truesdell (1962) has shown that the following conditions lead to Stefan's relations

(1) $$F_{kj} \to 0 \quad \text{if} \quad \rho_k \to 0 \tag{6.28}$$

and

(2) $$F_{kj} \text{ is independent of } \rho_i \quad \text{if} \quad i \neq k \text{ or } j \tag{6.29}$$

Condition (1) states that no constituent may exert a diffusive drag on the other constituents if it is not present in the mixture; condition (2) defines the special case of binary diffusive drags for which Stefan's relations are found to hold.

In the Maxwell–Stefan analysis, which is a hydrodynamic theory of diffusion, the diffusive drags are taken to be a function not only of the relative velocities but also of the concentration products $\rho_k \rho_j$. The *Maxwell–Stefan equations* for diffusion are

$$\rho \hat{\boldsymbol{p}}_k = \sum_{j=1}^{n} A_{kj} \rho_k \rho_j [\boldsymbol{u}_j - \boldsymbol{u}_k] \tag{6.30}$$

The symmetry relations

$$A_{kj} = A_{jk} \qquad k = 1, 2, \ldots, n \tag{6.31}$$

are equivalent to Eqns (6.27).

The constitutive equations for diffusion (6.24) and (6.30) are presented here in the *friction coefficient formalism* (Tyrrell, 1963): the coefficients F_{kj} and A_{kj} characterise the diffusive frictions between the components and are independent of the choice of reference frame. These equations express the diffusive forces as functions of the diffusion velocities or diffusion flows. It is often useful to express the diffusion flows as functions of the diffusion forces.

B. Inversion of the Constitutive Equations for Diffusion

In order to express the diffusion fluxes as functions of the diffusive frictional forces it is necessary to invert the constitutive equations. For this Truesdell

(1962) obtains the result

$$\rho_k(\boldsymbol{u}_k)_M = \boldsymbol{j}_k = \rho \sum_{j=1}^{n} G_{kj}(\hat{\boldsymbol{p}}_j - \hat{\boldsymbol{p}}_k) \tag{6.32}$$

in which the G_{kj} satisfy the condition

$$\sum_{j=1}^{m} (G_{kj} - G_{jk}) = 0 \tag{6.33}$$

but depend on the choice of reference-frame for the diffusion flows.

C. Generalised Diffusion Equations

The preceding equations are perfectly general and may be applied to an arbitrary class of isotropic continuous medium. We shall now consider diffusion in mixtures of perfect fluids as in the Maxwell–Stefan theory (Truesdell, 1962), i.e. Eqn (6.17) becomes

$$\rho\hat{\boldsymbol{p}}_k = \rho_k(\boldsymbol{a}_k - \hat{\boldsymbol{X}}_k) + \text{grad } p_k \tag{6.34}$$

so that from Eqn (6.32), if we restrict attention to a system in the absence of external forces, and neglect accelerations as is customary in theories of diffusion,

$$\boldsymbol{j}_k = -\sum_{j=1}^{m} G_{kj} \text{ grad } (p_k - p_j) \tag{6.35}$$

This is a diffusion equation expressed in terms of mechanical variables: it illustrates the fact that it is pressure gradients that are responsible for fluid motions (Truesdell, 1962).

If a comparison is to be made with Fick's Laws, Eqn (6.35) must be written in terms of nonmechanical variables. *This requires the introduction of thermodynamic assumptions.*

If each component has its own independent thermal equation of state

$$p_k = p_k(\rho_k, T) \qquad k = 1, 2, \ldots, m \tag{6.36}$$

then

$$\text{grad } p_k = \left(\frac{\partial p_k}{\partial \rho_k}\right)_T \text{grad } \rho_k + \left(\frac{\partial p_k}{\partial T}\right)_{\rho_k} \text{grad } T \tag{6.37}$$

For an isothermal system Eqn (6.35) becomes

$$\boldsymbol{j}_k = -\sum_{j=1}^{n} G_{kj}\left[\left(\frac{\partial p_k}{\partial \rho_k}\right)_T \text{grad } \rho_k - \left(\frac{\partial p_j}{\partial \rho_j}\right)_T \text{grad } \rho_j\right] \tag{6.38}$$

For a binary mixture of constant total density Eqn (6.38) reduces to a form which is directly comparable with Fick's first law. Since

$$\text{grad } \rho = \text{grad } \rho_1 + \text{grad } \rho_2 = 0 \tag{6.39}$$

we find

$$j_1 = -G_{12}\left[\left(\frac{\partial p_1}{\partial \rho_1}\right)_T + \left(\frac{\partial p_2}{\partial \rho_2}\right)_T\right] \text{grad } \rho_1 \tag{6.40}$$

Eqn (6.40) has the form of Fick's first law and describes a binary diffusion process governed by the single diffusion coefficient

$$D = G_{12}\left[\left(\frac{\partial p_1}{\partial \rho_1}\right)_T + \left(\frac{\partial p_2}{\partial \rho_2}\right)_T\right] \tag{6.41}$$

Even in this simple example the diffusion coefficient D is dependent on the thermodynamic properties of the components. The constancy of D is dependent on the behaviour of the thermodynamic quantities in Eqn (6.41) as well as on the coefficient G_{12}.

The treatment discussed here can be developed to give the same diffusion equations as may be derived from nonequilibrium thermodynamics: it is necessary to assume that the momentum supplies may include the effect of forces of a thermodynamic character and that each component possesses its own caloric equation of state, the different components enjoying a common temperature at a given time and place (Truesdell, 1962).

There is also a close relationship between this treatment and the generalised transport equations of Hirschfelder *et al.* (1964), as has been pointed out by Truesdell (1962).

In at least one instance, an analysis based on closely related generalised Stefan–Maxwell equations (Onsager, 1945); Lightfoot *et al.* (1962) has been applied to a problem of mass transport through an ion-exchange membrane (Scattergood and Lightfoot, 1968). This approach also involves thermodynamic assumptions.

We proceed now to an examination of the nonequilibrium thermodynamic theories of transport processes. As an essential preliminary we discuss the nature of the thermodynamic flows and forces which enter these theories.

REFERENCES

Bearman, R. J. and Kirkwood, J. G. (1958). *J. Chem. Phys.*, **28,** 136.
Bird, R. B., Stewart, W. E. and Lightfoot, E. N. (1964). "Transport Phenomena." John Wiley, New York; Toppan Company Ltd., Tokyo.
De Groot, S. R. and Mazur, P. (1962). "Nonequilibrium Thermodynamics." North-Holland Publishing Co., Amsterdam.
Fick, A. (1855). *Annln Phys.*, **94,** 594.
Fitts, D. D. (1962). "Nonequilibrium Thermodynamics." McGraw-Hill, New York.

Hirschfelder, J. O., Curtiss, C. F., and Bird, R. B. (1964). "Molecular Theory of Gases and Liquids." Reprinted with notes and corrections. John Wiley, New York; Toppan Co., Tokyo.

Lightfoot, E. N., Cussler, Jr., E. L., and Rettig, R. L. (1962). *Amer. Inst. Chem. Eng. J.*, **8,** 708.

Maxwell, J. C. (1860). *In* "Collected Papers," (Ed. W. D. Niven). Cambridge University Press (1890). Cf. Truesdell (1962).

Noll, W. (1955). *J. rat. Mech. Analysis*, **4,** 627. Cf. Truesdell (1957).

Onsager, L. (1945). *Ann. N.Y. Acad. Sci.*, **46,** 241.

Scattergood, E. M. and Lightfoot, E. N. (1968). *Trans. Faraday Soc.*, **64,** 1135.

Stefan, J. (1871). *Sber. Akad. Wiss. Wien*, **63,** Cf. Truesdell (1962).

Truesdell, C. (1957). *Atti Accad. nat. Lincei Rc.*, **22,** 33, 158.

Truesdell, C. (1962). *J. Chem. Phys.*, **37,** 2336.

Tyrrell, H. J. V. (1963). *J. Chem. Soc.*, **300,** 1599.

Part II The Formalism of Nonequilibrium Thermodynamics

Chapter 7 Thermodynamic Flows and Forces

In this Chapter we review briefly some of the properties of the internal energy U and of the entropy S. A discussion of irreversible processes in an isolated composite system leads to the introduction of the concept of a thermodynamic force, and of a thermodynamic flow.

The assumptions necessary for a thermodynamic analysis of the behaviour of real discontinuous systems are presented, together with an analysis of the Onsager relations in such systems.

We discuss here only a very simple type of macroscopic thermodynamic system. The influence of external fields (e.g. electrical, magnetic or gravitational fields) is negligible and surface phenomena may be ignored. The systems are macroscopically homogeneous, isotropic and uncharged. No chemical reactions take place in these systems (Callen, 1960).

I. INTERNAL ENERGY

The total energy E of a system includes its macroscopic kinetic energy, which may be ignored in equilibrium studies, the potential energy arising from external fields and the internal energy U. The internal energy is stored in the kinetic or thermal energy of molecules, and in their potential energy of mutual interaction. Only differences of energy have physical significance, and the existence of some arbitrary reference state is always implied in discussions of the energy of a system. We shall not pursue this point here. (Prigogine, 1961; De Groot, 1959; Haase, 1963).

When a closed adiabatic system passes from a state 1 to a state 2, the work W done on the system is (Guggenheim, 1957)

$$W = U(2) - U(1) = \Delta U \tag{7.1}$$

Eqn (7.1) expresses the principle of conservation of energy.

If the closed system is surrounded instead by diathermal walls, it is necessary to take into account the quantity of heat Q absorbed from the surroundings. Q is defined by

$$Q = \Delta U - W \tag{7.2}$$

which may be re-written as

$$\Delta U = Q + W \tag{7.3}$$

For an infinitesimal change

$$dU = đQ + đW \tag{7.4}$$

and for a finite process

$$U(2) - U(1) = \int_1^2 dU = \int_1^2 đQ + \int_1^2 đW \tag{7.5}$$

dU is a total differential or perfect differential; $đQ$ and $đW$ are not total differentials because there are no functions of state corresponding to Q or to W: the integrals $\int_1^2 đQ$ and $\int_1^2 đW$ depend on the "path" which connects states 1 and 2.

The detailed thermodynamic analysis of a system depends on the nature of the work term W.

If the only work performed on the system is the reversible work of volume change, $W = -p\, dV$, in which p is the thermodynamic pressure and V is the volume of the system, then from Eqn (7.4)

$$dU = dQ - p\, dV \tag{7.6}$$

Equation (7.6) is generalised to open systems by introducing an "energy flow" $đ\theta$ to represent the combined effect of heat and mass transfer from the surroundings (Prigogine, 1961).

$$dU = đ\theta - p\, dV \tag{7.7}$$

There is no unique way of splitting $đ\theta$ into a heat transfer and a contribution from mass transfer.

II. THE ENTROPY FUNCTION

When a closed system absorbs a quantity of heat $đQ$ in a reversible process at the thermodynamic temperature T, the entropy S of the system increases by the amount

$$dS = đQ/T \quad \text{(reversible process)} \tag{7.8}$$

The entropy S is an extensive function of state and dS is a perfect differential.

If a process is irreversible, classical thermodynamics offers only the second-law inequality

$$dS > đQ/T \quad \text{(irreversible process)} \tag{7.9}$$

From Eqns (7.6) and (7.8) we find for a reversible process

$$dS = \left(\frac{1}{T}\right) dU + \left(\frac{p}{T}\right) dV \quad \text{(closed system)} \tag{7.10}$$

When Eqn (7.10) is extended to open multicomponent systems we obtain the *Gibbs equation*

$$dS = \left(\frac{1}{T}\right) dU + \left(\frac{p}{T}\right) dV - \sum_{k=1}^{n} \left(\frac{\mu_k}{T}\right) dN_k \quad \text{(open system)} \tag{7.11}$$

in which μ_k is the *chemical potential* of component k and N_k is the number of moles of component k in the system.

The entropy S, like the other thermodynamic functions of state and state variables, is strictly defined only for equilibrium states of the system. The entropy change dS which occurs when a system passes from one equilibrium state to a neighbouring equilibrium state may be split into two distinct parts (Prigogine, 1961; Guggenheim, 1957)

$$dS = d_I S + d_E S \tag{7.12}$$

$d_E S$ represents the entropy change which results from reversible interactions with the environment; it is the *entropy flow* from the surroundings. $d_I S$ is the entropy change which arises from irreversible processes inside the system; it is the *entropy production*.

There will prove to be a close analogy between the splitting of the entropy production in Eqn (7.12) and the analysis of the rate of change of an extensive quantity in the continuous systems of Chapter 4. The entropy production $d_I S$ is in this sense obtained by integrating the local entropy production ϕ_S over the volume of the homogeneous system. The entropy flow $d_E S$ is obtained by integrating the local entropy flux from the surroundings over the enclosing surface of the homogeneous system.

The second law inequality of Eqn (7.9) is now equivalent to the conditions

$$d_I S > 0 \quad \text{(irreversible process)} \tag{7.13}$$

For a reversible process $d_I S = 0$.

Equation (7.13) offers the only general criterion for the occurrence of an irreversible process; for this reason the entropy function S plays a central role in the thermodynamics of irreversible processes (De Groot, 1959; Prigogine, 1961).

The entropy S of a homogeneous, multicomponent fluid mixture may be expressed as a single-valued, continuous and differentiable function of the internal energy U, the volume V and the mole numbers N_1, N_2, . . . ,

$N_k, \ldots, N_n$ of the n independent components of the mixture (Callen, 1960; Tisza, 1966).

$$S = S(U, V, N_1, N_2, \ldots, N_k, \ldots, N_n) \tag{7.14}$$

The total differential of the entropy S is

$$dS = \left(\frac{\partial S}{\partial U}\right)_{V,N_k} dU + \left(\frac{\partial S}{\partial V}\right)_{U,N_k} dV + \sum_{k=1}^{m} \left(\frac{\partial S}{\partial N_k}\right)_{U,V,N_j} dN_k \tag{7.15}$$

A comparison of Eqns (7.11) and (7.15) leads to the following thermodynamic definitions.

$$\left(\frac{\partial S}{\partial U}\right)_{V,N_k} = \frac{1}{T} \geqslant 0 \tag{7.16}$$

$$\left(\frac{\partial S}{\partial V}\right)_{U,N_k} = \frac{p}{T} \tag{7.17}$$

$$\left(\frac{\partial S}{\partial N_k}\right)_{U,V,N_j} = -\frac{\mu_k}{T} \tag{7.18}$$

The intensive state variables (μ_k, p, T) appear as the partial derivatives of Eqn (7.15). It is of course possible to concentrate attention on extensive functions of state other than the entropy S, so that other definitions of the intensive state variables are possible, for example

$$\mu_k = -T\left(\frac{\partial S}{\partial N_k}\right)_{U,V,N_j} = \left(\frac{\partial U}{\partial N_k}\right)_{S,V,N_j} = \left(\frac{\partial H}{\partial N_k}\right)_{S,p,N_j}$$
$$= \left(\frac{\partial A}{\partial N_k}\right)_{T,V,N_j} = \left(\frac{\partial G}{\partial N_k}\right)_{T,p,N_j} = \bar{G}_k \cdots (j \neq k) \tag{7.19}$$

H is the *enthalpy* ($H = U + PV$); A is the *Helmholtz function* ($A = U - TS$); G is the *Gibbs function* ($G = H - TS$) and $\bar{G}_k$ is the partial molar Gibbs function. The following properties of the chemical potentials will be useful later

$$\left(\frac{\partial(\mu_k/T)}{\partial T}\right)_{p,N_k} = \frac{\bar{H}_k}{T^2}; \quad \left(\frac{\partial \mu_k}{\partial p}\right)_{T,N_k} = \bar{v}_k; \quad \left(\frac{\partial \mu_k}{\partial T}\right)_{p,N_k} = -\bar{S}_k \tag{7.20}$$

$\bar{S}_k$ is the partial molar entropy of component k, $\bar{v}_k$ is its partial molar volume and $\bar{H}_k$ its partial molar enthalpy.

$$\bar{S}_k = \left(\frac{\partial S}{\partial N_k}\right)_{p,T,N_j}; \quad \bar{v}_k = \left(\frac{\partial V}{\partial N_k}\right)_{p,T,N_j}; \quad \bar{H}_k = \left(\frac{\partial H}{\partial N_k}\right)_{p,T,N_j} \tag{7.21}$$

Suppose we introduce generalised independent extensive quantities X_i, which may be functions of state or state variables, into Eqn (7.14)

$$S = S(X_1, X_2, \ldots, X_i, \ldots, X_n) \tag{7.22}$$

Then

$$dS = \sum_{i=1}^{n} \left(\frac{\partial S}{\partial X_i}\right)_{X_j} dX_i = \sum_{i=1}^{n} F_i\, dX_i \tag{7.23}$$

in which we have the generalised intensive quantities F_i.

$$F_i = \left(\frac{\partial S}{\partial X_i}\right)_{X_j} \tag{7.24}$$

The entropy S is a first order, homogeneous function of the X_i, i.e.

$$S(\lambda X_1, \lambda X_2, \ldots, \lambda X_i, \ldots, \lambda X_n) = \lambda S(X_1, X_2, \ldots, X_i, \ldots, X_n) \tag{7.25}$$

where λ is a positive scale factor which represents an arbitrary increase in the size of the system. From Eqn (7.25) it is possible to deduce the *Euler relation* (Callen, 1960)

$$S = \sum_{i=1}^{n} F_i X_i \tag{7.26}$$

Taking an infinitesimal variation of Eqn (7.26)

$$dS = \sum_{i=1}^{n} F_i\, dX_i + \sum_{i=1}^{n} X_i\, dF_i \tag{7.27}$$

A comparison with Eqn (7.23) shows that

$$\sum_{i=1}^{n} X_i\, dF_i = 0 \tag{7.28}$$

The intensive state variables F_i are *not* independent. Equation (7.28) is a generalised *Gibbs–Duhem equation*. It reflects the *homogeneity* of the equilibrium state.

III. IRREVERSIBLE PROCESSES IN AN ISOLATED COMPOSITE SYSTEM

A. Quasi-Static Processes

Consider an isolated composite system which is comprised of two isolated sub-systems ϕ and σ. Each sub-system is in internal thermodynamic equilibrium and its entropy (S^ϕ or S^σ) is well-defined. The total entropy S of the composite system is also well-defined

$$S = S^\phi + S^\sigma \tag{7.29}$$

The isolation of the composite system places *external constraints* on the extensive quantities X_i

$$X_i = X_i^\phi + X_i^\sigma = \text{const.} \tag{7.30}$$

The isolation of each sub-system represents an *internal constraint* which prevents interactions between the sub-systems; no internal processes are possible. Suppose we remove the internal isolation of the sub-systems, so that infinitesimal transfers may take place between them, and then restore the isolation.

When each sub-system has regained a state of internal equilibrium, the changes $d_I X_i^\phi$ and $d_I X_i^\sigma$ in the extensive properties are well-defined and are subject to the conditions

$$d_I X_i^\sigma = -d_I X_i^\phi \tag{7.31}$$

We have for the isolated composite system.

$$d_I S = (d_I S^\phi + d_I S^\sigma) \geqslant 0 \tag{7.32}$$

so that, with the help of Eqns (7.23) and (7.31)

$$d_I S = \sum_{i=1}^{n} (F_i^\phi - F_i^\sigma)\, d_I X_i^\phi \tag{7.33}$$

or

$$d_I S = \sum_{i=1}^{n} \mathscr{F}_i\, d_I X_i^\phi \tag{7.34}$$

in which the quantity $\mathscr{F}_i$

$$\mathscr{F}_i = \Delta F_i = (F_i^\phi - F_i^\sigma) = \left(\frac{\partial S^\phi}{\partial X_i^\phi}\right)_{X_j^\phi} - \left(\frac{\partial S^\sigma}{\partial X_i^\sigma}\right)_{X_j^\sigma} = \left(\frac{\partial S}{\partial X_i^\phi}\right)_{X_i} \tag{7.35}$$

is a *thermodynamic force*, or *thermodynamic affinity* (Callen, 1960; Tisza, 1966). $\mathscr{F}_i$ provides a measure of the "driving-force" behind the internal process which gives rise to the change $d_I X_i^\phi$ in X_i^ϕ. Note that the affinity $\mathscr{F}_i$ is equal to the difference between the intensive quantities F_i^ϕ and F_i^σ.

Suppose that no internal process occurs when the internal constraints on the ith quantity X_i are removed. Then $d_I X_i^\phi = 0$ and $d_I S = 0$ and the sub-systems must have been in mutual equilibrium with respect to the quantity X_i. This equilibrium state is characterised by a constrained maximum of the total entropy S (Callen, 1960; Tisza, 1966), so that for a virtual displacement $\delta_I X_i^\phi$ from the equilibrium value of X_i^ϕ

$$\delta_I S = \Delta F_i \cdot \delta_I X_i^\phi = 0 \tag{7.36}$$

The only way in which Eqn (7.36) may be satisfied for an arbitrary displacement $\delta_I X_i^\phi$ is by the condition

$$\mathscr{F}_i = \Delta F_i = 0 \quad \text{(\textit{internal equilibrium} with respect to the parameter } X_i\text{)} \tag{7.37}$$

The thermodynamic affinity ΔF_i reduces to zero at equilibrium.

Suppose now that a "*spontaneous*" *irreversible process* occurs on a temporary removal of the internal constraint, i.e.

$$\delta_I S = \Delta F_i \cdot \delta_I X_i^\phi > 0 \tag{7.38}$$

The necessary condition for a spontaneous process leading to an increase in X_i^ϕ is therefore

$$\Delta F_i > 0 \quad \text{(irreversible process in which } \delta X_i^\phi > 0) \tag{7.39}$$

If the thermodynamic affinity ΔF_i is *positive*, then a "spontaneous" irreversible process may occur on removal of the internal constraint. This process will increase X_i^ϕ at the expense of X_i^σ. We have in effect an *irreversible transfer* of the quantity X_i from the sub-system σ to sub-system ϕ.

The tendency of the entropy to increase as a result of irreversible processes determines the direction in which an irreversible process may occur.

The progressive incremental removal and replacement of the internal constraints in the composite system makes it possible to carry out an irreversible process in a *quasi-static* manner; provided that each sub-system is allowed to regain *internal equilibrium* after each incremental transfer, the thermodynamic variables and the thermodynamic affinities remain well-defined at all stages of the process. The time t does *not* enter as a variable in this quasi-static analysis of an irreversible process (Tisza, 1966).

B. Real Processes

1. Entropy Production

In order to develop a thermodynamics of irreversible processes, or a non-equilibrium thermodynamics, one may postulate the existence of real irreversible processes which occur so very slowly that the sub-systems ϕ and σ are at all times in individual internal equilibrium, even though they might not be in equilibrium with one another. The time-scale of the irreversible processes is assumed to be very long by comparison with the time necessary for the re-attainment of internal equilibrium within a sub-system.

This first postulate may be called *the postulate of local equilibrium*, since it is supposed that a state of local internal equilibrium exists within each sub-system, even though irreversible processes take place in the form of transfers between the sub-systems. One might visualise two reservoirs ϕ and σ which connect via a membrane or through a fine capillary. The exchange of energy, volume or of matter across the membrane or capillary may take placc so slowly that each reservoir maintains a substantially uniform temperature, pressure and composition during the real irreversible process.

The time t now enters as a natural variable and we may calculate *the rate of production of entropy* $d_I S/dt$ from Eqn (7.34)

$$\frac{d_I S}{dt} = \sum_{i=1}^{n} \mathscr{F}_i \frac{d_I X_i^{\phi}}{dt} = \sum_{i=1}^{n} \mathscr{F}_i \mathscr{I}_i \tag{7.40}$$

It is characteristic of nonequilibrium thermodynamics that the rate of production of entropy $d_I S/dt$ by irreversible processes may be expressed as the sum of products $\mathscr{F}_i \mathscr{I}_i$ in which $\mathscr{F}_i$ is the thermodynamic force associated with, or conjugate to, the thermodynamic flow $\mathscr{I}_i$.

In this instance the thermodynamic flows $\mathscr{I}_i$ are the time derivatives $d_I X_i^{\phi}/dt$ of the extensive state variables X_i^{ϕ}. The thermodynamic forces are the differences between the intensive state variables F_i^{ϕ} and F_i^{σ}. The ΔF_i are not necessarily independent, because the F_i are subject to the restrictions of the Gibbs–Duhem equation (Eqn 7.28). There may also be restrictions on the flows $\mathscr{I}_i$ so that they are not necessarily independent.

The type of system to which Eqn (7.40) applies is known as a *discontinuous system* because the values of the intensive state variables F_i undergo in general a discontinuous change as one passes from sub-system σ to sub-system ϕ.

The behaviour of a discontinuous system is a limiting form of behaviour which can be attained by a real system in approximation only. Nevertheless such behaviour is of theoretical interest and provides a standard of comparison for real systems.

2. Phenomenological Equations

The postulate of local equilibrium is the first fundamental postulate of nonequilibrium thermodynamics. This postulate leads to Eqn (7.40) for the rate of production of entropy during irreversible processes in discontinuous systems, and is equivalent to the assumption that the Gibbs equation may be used to calculate entropy changes in nonequilibrium systems. The postulate is to be justified by the success of nonequilibrium thermodynamics in describing experimental behaviour.

A second postulate is however necessary in order to relate the flows $\mathscr{I}_i$ to the forces $\mathscr{F}_i$. The simplest general assumption is that the flows $\mathscr{I}_i$ are linear homogeneous functions of the forces $\mathscr{F}_i$, i.e. we may write *the phenomenological equations*

$$\mathscr{I}_i = \sum_{j=1}^{n} \mathscr{L}_{ij} \mathscr{F}_j, \ldots, i = 1, 2, \ldots, n \tag{7.41}$$

in which the *phenomenological coefficients* $\mathscr{L}_{ij}$ represent the dependence of the ith flow upon the jth force

$$\mathscr{L}_{ij} = \left(\frac{\partial \mathscr{I}_i}{\partial \mathscr{F}_i}\right) \tag{7.42}$$

According to Eqn (7.41) the flows $\mathscr{I}_i$ vanish when the forces $\mathscr{F}_i$ vanish, as they should do. The coefficients $\mathscr{L}_{ij}$ are assumed independent of the $\mathscr{F}_j$, but they are not necessarily constants; they may be functions of the local intensive variables F_i.

This linear relationship between the flows and the forces is an approximation which is most likely to be valid for systems which are "*not very far*" *from equilibrium*. It is implicitly assumed that the system exhibits no "memory effects" in that it is the instantaneous values of the forces $\mathscr{F}_i$ which determine the instantaneous values of the flows $\mathscr{I}_i$, i.e. the system is assumed to be a Markoffian system (Callen, 1960). Once again, the justification for this postulate must be sought in comparisons with experiment.

The main coefficients $\mathscr{L}_{ii}$ represent the dependence of a flow $\mathscr{I}_i$ on its conjugate force $\mathscr{F}_i$. The cross-coefficients $\mathscr{L}_{ij}$ represent the *coupling effects* by which the flows $\mathscr{I}_i$ and $\mathscr{I}_j$ may interact. The coupling effects are included in this formalism for greater generality. It is for experiment or for molecular theories to decide if these effects exist and are significant.

The phenomenological coefficients are uniquely determined by the flows $\mathscr{I}_i$ *if and only if* the forces $\mathscr{F}_j$ are linearly independent. Consider the simple set of phenomenological equations

$$\begin{aligned} \mathscr{I}_1 &= \mathscr{L}_{11}\mathscr{F}_1 + \mathscr{L}_{12}\mathscr{F}_2 + \mathscr{L}_{13}\mathscr{F}_3 \\ \mathscr{I}_2 &= \mathscr{L}_{21}\mathscr{F}_1 + \mathscr{L}_{22}\mathscr{F}_2 + \mathscr{L}_{23}\mathscr{F}_3 \\ \mathscr{I}_3 &= \mathscr{L}_{31}\mathscr{F}_1 + \mathscr{L}_{32}\mathscr{F}_2 + \mathscr{L}_{33}\mathscr{F}_3 \end{aligned} \tag{7.43}$$

and suppose that the $\mathscr{F}_j$ are linearly dependent, i.e.

$$\alpha_1\mathscr{F}_1 + \alpha_2\mathscr{F}_2 + \alpha_3\mathscr{F}_3 = 0 \tag{7.44}$$

in which α_1, α_2 and α_3 are arbitrary parameters; any one of the forces $\mathscr{F}_j$ can be expressed linearly in terms of the remaining ones.

We may add the left-hand side of Eqn (7.44) to the right-hand side of each of the phenomenological equations (7.44) to give the new set

$$\begin{aligned} \mathscr{I}_1 &= (\mathscr{L}_{11} + \alpha_1)\mathscr{F}_1 + (\mathscr{L}_{12} + \alpha_2)\mathscr{F}_2 + (\mathscr{L}_{13} + \alpha_3)\mathscr{F}_3 \\ \mathscr{I}_2 &= (\mathscr{L}_{21} + \alpha_1)\mathscr{F}_1 + (\mathscr{L}_{22} + \alpha_2)\mathscr{F}_2 + (\mathscr{L}_{23} + \alpha_3)\mathscr{F}_3 \\ \mathscr{I}_3 &= (\mathscr{L}_{31} + \alpha_1)\mathscr{F}_1 + (\mathscr{L}_{32} + \alpha_2)\mathscr{F}_2 + (\mathscr{L}_{33} + \alpha_3)\mathscr{F}_3 \end{aligned} \tag{7.45}$$

The linear dependence of the forces $\mathscr{F}_j$ therefore means that there is more than one way of expressing the flows $\mathscr{I}_i$ as linear functions of the forces $\mathscr{F}_j$. The phenomenological coefficients in Eqns (7.43) and (7.45) are the same only if $\alpha_1, \alpha_2, \alpha_3$ are zero, i.e. only if the forces $\mathscr{F}_j$ are linearly independent.

3. The Onsager Reciprocal Relations

A fundamental theorem of nonequilibrium thermodynamics, due to Onsager (1931), states that for a "proper choice" of the flows and forces the phenomenological coefficients will obey the *Onsager reciprocal relations*

$$\mathscr{L}_{ij} = \mathscr{L}_{ji} \quad (i, j = 1, 2, \ldots) \tag{7.46}$$

Equation (7.46) effects a significant reduction in the number of independent phenomenological coefficients and expresses a very important symmetry of the coupling-phenomena.

IV. ONSAGER'S RECIPROCITY THEOREM

A careful discussion of the Onsager reciprocity theorem has been given by Yourgrau *et al.* (1966). This theorem is based on the statistical nature of the thermodynamic properties of real systems, on the principle of microscopic reversibility, and on the assumption that a system responds to artificially induced disturbances in the same way as it responds to the inevitable statistical fluctuations in its local properties.

Consider an isolated system whose state is determined by a set of independent local thermodynamic state variables A_i, $(i = 1, 2, \ldots)$. These variables will be assumed to be even functions of the local molecular velocities—they may be local temperatures, pressures, concentrations etc.—and they are subject to statistical fluctuations in their values. The entropy S of the system is determined by the A_i

$$S = S(A_1, A_2, \ldots) \tag{7.47}$$

If A_i^0 is the equilibrium value of A_i, then the quantity

$$\alpha_i = A_i - A_i^0 \tag{7.48}$$

is the deviation of A_i from its equilibrium value. The α_i disappear at equilibrium. They are the *Onsager coordinates* of the system.

We now expand the function $S = S(\alpha_1, \alpha_2, \alpha_3, \ldots)$ about the equilibrium state, of entropy S^0, in a Taylor Series

$$-\Delta S = S - S^0 = \sum_i \left(\frac{\partial S}{\partial \alpha_i}\right)^0 \alpha_i + \frac{1}{2}\sum_i \sum_j \left(\frac{\partial^2 S}{\partial \alpha_i \, \partial \alpha_j}\right)^0 \alpha_i \alpha_j + \cdots \tag{7.49}$$

If the system remains always near to equilibrium, we may ignore terms of higher order than the quadratic terms. Since the entropy is a maximum in the equilibrium state, each of the linear terms in Eqn (7.49) vanishes (the partial derivatives are taken at the equilibrium state for which $S = S^0$). In addition, the sum of the quadratic terms must be negative.

If we use the definition

$$g_{ij} = \left(\frac{\partial^2 S}{\partial\alpha_i\,\partial\alpha_j}\right)^0$$

then Eqn (7.49) takes the form

$$\Delta S = -\frac{1}{2}\sum_i\sum_j g_{ij}\alpha_i\alpha_j \tag{7.51}$$

If now we define the thermodynamic flows $\mathscr{I}_i$ as the time derivatives of the independent Onsager coordinates α_i

$$\mathscr{I}_i = \frac{\partial\alpha_i}{\partial t} \tag{7.52}$$

and if we define the thermodynamic forces $\mathscr{F}_i$ as

$$\mathscr{F}_i = \frac{\partial(\Delta S)}{\partial\alpha_i} = \frac{\partial_I S}{\partial\alpha_i} = -\sum_j g_{ij}\alpha_j \tag{7.53}$$

Then the rate of production of entropy is

$$\frac{\partial_I S}{\partial t} = \sum_i \mathscr{I}_i\mathscr{F}_i \tag{7.54}$$

which is a bilinear form in the flows and the forces.

Since the system is near to equilibrium, there will be a region in which the flows $\mathscr{I}_i$ may be taken to be linearly related to the forces $\mathscr{F}_i$

$$\mathscr{I}_i = \sum_j \mathscr{L}_{ij}\mathscr{F}_j \tag{7.55}$$

Onsager's theorem states that *for the independent flows and forces defined by Eqns (7.52) and (7.53)* the phenomenological coefficients in Eqn (7.55) obey the Onsager reciprocal relations

$$\mathscr{L}_{ij} = \mathscr{L}_{ji} \qquad i = 1, 2, \ldots \tag{7.56}$$

The proof of this result makes use of the principle of microscopic reversibility, according to which any molecular process and its reverse takes place on the average with the same frequency. (Yourgrau *et al.*, 1966). An alternative and simpler proof is given by Lothe (1966).

We shall follow Coleman and Truesdell (1960) and Yourgrau *et al.* (1966) in summarising the essential content of Onsager's theorem.

Suppose we have a set of n thermodynamic flows $\mathscr{I}_i$ which are linearly related to n thermodynamic forces $\mathscr{F}_j$ (Eqn 7.55)

If,

(1) The flows $\mathscr{I}_i$ are the time-derivatives of independent Onsager coordinates α_i (Eqn 7.52)

(2) The α_i are related to the entropy change ΔS by Eqn (7.51)
(3) The forces $\mathcal{F}_j$ are defined in accordance with Eqn (7.53)

and if,

(4) The α_i are even functions of the particle velocities
(5) The equations of motion are reversible,

then the phenomenological coefficients $\mathcal{L}_{ij}$ obey the Onsager reciprocal relations.

Conditions (4) and (5) are statistical-mechanical in origin. They become important if magnetic fields and Coriolis forces must be taken into account (Casimir, 1945; Yourgrau *et al*., 1966; Fitts, 1962; De Groot and Mazur, 1962).

V. LINEAR TRANSFORMATIONS OF THE FLOWS AND FORCES

Suppose we have a set of linearly independent flows and forces which satisfy equations (7.54) and (7.55).

Onsager's theorem leads to the reciprocal relations of Eqn (7.56) *if and only if* the $\mathcal{J}_i$ and the $\mathcal{F}_j$ satisfy the additional conditions stated earlier.

The mere fact that the $\mathcal{J}_i$ and the $\mathcal{F}_j$ satisfy Eqns (7.54) and (7.55) does not in itself lead to the reciprocal relations for the phenomenological coefficients.

Suppose for example that the $\mathcal{J}_i$ and the $\mathcal{F}_j$ obey Eqns (7.54) to (7.56). Then it is possible by linear combination of the $\mathcal{J}_i$ and the $\mathcal{F}_i$ to construct new flows $\mathcal{J}_i^1$ and new forces $\mathcal{F}_i^1$ which also obey Eqns (7.54) and (7.55) but which do *not* give reciprocal relations. Conversely, if a set of flows $\mathcal{J}_i$ and a set of forces $\mathcal{F}_j$ obey Eqns (7.54) and (7.55) but not Eqn (7.56), it is always possible by a mere linear combination of flows and forces to find a new set of flows $\mathcal{J}_i$ and forces $\mathcal{F}_j$ for which all three equations are valid (Coleman and Truesdell, 1960).

Suppose we have a set of linearly independent flows $\mathcal{J}_i$ and linearly independent forces $\mathcal{F}_j$ for which the reciprocal relations are valid. Then it is mathematically possible to construct an infinite number of other sets of linearly independent flows and forces for which reciprocal relations also hold (Meixner and Reik, 1959; Coleman and Truesdell, 1960).

The new forces are to be defined by linear transformations of the form

$$\mathcal{F}_i^{11} = \sum_i a_{ij}\mathcal{F}_j \tag{7.57}$$

in which the a_{ij} are arbitrary coefficients.

The new flows are

$$\mathcal{J}_i^{11} = \sum_j b_{ij}\mathcal{J}_j \tag{7.58}$$

and, for a given choice of the a_{ij}, it is always possible to choose the coefficients b_{ij} in such a way as to obtain reciprocal relations $\mathscr{L}_{ij}^{11} = \mathscr{L}_{ji}^{11}$ for the new flows and forces. Only this type of symmetry-preserving transformation is really suitable for the selection of alternative flows and forces (Coleman and Truesdell, 1960; Andrews, 1967).

The concept of symmetry of the phenomenological coefficients arises naturally from the matrix representation, i.e.

$$\begin{pmatrix} \mathscr{I}_1 \\ \mathscr{I}_2 \\ \mathscr{I}_3 \end{pmatrix} = \begin{pmatrix} \mathscr{L}_{11} & \mathscr{L}_{12} & \mathscr{L}_{13} \\ \mathscr{L}_{21} & \mathscr{L}_{22} & \mathscr{L}_{23} \\ \mathscr{L}_{31} & \mathscr{L}_{32} & \mathscr{L}_{33} \end{pmatrix} \begin{pmatrix} \mathscr{F}_1 \\ \mathscr{F}_2 \\ \mathscr{F}_3 \end{pmatrix} \tag{7.59}$$

The matrix of phenomenological coefficients is symmetric when the corresponding non-diagonal components are equal.

These are the cross coefficients. The main coefficients lie on the diagonal itself. The matrix of phenomenological coefficients is a square ($n \times n$) matrix since the number of flows is in general equal to the number of forces.

It can be shown mathematically that a linear homogeneous dependence both of the flows $\mathscr{I}_i$ and of the forces $\mathscr{F}_j$ does not necessarily invalidate the reciprocal relations because, although the $\mathscr{L}_{ij}$ are then not uniquely defined, the freedom which exists in the definition of the $\mathscr{L}_{ij}$ can always be used to ensure that the reciprocal relations are satisfied (De Groot and Mazur, 1962). It can also be demonstrated that a linear homogeneous dependence of the flows $\mathscr{I}_i$ alone will leave the validity of the Onsager reciprocal relations unimpaired. (De Groot and Mazur, 1962).

There is so much mathematical freedom in the definition of the flows and forces that reciprocal relations deduced from Eqns (7.54) and (7.55) alone are of doubtful physical significance in the context of the Onsager reciprocity theorem.

It is generally very difficult to establish that a given choice of flows and forces will satisfy all the physical requirements of the Onsager theorem. (Coleman and Truesdell, 1960). Therefore it is probably better to adopt, as an additional postulate, the validity of the Onsager reciprocal relations for certain "physically realistic" flows and forces which satisfy Eqns (7.54) and (7.55). This then constitutes a third fundamental postulate of nonequilibrium thermodynamics, and is to be justified by comparison with experiment (Miller, 1960) or by appeal to molecular theories (Fitts, 1962; De Groot and Mazur, 1962; Wei, 1966; Andrews, 1967).

REFERENCES

Andrews, F. C. (1967). *Ind. Eng. Chem. Fundamentals.*, **6**, 48.
Callen, H. B. (1960). "Thermodynamics." John Wiley, Inc., New York.

Casimir, H. B. G., (1945). *Revs. mod. Phys.*, **17,** 343.

Coleman, B. D. and Truesdell, C., (1960). *J. Chem. Phys.*, **33,** 28.

Fitts, D. D. (1962). "Nonequilibrium Thermodynamics." McGraw-Hill, New York.

De Groot, S. R. (1959). "Thermodynamics of Irreversible Processes," North-Holland Publishing Co., Amsterdam.

De Groot, S. R. and Mazur, P. (1962). "Nonequilibrium Thermodynamics." North-Holland Publishing Co., Amsterdam.

Guggenheim, E. A. (1957). "Thermodynamics." 3rd Edn., North-Holland Publishing Co., Amsterdam.

Haase, R. (1963). "Thermodynamik der irreversiblen Prozesse." Dr. Dietrich Steinkopff Verlag, Darmstadt.

Lothe, J. (1966). *J. Chem Phys.*, **45,** 2678.

Manes, M. (1963). *J. Chem. Phys.*, **39,** 456.

Meixner, J. and Reik, H. G. (1959). "Thermodynamik der irreversiblen Prozesse." *In* "Handbuch der Physik" Vol. 3, Part 2. Ed. S. Flügge, Springer-Verlag, Berlin.

Miller, D. G. (1960). *Chem. Revs.* **60,** 15.

Onsager, L. (1931). *Phys. Rev.* **37,** 405; **38,** 2265.

Prigogine, I. (1961). "Introduction to Thermodynamics of Irreversible Processes." 2nd Edn. Interscience Publishers, New York.

Tisza, L. (1966). "Generalised Thermodynamics." M.I.T. Press, Cambridge, Massachusetts.

Wei, J. (1966). *Ind. Eng. Chem.*, **58,** 55.

Yourgrau, W., Van der Merve, A. and Raw, G. (1966). "A Treatise on Irreversible and Statistical Thermophysics." McGraw-Hill, New York.

Chapter 8 Discontinuous Systems

The thermodynamic flows and forces of Chapter 7 are those to which Onsager's reciprocity theorem refers, but in discussing real systems other flows and forces are commonly used. The new flows and forces are obtained in such a way that the entropy production remains the same, and linear phenomenological equations can be written, but the validity of the reciprocal relations requires careful examination. The various transformations are discussed in detail in other texts (Prigogine, 1961; De Groot, 1959; De Groot and Mazur, 1962) but we shall consider only one possibility here.

I. OPEN COMPOSITE SYSTEMS

Suppose the sub systems ϕ and σ of Chapter 7 are open to exchange of matter, energy and volume with the environment. Then the entropy change for the composite system may in analogy with Eqn (7.12) be resolved into an *entropy flow* d_ES/dt and an *entropy production* d_IS/dt

$$\frac{dS}{dt} = \frac{d_ES}{dt} + \frac{d_IS}{dt} \tag{8.1}$$

The entropy flow is calculated using the Gibbs equation and represents the reversible interactions with the environment. In general the pure volume changes are assumed to occur reversibly by interaction with the environment ($d_IV^\phi = d_IV^\sigma = 0$) and the only "volume flows" of interest turn out to be those associated with the flow of chemical components from one sub system to the other.

The entropy production relates to the irreversible processes in which energy and matter "flow" from one sub-system to the other. If the volume changes are taken as part of the external entropy flow and if the *second law heat flux* $\mathscr{J}_{Q2}$ is introduced we can write (Prigogine, 1961; De Groot, 1959)

$$\frac{d_IS}{dt} = \Delta\left(\frac{1}{T}\right)\mathscr{J}_{Q2} + \sum_{k=1}^{n}\left(\frac{A_k}{T^\sigma}\right)\mathscr{J}_k \tag{8.2}$$

in which the thermodynamic force for "heat flow" is

$$\mathscr{F}_{Q2} = \Delta\left(\frac{1}{T}\right) = \frac{1}{T^\phi} - \frac{1}{T^\sigma} \tag{8.3}$$

and the thermodynamic force for "mass flow" is

$$\mathscr{F}_k = \frac{A_k}{T} = -\frac{(\Delta\mu_k)_T}{T} = -\frac{(\mu_k^\phi - \mu_k^\sigma)_T}{T^\sigma} \tag{8.4}$$

A_k is customarily known as the *affinity of mass transfer* for component k. The chemical potential difference

$$(\Delta\mu)_T = (\mu_k^\phi - \mu_k^\sigma)_T \tag{8.5}$$

is taken at constant temperature $T = T^\sigma$ and represents the chemical potential difference in an equivalent isothermal system, i.e. one in which the mole numbers N_k^ϕ, N_k^σ and the pressures p^ϕ and p^σ retain their existing values, but in which $T^\phi = T^\sigma$.

The heat flow $\mathscr{I}_{Q2}$ is defined as positive for a heat flow from sub system σ to sub system ϕ. The mass flows $\mathscr{I}_k$ are defined by

$$\mathscr{I}_k \equiv \frac{d_I N_k^\phi}{dt} \tag{8.6}$$

and relate only to the internal mass transfers between the two sub systems.

For a spontaneous "heat flow" to sub system ϕ we require [Eqn (7.38)]

$$\Delta\left(\frac{1}{T}\right) > 0 \quad \text{or} \quad T^\sigma > T^\phi \tag{8.7}$$

For a spontaneous "mass flow" to sub system ϕ we normally expect

$$\frac{A_k}{T} > 0 \quad \text{or} \quad (\mu_k^\sigma)_{T^\sigma} > (\mu_k^\phi)_{T^\sigma} \tag{8.8}$$

A positive value of the affinity means that a spontaneous transfer to sub system ϕ is possible. The affinities are zero at equilibrium if there are no unusual constraints on the internal transfers.

We have also [cf. Eqns (7.18) and (7.19)]

$$A_k = T\left(\frac{\partial_I S}{\partial N_k^\phi}\right)_{U,V,N_j} = -\left(\frac{\partial_I G}{\partial N_k^\phi}\right)_{T,p,N_j} \tag{8.9}$$

since A_k is the thermodynamic affinity which would be obtained on the basis of the *dissipation function* Td_IS/dt, i.e. for mass flow only in an isothermal system at constant pressure

$$-\frac{\partial_I G}{\partial t} = T\frac{d_I S}{dt} = \sum_k A_k \mathscr{I}_k \tag{8.10}$$

II. COUPLING OF HEAT AND MASS TRANSFER IN SINGLE-COMPONENT SYSTEMS

For a single-component system

$$\frac{d_I S}{dt} = \left[\Delta\left(\frac{I}{T}\right)\mathscr{I}_{Q2} + \frac{A_k}{T^\sigma}\mathscr{I}_k\right] \geqslant 0 \tag{8.11}$$

and the phenomenological equations are

$$\begin{aligned} \mathscr{I}_k &= \mathscr{L}_{kk}(A_k/T^\sigma) + \mathscr{L}_{kQ}\,\Delta\left(\frac{I}{T}\right) \\ \mathscr{I}_{Q2} &= \mathscr{L}_{Qk}(A_k/T^\sigma) + \mathscr{L}_{QQ}\,\Delta\left(\frac{I}{T}\right) \end{aligned} \tag{8.12}$$

The phenomenological coefficients are postulated to obey the reciprocal relations $\mathscr{L}_{kQ} = \mathscr{L}_{Qk}$ (Miller, 1960). There is a further restriction on the phenomenological coefficients which arises from the second law inequality

$$\frac{d_I S}{dt} = [\mathscr{F}_{Q2}\cdot\mathscr{I}_{Q2} + \mathscr{F}_k\mathscr{I}_k] \geqslant 0 \tag{8.13}$$

If we substitute from Eqns (8.12) into Eqn (8.13) we find that

$$\mathscr{L}_{QQ}(\mathscr{F}_{Q2})^2 + (\mathscr{L}_{Qk} + \mathscr{L}_{kQ})\mathscr{F}_{Q2}\cdot\mathscr{F}_k + \mathscr{L}_{kk}(\mathscr{F}_k)^2 \geqslant 0 \tag{8.14}$$

Equation (8.14) must be positive for all positive or negative values of the variables $\mathscr{F}_{Q2}$ and $\mathscr{F}_k$, except at equilibrium when $\mathscr{F}_{Q2} = \mathscr{F}_k = 0$ and the entropy production vanishes. The phenomenological coefficients must therefore satisfy the inequalities (Prigogine, 1961)

$$\mathscr{L}_{QQ}, \mathscr{L}_{kk} > 0; \qquad (\mathscr{L}_{Qk} + \mathscr{L}_{kQ})^2 < 4\mathscr{L}_{QQ}\mathscr{L}_{kk} \tag{8.15}$$

so that if the reciprocal relations hold

$$\mathscr{L}_{Qk}^2 = \mathscr{L}_{kQ}^2 < \mathscr{L}_{QQ}\cdot\mathscr{L}_{kk} \tag{8.16}$$

The main coefficients $\mathscr{L}_{QQ}$, $\mathscr{L}_{kk}$ are always positive, but the cross-coefficients $\mathscr{L}_{kQ}$, $\mathscr{L}_{Qk}$ may have any sign.

If the single-component system is isothermal the force $\mathscr{F}_{Q2}$ disappears, but the flow of heat $\mathscr{I}_{Q2}$ may remain. We have the phenomenological equations

$$\begin{aligned} \mathscr{I}_k &= \mathscr{L}_{kk}\left(\frac{A^k}{T^\sigma}\right) \\ \mathscr{I}_{Q2} &= \mathscr{L}_{Qk}\left(\frac{A_k}{T^\sigma}\right) \end{aligned} \tag{8.17}$$

The heat flow $\mathscr{I}_{Q2}$ does not disappear unless the coefficient $\mathscr{L}_{Qk}$ is zero, i.e. *the transfer of matter is accompanied in general by a transfer of heat*. The quantity Q^* defined by

$$\left(\frac{\mathscr{I}_{Q2}}{\mathscr{I}_k}\right)_{\Delta T=0} = \frac{\mathscr{L}_{Qk}}{\mathscr{L}_{kk}} = Q^* \tag{8.18}$$

is known as the *heat of transfer*. Q^* provides a measure of the transfer of heat which is associated with unit transfer of mass in a single-component isothermal system.

For the *stationary state* in which $\mathscr{I}_k = 0$ but in which $\mathscr{I}_{Q2}$ does not disappear we may, with the help of Eqns (8.12) and (8.18), obtain the result

$$\frac{A_k T^{\phi}}{\Delta T} = Q^* \tag{8.19}$$

Equations (8.18) and (8.19) provide in principle a means of investigating the coupling between heat and mass transfer in such a discontinuous system.

The attainment of thermodynamic equilibrium is characterised by the simultaneous disappearance of both the flows and the forces, provided that there are no special constraints on the flows.

III. CHEMICAL REACTION AND THE EXTENT OF REACTION ξ

We now consider chemical reactions which lead to changes in the mole numbers N_k, $k = 1, 2, \ldots, n$. Prigogine (1961). The total number of moles in a reacting system is not conserved, but the total mass is. The conservation of mass is expressed by the stoichiometric equation for the reaction. Let M_k both represent the molar mass of component k and represent component k symbolically. The stoichiometric equation for the ith reaction is ($i = 1, 2, \ldots, s$)

$$\sum_{k=1}^{m} \nu_{ki} M_k = 0 \tag{8.20}$$

and ν_{ki} is the stoichiometric coefficient with which component k enters reaction i. It represents the number of moles of component i which are produced in the reaction equation. ν_{ki} is positive if component k is a product and is negative if component k is a reactant. The mass of component k produced per stoichiometric unit of reaction is $\nu_{ki} M_k$ and the *extent of reaction* ξ_i is then unity. When no reaction has occurred, $\xi_i = 0$. In general

$$d_i m_k = \nu_{ki} M_k \, d\xi_i \tag{8.21}$$

where $d_i m_k$ is the mass of component k produced by a change $d\xi_i$ in the extent of reaction of reaction i. Equation (8.21) holds for each species $k = 1, 2, \ldots, n$ since the extent of reaction ξ_i is independent of k: it characterises the reaction as a whole. The conservation of the total mass m in each chemical reaction i requires that

$$d_i m = \sum_{k=1}^{n} d_i m_k = \sum_{k=1}^{n} (\nu_{ki} M_k)\, d\xi_i = 0 \tag{8.22}$$

Equation (8.20) follows from Eqn (8.22) since Eqn (8.22) must hold for an arbitrary value of $d\xi_i$.

The rate of accumulation of component k in reaction i is a function of the *chemical reaction rate* $d\xi_i/dt$

$$\frac{d_i m_k}{dt} = \nu_{ki} M_k \frac{d\xi_i}{dt} \tag{8.23}$$

In terms of the mole numbers N_k,

$$\frac{d_i N_k}{dt} = \nu_{ki} \frac{d\xi_i}{dt} \tag{8.24}$$

The rate of production of entropy by reaction i is

$$\begin{aligned} \frac{d_I S}{dt} &= \sum_{k=1}^{n} \left(\frac{\partial_I S}{\partial N_k}\right)_{U,V,N_j} \cdot \frac{d_i N_k}{dt} = -\sum_{k=1}^{n} \left(\frac{\mu_k}{T}\right) \frac{d_i N_k}{dt} \\ &= -\frac{1}{T}\left(\sum_{k=1}^{n} \nu_{ki}\mu_k\right) \cdot \frac{d\xi_i}{dt} \end{aligned} \tag{8.25}$$

It appears as the product of the chemical reaction rate with the *chemical affinity* $-1/T\left(\sum_{k=1}^{n} \nu_{ki}\mu_k\right)$. Following De Donder, however, it is conventional to define the Affinity A_i of a chemical reaction i as

$$A_i = -\sum_{k=1}^{n} \nu_{ki}\mu_k \tag{8.26}$$

The total rate of production of entropy is therefore

$$\frac{d_I S}{dt} = \sum_{i=1}^{s} \frac{A_i}{T} \cdot \frac{d\xi_i}{dt} \geqslant 0 \tag{8.27}$$

At equilibrium the chemical reaction rates are zero and the entropy production disappears. If there are no restrictions on the ξ_i, then the affinities A_i also disappear at equilibrium.

The term "chemical reaction" may include processes such as the passage of a component from one sub-system to another, or even more general physico-chemical transformations (Prigogine, 1961) (cf. Eqn 8.10).

If we have two reactions for which

$$\frac{d_I S}{dt} = \left[\frac{A_1}{T}\frac{d\xi_1}{dt} + \frac{A_2}{T}\frac{d\xi_2}{dt}\right] \geqslant 0 \tag{8.28}$$

it is possible for one of the reactions to proceed in a direction which *opposes* its own affinity, without necessarily violating the second-law inequality, i.e. we may have simultaneously

$$\frac{A_1}{T}\cdot\frac{d\xi_1}{dt} < 0 \quad \text{and} \quad \frac{A_2}{T}\cdot\frac{d\xi_2}{dt} > 0 \tag{8.29}$$

if the entropy production of reaction 2 more than compensates for the "entropy consumption" of reaction 1.

Such sets of "coupled chemical reactions" may be important in biological systems in which the mass transfer of a species may take place in the opposed direction to the chemical potential gradient (Katchalsky and Curran, 1965).

For the discussion of continuous systems it is usual to adopt mass units rather than molar units (Fitts, 1962; De Groot and Mazur, 1962). For each stoichiometric unit of reaction $i(d\xi_i = 1)$ the total mass of products is

$$a_i = \sum_{\text{products}} \nu_{ki} M_k \tag{8.30}$$

and we may regard each stoichiometric unit of reaction i as equivalent to a_i grams of chemical reaction.

The extent of reaction $d\lambda_i$ in units of grams of chemical reaction per gram of original reactants is

$$d\lambda_i = a_i\, d\xi_i/m \tag{8.31}$$

The mass of component k produced per gram of reaction i is

$$\hat{\nu}_{ki} = \nu_{ki} M_k/a_i \tag{8.32}$$

so that we may replace Eqn (8.21) by the equation

$$d_i m_k = m\hat{\nu}_{ki}\, d\lambda_i \tag{8.33}$$

The rate of production of entropy per unit mass by reaction i is, since the mass fraction $W_k = m_k/m$

$$\frac{1}{m}\left(\frac{d_I S}{dt}\right)_i = -\sum_{k=1}^{n}\left(\frac{\hat{\mu}_k}{T}\right)\frac{d_i W_k}{dt} \tag{8.34}$$

in which $\hat{\mu}_k$ is the *partial specific Gibbs function*, or chemical potential per unit mass, for component k.

If we define the specific affinity $\hat{A}_i$ of reaction i by analogy to Eqn (8.26) as

$$\hat{A}_i = -\sum_{k=1}^{n} \hat{\nu}_{ki}\hat{\mu}_k = A_i/a_i \tag{8.35}$$

then Eqn (8.34) takes the expected form

$$\frac{1}{m}\left(\frac{d_I S}{dt}\right)_i = \left(\frac{d_I \hat{S}}{dt}\right)_i = \frac{\hat{A}_i}{T} \cdot \frac{d\lambda_i}{dt} \tag{8.36}$$

and we note the relationships (Prigogine, 1961)

$$\hat{A}_i = T\left(\frac{\partial \hat{S}}{\partial \lambda_i}\right)_{U,V,\lambda_j} = -\left(\frac{\partial \hat{G}}{\partial \lambda_i}\right)_{p,T,\lambda_j} \tag{8.37}$$

and

$$A_i = T\left(\frac{\partial S}{\partial \xi_i}\right)_{U,V,\zeta_j} = -\left(\frac{\partial G}{\partial \xi_i}\right)_{p,T,\zeta_j} \tag{8.38}$$

The *extent of reaction* (ξ_i or λ_i) is *a new variable of state* which expresses in a compact form the changes in the mole numbers N_k, or in the mass fractions W_k. For a homogeneous system the entropy per unit mass (S/m) is identical with the specific entropy $\hat{S}$, and the Gibbs function per unit mass (G/m) is identical with the specific Gibbs function $\hat{G}$.

IV. ISOTHERMAL MULTICOMPONENT SYSTEMS

A. Electrochemical Systems

The individual ionic components of an electrolyte mixture are not accessible in an isolated state and they must normally be accompanied by other ions of opposite charge. From this point of view the individual ionic species do *not* qualify as thermodynamic components in terms of which the composition and thermodynamic behaviour of the mixture may be described. Only certain specially selected neutral combinations of ions are really appropriate for a thermodynamic description of such a system.

It has, however, become conventional to treat the individual ionic species as components of the system in discussion of electrochemical systems. Since these species are charged it is necessary to take into account the electrical work that must be done when introducing an ion of ionic valency z_k, (which includes the sign of the ionic charge), into a region of electrical potential ψ. Although there is no unique way of separating the electrical work terms from the "chemical" work terms for ionic species, this is usually done by the formal introduction of the electrochemical potentials $\tilde{\mu}_k$ for the ionic species (Guggenheim, 1957; Prigogine, 1961).

$$\tilde{\mu}_k = \mu_k + z_k F\psi \tag{8.39}$$

F is the *Faraday* (coulombs per equivalent), ψ is the electrical potential (volts) and z_k is the ionic valency. μ_k represents a "chemical" contribution to the total electrochemical potential $\tilde{\mu}_k$.

The *electrochemical potential difference* $(\Delta\tilde{\mu}_k)_T$ in an isothermal composite system is influenced by the electrical potential difference $(\Delta\psi = \psi^\phi - \psi^\sigma)$

$$(\Delta\tilde{\mu}_k)_T = (\Delta\mu_k)_T + z_k F\,\Delta\psi \tag{8.40}$$

The chemical potential difference $(\Delta\mu_k)_T$ is a function of the pressure difference $\Delta p = p^\phi - p^\sigma$ between the two phases. If Δp is sufficiently small and $\bar{v}_k{}^\phi$, the *partial molar volume* of component k in phase ϕ, may be treated as constant Eqn (7.21) leads to the result

$$(\Delta\mu_k)_T = (\Delta\mu_k)_{T,p} + \bar{v}_k\phi\,\Delta p \tag{8.41}$$

The *electrochemical affinity* $\tilde{A}_k$ for the transfer of an ionic component k from sub-system σ to sub-system ϕ is defined as (Prigogine, 1961)

$$\tilde{A}_k = -(\Delta\tilde{\mu}_k)_T = -\{(\Delta\mu_k)_{T,p} + \bar{v}_k{}^\phi\,\Delta_p + z_k F\,\Delta\psi\} \tag{8.42}$$

and is seen to consist of three separate contributions. $(\Delta\mu_k)_{T,p}$ represents the effect of *differences of composition* between phase ϕ and phase σ; $\bar{v}_k{}^\phi\,\Delta p$ takes into account *pressure differences* and $z_k F\,\Delta\psi$ takes into account *electrical potential differences*. This separation into three components has physical meaning only if the three contributions can be separately measured and independently altered.

Consider a closed isothermal composite system in which ionic species are transported from sub-system σ to sub-system ϕ. The entropy production is (Prigogine, 1961)

$$\frac{d_I S}{dt} = \sum_{k=1}^{n} \frac{\tilde{A}_k}{T} \cdot \mathscr{I}_k \tag{8.43}$$

If the "flow" of electrical charge I is defined as

$$I = F \sum_{k=1}^{n} z_k \mathscr{I}_k \tag{8.44}$$

and the "flow" of volume $\mathscr{I}_v$ which is associated with the mass flows is defined as

$$\mathscr{I}_v = \sum_{k=1}^{n} \bar{v}_k{}^\phi \mathscr{I}_k \tag{8.45}$$

then the entropy production (8.43) may be resolved into three distinct contributions

$$\frac{d_I S}{dt} = -\frac{\Delta\psi}{T} \cdot I - \frac{\Delta p}{T} \cdot \mathscr{I}_v - \sum_{k=1}^{n} \frac{(\Delta\mu_k)_{T,p}}{T} \cdot \mathscr{I}_k \tag{8.46}$$

Both $\mathscr{I}_v$ and I are directly related to the mass flows $\mathscr{I}_k$ and in this sense can hardly be regarded as representing independent irreversible processes. However, it is in principle possible to vary $(\Delta\mu_k)_{T,p}$ Δp and $\Delta\psi$ independently, and phenomenological equations based on Eqn (8.46) lead to possibilities of "*thermodynamic coupling*" between $\mathscr{I}_v$, I and the $\mathscr{I}_k$ which are not explicitly apparent in phenomenological equations based on the entropy production of Eqn (8.43).

In the remainder of this chapter we shall consider only an entropy production of the type of Eqn (8.43). The implications of Eqn (8.46) will be examined in Chapter 13.

The entropy production disappears at equilibrium

$$\frac{d_I S}{dt} = \sum_{j=1}^{n} \frac{\tilde{A}_k}{T} \cdot \mathscr{I}_k = 0 \tag{8.47}$$

and the flows $\mathscr{I}_k$ also vanish

$$\mathscr{I}_k = \sum_{j=1}^{n} \mathscr{L}_{kj}\tilde{A}_j = 0 \tag{8.48}$$

Equation (8.47) implies the following restriction on virtual displacements δN_k^ϕ from the equilibrium composition of sub-system ϕ

$$\sum_{k=1}^{n} \tilde{A}_k \, \delta N_k^\phi = 0 \tag{8.49}$$

If Eqn (8.49) is to apply for arbitrary independent virtual displacements δN_k^ϕ, the equilibrium conditions must take the form

$$\tilde{A}_k = 0 \qquad (k = 1, 2, \ldots, n) \tag{8.50}$$

The equilibrium values of the $\tilde{A}_k$ are uniquely defined by Eqn (8.49) only if the virtual displacements δN_k^ϕ are linearly independent. The equilibrium conditions (8.50) are those which would be obtained for an isolated composite system from the requirement that the entropy S have a maximum value at equilibrium, subject to the existing constraints (Chapter 7). When the $\tilde{A}_k$ are all zero it follows from Eqn (8.48) that the flows $\mathscr{I}_k$ are all zero.

If a given flow $\mathscr{I}_j$ is prevented from occurring, then the corresponding phenomenological coefficients are zero

$$\mathscr{L}_{jk} = 0 \qquad (k = 1, 2, \ldots, n; \text{ "constrained flow" } \mathscr{I}_j) \tag{8.51}$$

and at equilibrium we may have

$$\tilde{A}_j \neq 0 \qquad (\text{"constrained flow" } \mathscr{I}_j) \tag{8.52}$$

However, the affinities $\tilde{A}_k$ will vanish at equilibrium *for those components which are free to attain an equilibrium distribution and which correspond to linearly independent flows* $\mathscr{I}_k$, i.e.

$$\tilde{A}_k = -[(\Delta\mu_k)_{T,p} + \bar{v}_k^\phi \,\Delta p + z_k F \,\Delta\psi] = 0 \tag{8.53}$$

If some components are not free to attain an equilibrium distribution, as may happen when a semi-permeable membrane separates two solutions and opposes the transfer of certain components, an electrical potential difference $\Delta\psi$ and a pressure difference Δp are often established across the membrane at equilibrium, *and in this way the equilibrium distributions of the unconstrained components are modified by the distribution of the constrained components.* Since at equilibrium

$$-(\Delta\mu_k)_{T,p} = \bar{v}_k^{\phi}\,\Delta p + z_k F\,\Delta\psi \tag{8.54}$$

the equilibrium distributions of the unconstrained components can be used in favourable circumstances to determine Δp and $\Delta\psi$, i.e. we obtain the classical thermodynamic results (Guggenheim, 1957).

$$\Delta\psi = -\frac{(\Delta\mu_k)_{T,p}}{z_k F}\cdots(\bar{v}_k^{\phi}\,\Delta p \ll (\Delta\mu_k)_{T,p}) \tag{8.55}$$

and

$$\Delta p = -\frac{(\Delta\mu_k)_{T,p}}{\bar{v}_k^{\phi}}\cdots(z_k F\,\Delta\psi \ll (\Delta\mu_k)_{T,p}) \tag{8.56}$$

If the chemical potential differences $(\Delta\mu_k)_{T,p}$ are known as functions of the compositions of the phases it is possible to calculate the magnitude of $\Delta\psi$ and Δp. In this particular form of thermodynamic equilibrium the "forces" $\Delta\psi$ and Δp do not disappear. For ionic systems with $\Delta\psi \neq 0$ and $\Delta p \neq 0$ we have a *Donnan Membrane Equilibrium* (Donnan, 1934) and for nonionic systems with $\Delta p \neq 0$ we have an *Osmotic Equilibrium* (Guggenheim, 1957). The *Donnan Potential* $\Delta\psi$ cannot, strictly speaking, be measured but its use can be justified in terms of the physical picture that is obtained of the membrane processes (cf. Chapter 13).

The phenomenological equations which are obtained on the basis of the "splitting" in Eqn (8.46) will be examined in more detail in Chapter 13. In the remainder of this chapter the phenomenological equations based on Eqn (8.43) will continue to be used.

B. Phenomenological Equations

In the abstract theoretical discussion of a discontinuous composite system in Chapter 7, the "flows" were the time derivatives of scalar quantities and there was no basis on which to distinguish between the different types of flow when writing the phenomenological equations. It was in principle possible for any of the different flows to interact.

A true discontinuous system represents a limiting type of system with which a real system may be compared. A system is either a true discontinuous system, or it is not discontinuous and the discontinuous formalism may be used to describe its behaviour only in a formal sense. A proper description of the system would have to examine the behaviour in the regions in which gradients of the variables are found.

A perfectly discontinuous system is unlikely to exist in practice and the transfers between the sub-systems will occur via a membrane, a capillary or through a finite interfacial region. The flows within these continuous regions may be vector or tensor in character and so there may be some grounds for using "Curie's principle" to distinguish between these different types of flow when phenomenological equations are written, at least for transport through an *isotropic* membrane system, (Prigogine, 1961; De Groot, 1959; De Groot and Mazur, 1962).

It is usual to suppose that the "vectorial" flows of matter and of energy may interact with each other, but that they may not interact with the scalar chemical reaction "flows." It is also postulated that the chemical reaction flows may interact with each other only if these flows take place in the same sub-system.

On this basis the entropy production falls into three separate contributions, each of which separately satisfies the second law inequality, i.e.

$$\left(\frac{d_I S}{dt}\right)_{tr} = \left[\Delta\left(\frac{1}{T}\right)\mathscr{I}_{Q2} + \sum_{k=1}^{n} \frac{\tilde{A}_k}{T^\sigma}\cdot \mathscr{I}_k\right] \geqslant 0 \tag{8.57}$$

$$\left(\frac{d_I S}{dt}\right)_r^\phi = \frac{1}{T^\phi}\sum_{i=1}^{s} A_i^\phi \cdot \frac{d\xi_i^\phi}{dt} \leqslant 0 \tag{8.58}$$

$$\left(\frac{d_I S}{dt}\right)_r^\sigma = \frac{1}{T^\sigma}\sum_{i=1}^{s} A_i^\sigma \frac{d\xi_i^\sigma}{dt} \geqslant 0 \tag{8.59}$$

Equations (8.58) and (8.59) imply a local formulation of the second law inequality, in the following sense. For a composite system we already have the global formulation

$$d_I S = (d_I S^\phi + d_I S^\sigma) \geqslant 0 \tag{8.60}$$

which places no specific restrictions on $d_I S^\phi$ or on $d_I S^\sigma$ taken separately. A stronger local formulation of the second law inequality might take the form (Prigogine, 1961)

$$d_I S^\phi \geqslant 0; \qquad d_I S^\sigma \geqslant 0 \tag{8.61}$$

and so forbid any coupling process whereby the absorption of entropy in one part of a system may be compensated by the excess production of entropy in another part of the system.

The phenomenological equations for the "vectorial" flows are

$$\begin{aligned} \mathscr{I}_k &= \sum_j \mathscr{L}_{kj}\left(\frac{\tilde{A}_j}{T^\sigma}\right) + \mathscr{L}_{kQ}\,\Delta\left(\frac{1}{T}\right) \\ \mathscr{I}_{Q2} &= \sum_k \mathscr{L}_{Qk}\left(\frac{\tilde{A}_k}{T^\sigma}\right) + \mathscr{L}_{QQ}\,\Delta\left(\frac{1}{T}\right) \end{aligned} \tag{8.62}$$

For chemical reaction in phase ϕ we have

$$\frac{d\xi_i^\phi}{dt} = \sum_j \mathscr{L}_{ij}^\phi\left(\frac{A_i^\phi}{T^\phi}\right) \tag{8.63}$$

and for chemical reaction in phase σ

$$\frac{d\xi_i^\sigma}{dt} = \sum_j \mathscr{L}_{ij}^\sigma\left(\frac{A_i^\sigma}{T^\sigma}\right) \tag{8.64}$$

The linear phenomenological equations (8.63) and (8.64) for chemical reaction are obeyed only in a very narrow region near to chemical equilibrium, so that empirical kinetic equations are more useful in describing normal chemical reactions (Fitts, 1962). In this particular respect the theory of nonequilibrium thermodynamics is unrewarding.

Provided that the chemical potentials of all components remain well-defined at all times in each sub-system, there appear to be no special restrictions on the application of nonequilibrium thermodynamics to problems of simultaneous mass transfer and chemical reaction.

If, however, there are no internal processes whereby a sub-system may attain internal equilibrium, then the sub-system will not attain internal equilibrium before it has attained equilibrium with its surroundings (Hill and Plesner, 1964, 1965) and an approach based on nonequilibrium thermodynamics will be invalid.

C. Activity, Activity Coefficients and the Chemical Potentials

1. Nonionic Systems

A discussion of the chemical potentials μ_k is simplified by the introduction of the absolute activities λ_k of the chemical components (Guggenheim, 1957)

$$RT \ln \lambda_k = \mu_k \tag{8.65}$$

where R is the gas constant.

If λ_k^0 is the *absolute activity* of component k in some arbitrary *reference state*, then

$$RT \ln \lambda_k^0 = \mu_k^0 \tag{8.66}$$

in which μ_k^0 is the *standard chemical potential* of component k in the reference state.

Introducing the *relative activity* a_k

$$a_k = \lambda_k/\lambda_k^0 \tag{8.67}$$

we have the general expression for the chemical potential

$$\mu_k = \mu_k^0 + RT \ln a_k \tag{8.68}$$

The quantities a_k and μ_k^0 are determined by the choice of the reference state (for which $\lambda_k = \lambda_k^0$). In general λ_k^0 may be a function of the temperature T and pressure p, so that $\mu_k^0 = \mu_k^0(T, p)$.

1. (a) *Mole-Fractional Activity Coefficients Based on Raoult's Law*
The *mole fraction* x_k of component k is the intensive variable

$$x_k = N_k/\sum_k N_k \tag{8.69}$$

If a component k behaves ideally in the sense that it conforms to *Raoult's Law* we have

$$\lambda_k = \lambda_k^* x_k \qquad \text{(Raoult's Law)} \tag{8.70}$$

where λ_k^* is the absolute activity of *pure component k at the temperature T and pressure p of experiment*

$$\lambda_k^* = \lambda_k^*(T, p) \tag{8.71}$$

The relative activity a_k^* of an *ideal system* on the basis of *Raoult's* Law is

$$a_k^* = \lambda_k/\lambda_k^* = x_k \tag{8.72}$$

or, in a nonideal system,

$$a_k^* = \lambda_k/\lambda_k^* = f_k^* x_k \tag{8.73}$$

in which f_k^* is the *mole-fractional activity coefficient* based on Raoult's Law.

We expect ideal behaviour, in the sense of adherence to Raoult's Law, in the limit as $x_k \to 1$

$$\lim_{x_k \to 1} f_k^* = 1 \tag{8.74}$$

It follows from the Gibbs–Duhem equation that the chemical potentials μ_k at constant T and p are not independent, so that the λ_k are not independent. If in a binary solution at constant T and p the "solvent" (0) obeys Raoult's Law, the Gibbs–Duhem equation predicts that the "solute" (1) will obey *Henry's Law*, i.e. if

$$\lambda_0 = \lambda_0^* x_0 \qquad \text{(Raoult's Law for "solvent")} \tag{8.75}$$

then

$$\lambda_1 = \lambda_1^{\ominus} x_1 \qquad \text{(Henry's Law for "solute")} \tag{8.76}$$

where in general

$$\lambda_1^{\ominus} = h_1 \lambda_1^* \tag{8.77}$$

in which h_1 is the *Henry's Law constant* for the solute.

The behaviour of the solute in a binary solution is in general described by Eqn (8.73) i.e.

$$\lambda_1 = \lambda_1^* f_1^* x_1 \tag{8.78}$$

with the limiting behaviour

$$\lim_{x_1 \to 1} f_1^* = 1 \qquad \text{(Raoult's Law obeyed by solute)} \tag{8.79}$$

and

$$\lim_{x_1 \to 0} f_1^* = h_1 \qquad \text{(Henry's Law obeyed by solute)} \tag{8.80}$$

Analogous limiting behaviour may be expected in multicomponent systems; at infinite dilution a nonionic solute species tends to obey Henry's Law (Kirkwood and Oppenheim, 1961; Varsányi and Huszár, 1966).

$$\lim_{x_k \to 0} f_k^* = h_k \tag{8.81}$$

In the preceding discussion it has been tacitly assumed that the components k are completely miscible. If this is not so a complication arises which has been discussed with reference to dyeing systems by Milicevic (1963). The form of Raoult's Law may be preserved for systems of limited miscibility if an appropriate choice of reference state is made.

1. (b) *Mole-Fractional Activity Coefficients Based on Henry's Law*

If component k is ideally dilute in that it obeys Henry's Law, we have

$$\lambda_k = \lambda_k^{\ominus} x_k \tag{8.82}$$

and the relative activity $a_k^{\ominus}$ on the basis of Henry's Law is for an ideal solution

$$a_k^{\ominus} = \lambda_k / \lambda_k^{\ominus} = x_k \tag{8.83}$$

For a nonideal solution

$$a_k^{\ominus} = \lambda_k / \lambda_k^{\ominus} = f_k^{\ominus} x_k \tag{8.84}$$

or

$$\lambda_k = \lambda_k^{\ominus} f_k^{\ominus} x_k \tag{8.85}$$

Since

$$\lambda_k^{\ominus} = h_k \lambda_k^* \tag{8.86}$$

we have

$$a_k^* = h_k a_k^{\ominus} \tag{8.87}$$

$$f_k^* = h_k f_k^{\ominus} \tag{8.88}$$

and the limiting behaviour

$$\lim_{x_k \to 1} f_k^{\ominus} = 1/h_k \tag{8.89}$$

and

$$\lim_{x_k \to 0} f_k^{\ominus} = 1 \tag{8.90}$$

In general

$$\begin{aligned} \mu_k &= \mu_k^{\ominus}(p, T) + RT \ln f_k^{\ominus} x_k \\ &= \mu_k^*(p, T) + RT \ln f_k^* x_k \end{aligned} \tag{8.91}$$

with

$$\mu_k^{\ominus}(p, T) = \mu_k^*(p, T) + RT \ln h_k(p, T) \tag{8.92}$$

Reverting to the general rotation of Eqn (8.68) we may write

$$\mu_k = \mu_k^0(p, T) + RT \ln f_k x_k \tag{8.93}$$

where f_k is a *mole-fractional activity coefficient*. The quantities $\mu_k^0(T, p)$ and f_k are determined by the choice of reference state for λ_k^0.

1. (c) *Alternative Concentration Units*

Let m_k be the *molal concentration* of component k and let C_k be its molar concentration. Then the following three equations are equivalent expressions for λ_k

$$\lambda_k = (\lambda_k^0)_x f_k x_k \tag{8.94}$$

$$\lambda_k = (\lambda_k^0)_m \gamma_k m_k \tag{8.95}$$

$$\lambda_k = (\lambda_k^0)_c y_k C_k \tag{8.96}$$

γ_k is a *molal activity coefficient* and y_k is a *molar activity coefficient*. Each choice of concentration unit corresponds to a distinct choice of reference state, i.e. in general

$$(\lambda_k^0)_x \neq (\lambda_k^0)_m \neq (\lambda_k^0)_c \tag{8.97}$$

It follows that we may write the three equivalent expressions

$$\mu_k = (\mu_k^0)_x + RT \ln f_k x_k \tag{8.98}$$

$$\mu_k = (\mu_k^0)_m + RT \ln \gamma_k m_k \tag{8.99}$$

and

$$\mu_k = (\mu_k^0)_c + RT \ln y_k C_k \tag{8.100}$$

for the chemical potential μ_k. In general

$$(\mu_k^0)_x \neq (\mu_k^0)_m \neq (\mu_k^0)_c \tag{8.101}$$

It is often convenient to base the definition of the reference state on Henry's Law, in which case

$$\lim_{C_k \to 0} y_k = \lim_{m_k \to 0} \gamma_k = \lim_{x_k \to 0} f_k = 1 \tag{8.102}$$

f_k is often termed the *rational activity coefficient* and γ_k is known as the *practical activity coefficient* (Harned and Owen, 1958). The use of the molal concentrations m_k is often preferable to the use of the molar concentrations C_k because the C_k vary with temperature and, to a smaller extent, with pressure.

If species $k = 0$ is chosen as the "solvent"

$$x_k = \frac{M_0 m_k}{M_0 \sum_{k=1}^{n-1} m_k + 1000} = \frac{M_0 C_k}{\sum_{k=1}^{n-1} C_k(M_0 - M_k) + 1000\rho} \tag{8.103}$$

M_0 is the molecular weight of the solvent; M_k is the molecular weight of component k; ρ is the mass density of the solution.

For the solute ($k = 1$) in a binary solution ($n = 2$)

$$x_1 = \frac{M_0 m_1}{M_0 m_1 + 1000} = \frac{M_0 C_1}{C_1(M_0 - M_1) + 1000\rho} \tag{8.104}$$

At infinite dilution

$$\lim_{\substack{m_1 \to 0 \\ C_1 \to 0}} x_1 = \frac{M_0 m_1}{1000} = \frac{M_0 C_1}{1000\rho_0} \tag{8.105}$$

where p_0 is the mass density of the solvent.

It follows that

$$\begin{aligned}(\mu_1^0)_x &= (\mu_1^0)_c - RT \ln\left(\frac{M_0}{1000\rho_0}\right) \\ &= (\mu_1^0)_m - RT \ln\left(\frac{M_0}{1000}\right)\end{aligned} \tag{8.106}$$

and in dilute aqueous solutions $(\mu_1^0)_c \approx (\mu_1^0)_m$.

2. Ionic Systems

Although it is conventional to define the electrochemical potential $\tilde{\mu}_k$ of an ion by Eqn (8.39), and to refer to corresponding single-ion activities, in practice only those combinations of the $\tilde{\mu}_k$ which correspond to electrically neutral combinations of ions have real physical significance. Consider an electrically neutral combination of ions in which we have $\nu_k = |z_k|$ ions of type j and $\nu_j = |z_j|$ ions of type k. The symbol $|z_k|$ represents the *modulus* of z_k, i.e. the numerical magnitude regardless of sign. This combination of ions corresponds to a fully dissociated molecule of a hypothetical "salt" $J\nu_k K\nu_j$ which we shall refer to as the species jk.

We define the quantities (Harned and Owen, 1958)

$$\mu_{jk} = \nu_k\tilde{\mu}_j + \nu_j\tilde{\mu}_k \tag{8.107}$$

$$\mu^0_{jk} = \nu_k\tilde{\mu}^0_j + \nu_j\tilde{\mu}^0_k \tag{8.108}$$

$$\nu_{jk} = \nu_j + \nu_k \tag{8.109}$$

and write Eqn (8.39) in the form

$$\tilde{\mu}_k = (\tilde{\mu}^0_k)_x + RT\ln f_k x_k + z_k F\psi \tag{8.110}$$

Using Eqns (8.107) to (8.109) we find

$$\mu_{jk} = (\mu^0_{jk})_x + RT\ln (f_j^{\nu_k} f_k^{\nu_j})(x_j^{\nu_k} x_k^{\nu_j}) \tag{8.111}$$

and the terms involving ψ, which is not directly measurable, disappear.

We may define a mean *ionic mole fraction* $x^{\pm}_{jk}$ by

$$x^{\pm}_{jk} = \sqrt{x_j^{\nu_k} \cdot x^{\nu}_{k_j}} = x_{jk}\sqrt[\nu_{jk}]{\nu_k^{\nu_k} \cdot \nu_j^{\nu_j}} \tag{8.112}$$

where x_{jk} is the mole fraction of species jk.

If we define a mean ionic mole-fractional activity coefficient $f^{\pm}_{jk}$ by

$$f^{\pm}_{jk} = \sqrt[\nu_{jk}]{f_j^{\nu_k} \cdot f_k^{\nu_j}} \tag{8.113}$$

then Eqn (8.111) takes the simpler form

$$\begin{aligned}\mu_{jk} &= (\mu^0_{jk})_x + RT\ln (f^{\pm}_{jk})^{\nu_{jk}}(x^{\pm}_{jk})^{\nu_{jk}} \\ &= (\mu^0_{jk})_x + \nu_{jk}RT\ln f^{\pm}_{jk} \cdot x^{\pm}_{jk}\end{aligned} \tag{8.114}$$

Completely analogous expressions may be written for each choice of concentration units if we define the following quantities.

The *mean ionic molality* $m^{\pm}_{jk}$ is

$$m^{\pm}_{jk} = \sqrt[\nu_{jk}]{m_j^{\nu_k} m_k^{\nu_j}} = m_{jk}\sqrt[\nu_{jk}]{\nu_k^{\nu_k}\nu_j^{\nu_j}} \tag{8.115}$$

where m_{jk} is the molal concentration of species jk.

The *mean ionic molal activity coefficient* $\gamma^{\pm}_{jk}$ is

$$\gamma^{\pm}_{jk} = \sqrt[\nu_{jk}]{\gamma_j^{\nu_k}\gamma_k^{\nu_j}} \tag{8.116}$$

The *mean ionic molarity* $C^{\pm}_{jk}$ is

$$C^{\pm}_{jk} = \sqrt[\nu_{jk}]{C_j^{\nu_k} C_k^{\nu_j}} = C_{jk}\sqrt[\nu_{jk}]{\nu_k^{\nu_k}\nu_j^{\nu_j}} \tag{8.117}$$

where C_{jk} is the molar concentration of species jk.

The *mean ionic molar activity coefficient* $y_{jk}^{\pm}$ is

$$y_{jk}^{\pm} = \sqrt[\nu_{jk}]{y_j^{\nu_k} y_k^{\nu_j}} \tag{8.118}$$

In general the discussion of electrolyte solutions is based on Henry's Law, the activity coefficients being so defined that

$$\lim_{x_{jk}^{\pm} \to 0} f_{jk}^{\pm} = \lim_{m_{jk}^{\pm} \to 0} \gamma_{jk}^{\pm} = \lim_{C_{jk}^{\pm} \to 0} y_{jk}^{\pm} = 1 \tag{8.119}$$

In electrolyte mixtures, however, these activity coefficients approach unity *only in the limit of zero ionic strength of the mixture.*

We have the three equivalent expressions

$$\mu_{jk} = (\mu_{jk}^0)_m + \nu_{jk} RT \ln (\gamma_{jk}^{\pm} \cdot m_{jk}^{\pm}) \tag{8.120}$$

$$\mu_{jk} = (\mu_{jk}^0)_x + \nu_{jk} RT \ln (f_{jk}^{\pm} \cdot x_{jk}^{\pm}) \tag{8.121}$$

$$\mu_{jk} = (\mu_{jk}^0)_c + \nu_{jk} RT \ln (y_{jk}^{\pm} C_{jk}^{\pm}) \tag{8.122}$$

in which the three standard chemical potentials are functions of the temperature T and the pressure p.

V. THE STANDARD AFFINITY OF MASS TRANSFER

The equilibrium condition for the unconstrained distribution of a component k between sub-systems ϕ and σ is given in Eqn (8.53).

From Eqn (8.68)

$$(\Delta\mu_k)_{T,p} = (\Delta\mu_k^0)_{T,p} + RT \ln a_k^{\phi}/a_k^{\phi} \tag{8.123}$$

The *standard affinity of mass transfer* $-(\Delta\mu_k^0)_{T,p}$ is a characteristic thermodynamic parameter for the equilibrium distribution of species k between sub-systems ϕ and σ and is defined by

$$-(\Delta\mu_k^0)_{T,p} = A_k^0 = (\mu_k^{0\sigma})_{T^\sigma,p^\sigma} - (\mu_k^{0\phi})_{T^\sigma,p^\sigma} \tag{8.124}$$

where the reference state used for both sub-systems is at the temperature T^σ and pressure p^σ of sub-system σ. $(\Delta\mu_k^0)_{T,p}$ is the standard chemical potential difference to be expected in an equivalent system at uniform temperature $T = T^\sigma$ and uniform pressure $p = p^\sigma$. For convenience in what follows we shall drop the subscripts T and p, but this particular choice of reference states will be retained. Eqn (8.53) may now be written in the form

$$\frac{a_k^{\phi}}{a_k^{\sigma}} = \exp\left\{-\frac{\Delta\mu_k^0 + \bar{v}_k^{\phi}\,\Delta p + z_k F\,\Delta\psi}{RT}\right\} \tag{8.125}$$

Each choice of concentration units corresponds to a different numerical value of the standard affinity e.g.

$$\frac{C_k^\phi}{C_k^\sigma} = \exp\left\{-\frac{(\Delta\mu_k^0)_c + \bar{v}_k^\phi\,\Delta p + z_k F\,\Delta\psi + RT\ln y_k^\phi/y_k^\sigma}{RT}\right\} \tag{8.126}$$

Equation (8.126) can be very helpful in the formal analysis of a problem but has limited physical significance unless the activity coefficient ratios and the individual terms within the brackets can be determined independently by experiment. Such a procedure does not seem to be possible for single ionic species (Guggenheim, 1957) and the discussion of ionic systems often requires the introduction of the mean ionic variables.

We may derive an expression for the equilibrium distribution of an arbitrary neutral ionic combination *jk*

$$\frac{(C_{jk}^{\pm})^\phi}{(C_{jk}^{\pm})^\sigma} = \frac{(y_{jk}^{\pm})^\sigma}{(y_{jk}^{\pm})^\phi}\exp\left\{-\frac{(\Delta\mu_{jk}^0)_c + \bar{v}_{jk}^\phi\,\Delta p}{\nu_{jk}RT}\right\} \tag{8.127}$$

The relative distribution of the ions *j* and *k* is given by the equation

$$\left(\frac{C_k^\phi}{C_k^\sigma}\right)^{\nu_j}\left(\frac{C_j^\phi}{C_j^\sigma}\right)^{\nu_k} = \left(\frac{(y_{jk}^{\pm})^\sigma}{(y_{jk}^{\pm})^\phi}\right)^{\nu_{jk}}\exp\left(-\frac{(\Delta\mu_{jk}^0)_c + \bar{v}_{jk}^\phi\,\Delta p}{RT}\right) \tag{8.128}$$

The standard affinity of mass transfer $-(\Delta\mu_{jk}^0)_c$ is a characteristic thermodynamic constant for the equilibrium distribution of species *jk*.

There are certain difficulties in the application of the preceeding equations to the distribution of a substance between an aqueous solution σ and a polymeric or fibrous substate ϕ. These will be examined in more detail in later chapters.

REFERENCES

Fitts, D. D. (1962). "Nonequilibrium Thermodynamics." McGraw-Hill, New York.
De Groot, S. R. (1959). "Thermodynamics of Irreversible Processes." North-Holland Publishing Co., Amsterdam.
De Groot, S. R. and Mazur, P. (1962). "Nonequilibrium Thermodynamics." North-Holland Publishing Co., Amsterdam.
Donnan, F. G. (1934). *Z. physik. Chem.*, **A168,** 369.
Guggenheim, E. A. (1957). "Thermodynamics," 3rd Edn. North-Holland Publishing Co., Amsterdam.
Harned, H. S. and Owen, B. B. (1958). "The Physical Chemistry of Electrolytic Solutions," 3rd Edn. Reinhold, New York.
Helfferich, F. (1962). "Ion Exchange." McGraw-Hill, New York.
Hill, T. L. and Plesner, I. W. (1964). *J. Chem. Phys.*, **41,** 1359.
Hill, T. L. and Plesner, I. W. (1965). *J. Chem. Phys.*, **43,** 267.
Kirkwood, J. G. and Oppenheim, I. (1961). "Chemical Thermodynamics," McGraw-Hill, New York.

Katchalsky, A., and Curran, P. F. (1965). "Nonequilibrium Thermodynamics in Biophysics." Harvard University Press, Cambridge, Massachusetts.

Milicevic, B. (1963). *Helv. Chim. Acta.*, **46,** 1466.

Miller, D. G. (1960). *Chem. Rev.*, **60,** 15.

Prigogine, I. (1961). "Introduction to Thermodynamics of Irreversible Processes." 2nd Edn., Interscience, New York.

Staverman, A. J. (1966). *Rheologica Acta.*, **7** (4), 283.

Varsanyi, G., and Huszar, K. (1966). *Periodica Polytechnica*, **10** (2), 117.

Vickerstaff, T. (1954). "The Physical Chemistry of Dyeing," 2nd Edn. Oliver and Boyd, London.

Chapter 9 Continuous Multicomponent Systems

I. LOCAL THERMODYNAMIC VARIABLES

A. Homogeneous Systems

If a system is homogeneous, we may replace a thermodynamic equation of the type

$$G = H - TS \tag{9.1}$$

in which extensive variables appear, by the analogous intensive form in which only intensive variables appear

$$\hat{G} = \hat{H} - T\hat{S} \tag{9.2}$$

Such an intensive form is suitable for the discussion of the local properties of an arbitrary volume element dV. The amount dX of an extensive property X associated with a volume element dV is (within the continuum approximation)

$$dX = (\rho\hat{X})\,dV = \sum_{k=1}^{n} (\rho_k\hat{X}_k)\,dV \tag{9.3}$$

in which the partial mass densities ρ_k and the partial specific quantities $\hat{X}_k$ have been introduced for each component k.

In terms of the mass fractions

$$\hat{X} = \sum_{k=1}^{n} W_k\hat{X}_k \tag{9.4}$$

and we have

$$\hat{X}_k = \left(\frac{\partial X}{\partial m_k}\right)_{pT} \tag{9.5}$$

where m_k is the mass of component k.

An intensive form of the Gibbs equation may be used in discussing the local behaviour in a continuous system

$$d\hat{S} = \left(\frac{1}{T}\right) d\hat{U} + \left(\frac{p}{T}\right) d\hat{V} - \sum_{k=1}^{n}\left(\frac{\hat{\mu}_k}{T}\right) dW_k \tag{9.6}$$

$\hat{S}$ is the local specific entropy, $\hat{U}$ is the local specific internal energy, $\hat{V}$ is the local specific volume ($\hat{V} = 1/\rho$) and $\hat{\mu}_k$ is the local partial specific Gibbs function (or chemical potential per unit mass).

The use of a *Gibbs–Duhem equation* for a volume element dV implies that dV is regarded as a *homogeneous region*

$$\hat{U}\, d\left(\frac{1}{T}\right) + \hat{V} d\left(\frac{p}{T}\right) - \sum_{k=1}^{n} W_k\, d\left(\frac{\hat{\mu}_k}{T}\right) = 0 \tag{9.7}$$

In such a region the intensive quantities T, p and $\hat{\mu}_k$ are no longer independent variables. In the development of the continuum theories the Gibbs–Duhem equation is often applied to the *gradients* of the intensive quantities, i.e.

$$\hat{U} \text{ grad}\left(\frac{1}{T}\right) + \hat{V} \text{grad}\left(\frac{p}{T}\right) - \sum_{k=1}^{n} W_k \text{ grad}\left(\frac{\hat{\mu}_k}{T}\right) = 0 \tag{9.8}$$

Objections have been raised against this procedure on the grounds that the Gibbs–Duhem equation reflects the homogeneity of an equilibrium state and may not therefore be applicable in systems which are not homogeneous (Truesdell, 1962). This criticism appears to be equivalent to a criticism of the use of the continuum approximation in conjunction with the assumption of local equilibrium.

B. Nonequilibrium Systems

When irreversible processes occur in continuous systems space gradients of the local intensive variables appear and the system is no longer homogeneous.

The vectorial flows of mass and energy that characterise irreversible processes in continuous systems result in the transfer of mass and energy from one volume element to another so that some analogy is possible with the discontinuous composite systems of Chapters 7 and 8.

If the rate of the vectorial transfers is slow by comparison with the rate at which a volume element dV may attain local internal equilibrium, we may postulate that the entropy of the volume element remains the same function of the extensive parameters of the volume element as at equilibrium. We may then apply Eqn (9.6) to a volume element of a continuous system in which irreversible processes are occurring and in which the intensive variables are no longer uniform in time and space.

This is the essential feature of *the assumption of local equilibrium* for irreversible processes in continuous systems: a volume element dV is treated as an effectively homogeneous region with well-defined thermodynamic properties. These properties are assigned to the point in space on which the volume element is centred.

In particular Eqn (9.6) is assumed to remain valid for a volume element which is followed along its centre of mass motion, i.e.

$$\frac{d\hat{S}}{dt} = \left(\frac{1}{T}\right)\frac{d\hat{U}}{dt} + \left(\frac{p}{T}\right)\frac{d\hat{V}}{dt} - \sum_{k=1}^{n}\left(\frac{\hat{\mu}_k}{T}\right)\frac{dW_k}{dt} \tag{9.9}$$

in which the time derivatives are all convected time derivatives.

In very simple systems the methods of statistical mechanics can reveal the range of validity of these assumptions.

From the molecular point of view we require that the distribution function of the system can be written as the sum of a local equilibrium distribution and a correction term which is small in some sense: the mean values of the number density, energy density and momentum density are to remain the same whether computed from the local equilibrium distribution or the exact equilibrium distribution (Andersen *et al.*, 1964).

From a purely phenomenological viewpoint, the evidence for the validity of these assumptions will lie in the correctness of the conclusions deduced from them. The assumption of local equilibrium is most likely to be justified for "slow" irreversible processes which are "near to equilibrium" and which are not associated with large gradients of the local intensive variables. It is currently stated that the usual transport processes satisfy these conditions, although most chemical reactions do not (Prigogine, 1961; De Groot and Mazur, 1962; Fitts, 1962).

There remains however the difficulty of the definition and measurement the temperature T and the pressure p, for example, in nonequilibrium situations. The temperature and pressure to be associated with a volume element are thermodynamically defined only for equilibrium states of the element: they are the values which would be measured if the volume element were isolated and allowed to reach true internal equilibrium (Yourgrau *et al.*, 1966). The mechanical definition of the pressure tensor $\mathbf{P}$ reduces to the form of an equilibrium hydrostatic pressure p only in non-elastic fluids at equilibrium (Chapter 5) (Hirschfelder *et al.*, 1964). Except at equilibrium, different kinds of thermometers will register different temperatures. Measurements of temperature and pressure in nonequilibrium situations are therefore in this sense empirical.

II. ENTROPY PRODUCTION AND ENTROPY FLOW

The assumption of local equilibrium makes is possible to write the equations

$$\frac{\partial(\rho S)}{\partial t} = -\operatorname{div} \boldsymbol{J}_s + \phi_s \tag{9.10}$$

ϕ_s is the local rate of production of entropy per unit volume and $\boldsymbol{J}_s$ is the total entropy flux vector.

The local entropy production ϕ_s is assumed to obey a local second law inequality

$$\phi_s \geqslant 0 \tag{9.11}$$

$\boldsymbol{J}_s$ includes a convective entropy flux $\rho\hat{S}\boldsymbol{u}$, so that the entropy flux vector $\boldsymbol{j}_s$ with respect to the local centre of mass is

$$\boldsymbol{j}_s = \boldsymbol{J}_s - \rho\hat{S}\boldsymbol{u} \tag{9.12}$$

and therefore

$$\rho\frac{d\hat{S}}{dt} = -\operatorname{div}\boldsymbol{j}_s + \phi_s \tag{9.13}$$

From Eqn (9.9), since $\hat{V} = 1/\rho$ for a fluid system,

$$\rho\frac{d\hat{S}}{dt} = \left(\frac{\rho}{T}\right)\frac{d\hat{U}}{dt} - \left(\frac{p}{\rho T}\right)\frac{d\rho}{dT} - \frac{\rho}{T}\sum_{k=1}^{n}\hat{\mu}_k\cdot\frac{dW_k}{dt} \tag{9.14}$$

The equations of conservation of energy, mass and momentum in a continuous system can be used to calculate all the terms on the right-hand side of Eqn (9.14).

The expression so obtained may be rearranged into the form of a sum of the negative divergence of an entropy flux vector $(-\operatorname{div}\boldsymbol{j}_s)$ and an entropy production ϕ_s as in Eqn (9.13). There is no unique way of making this separation and so there is no unique expression for ϕ_s. The entropy production ϕ_s may be put into the form of a sum of the scalar products of conjugated "thermodynamic" flows and forces. Since ϕ_s itself is not uniquely defined there is some arbitrariness in the definition of the "thermodynamic" flows and forces. We consider here only the definitions based on the use of the *second law heat flux* $\boldsymbol{j}_{Q2}$.

III. THE LOCAL ENTROPY PRODUCTION

By a rather complex analysis in which the accelerations of the diffusive motions are ignored and in which the kinetic energy of diffusion is neglected (diffusion being assumed to be a "slow process"), it is possible to derive the following result for the local rate of entropy production per unit volume in a fluid system having a symmetrical stress tensor (Fitts, 1962; De Groot and Mazur, 1962).

$$\begin{aligned}\phi_s = {} & \frac{1}{T}\boldsymbol{\sigma}\colon \operatorname{grad}\boldsymbol{u} + \boldsymbol{j}_{Q2}\cdot\operatorname{grad}\left(\frac{1}{T}\right)\\ & - \sum_{k=1}^{n}\boldsymbol{j}_k\cdot\frac{(\operatorname{grad}\hat{\mu}_k^1)_T}{T} + \rho\sum_{i=1}^{s}\frac{\hat{A}_i}{T}\cdot\frac{d\lambda_i}{dt}\end{aligned} \tag{9.15}$$

The dyadic product $(1/T)\boldsymbol{\sigma}$:grad $\boldsymbol{u}$ is the entropy production by the fluid flow processes which involve the second order tensor $\boldsymbol{\sigma}$.

The vectorial flows of mass and of heat give rise to the entropy productions $-\sum_{k=1}^{n} \boldsymbol{j}_k \cdot (\text{grad } \hat{\mu}'_k)_T/T$ and $\boldsymbol{j}_{Q2} \cdot \text{grad } (1/T)$, respectively.

The scalar chemical reaction flows give rise to the entropy production $\rho \sum_{i=1}^{s} (\hat{A}_i/T)\, d\lambda_i/dt$.

Each of these four distinct contributions to the entropy production may be regarded as the scalar product of a thermodynamic force with its conjugated thermodynamic flow, or as a summation of such products.

Whereas the thermodynamic forces in the discontinuous systems of Chapter 8 were the *scalar differences* $\Delta(1/T)$ and $-[(\Delta\hat{\mu}_k)_T]/T$ for example, in the continuous systems we have in their place the *vectorial gradients* grad $(1/T)$ and $-(\text{grad } \hat{\mu}_k^1)/T$, respectively. This comparison is summarised in Table I.

TABLE I. Thermodynamic Flows and Forces. A Comparison of Continuous and Discontinuous Systems

Irreversible Process	Thermodynamic Flows: Continuous systems	Thermodynamic Flows: Discontinuous systems	Thermodynamic Forces: Continuous systems	Thermodynamic Forces: Discontinuous systems
Viscous Momentum Flux	$\boldsymbol{\sigma}$		$\dfrac{\text{grad } \boldsymbol{u}}{T}$	
"Volume Flow"	$\boldsymbol{J}_v$	$\mathscr{I}_v = \dfrac{d_I V^\phi}{dt}$	$-\dfrac{\text{grad } p}{T}$	$-\dfrac{\Delta p}{T}$
Mass Flow (Diffusion)	$\boldsymbol{j}_k$	$\mathscr{I}_k = \dfrac{d_I N_k^\phi}{dt}$	$-\dfrac{(\text{grad } \hat{\mu}'_k)_T}{T}$	$-\dfrac{(\Delta\tilde{\mu}_k)_T}{T} = \dfrac{\tilde{A}_k}{T}$
"Heat flow"	$\boldsymbol{j}_{Q2}$	$\mathscr{I}_{Q2} = \dfrac{d_I Q_2^\phi}{dt}$	$\text{grad}\left(\dfrac{1}{T}\right)$	$\Delta\left(\dfrac{1}{T}\right)$
Chemical Reaction	$\rho \dfrac{d\lambda_i}{dt}$	$\dfrac{d\xi_i}{dt}$	$\dfrac{\hat{A}_i}{T} = -\dfrac{1}{T}\left(\dfrac{\partial \hat{G}}{\partial \lambda_i}\right)_{p,T}$	$\dfrac{A_i}{T} = -\dfrac{1}{T}\left(\dfrac{\partial G}{\partial \xi_i}\right)_{p,T}$

The choice of the diffusion forces $-(\text{grad } \hat{\mu}_k^1)/T$ is advantageous because they do not include in themselves the effects of the temperature gradients. They do however include the effects of the partial specific volume forces $\hat{\boldsymbol{X}}_k$ which are here assumed to be conservative forces i.e.

$$(\text{grad } \hat{\mu}_k^1)_T = (\text{grad } \hat{\mu}_k)_T - \hat{\boldsymbol{X}}_k \tag{9.16}$$

where $(\text{grad}\,\hat{\mu}_k)_T$ is the chemical potential gradient for an equivalent isothermal system having exactly the same gradients of velocity, composition and pressure.

$$\begin{aligned}(\text{grad}\,\hat{\mu}_k)_T &= \text{grad}\,\hat{\mu}_k - \left(\frac{\partial \hat{\mu}_k}{\partial T}\right)_p \text{grad}\,T \\ &= \text{grad}\,\hat{\mu}_k + \hat{S}_k\,\text{grad}\,T \qquad (9.17)\end{aligned}$$

If ψ_k is the partial specific potential for component k in the conservative force field $\hat{X}_k(r)$ then

$$\hat{\mu}_k^1 = \hat{\mu}_k + \psi_k \qquad (9.18)$$

For an electrical field associated with an electrical potential ψ

$$\hat{\mu}_k^1 = \hat{\mu}_k + l_k\psi$$

where l_k is the electrical charge per unit mass of component k and $\hat{\mu}_k^1$ is now the *specific electrochemical potential* of component k.

REFERENCES

Andersen, H. C., Oppenheim, I., Shuler, K. E., and Weiss, G. H. (1964). *J. Chem. Phys.*, **41,** 3012.

Callen, H. B. (1960). "Thermodynamics." John Wiley, New York.

De Groot, S. R. (1951). "Thermodynamics of Irreversible Processes," North-Holland Publishing Co., Amsterdam.

De Groot, S. R., and Mazur, P. (1962). "Nonequilibrium Thermodynamics." North-Holland Publishing Co., Amsterdam.

Fitts, D. D. (1962). "Nonequilibrium Thermodynamics." McGraw-Hill, New York.

Hirschfelder, J. O., Curtiss, C. F., and Bird, R. B. (1964). "Molecular Theory of Gases and Liquids." Reprinted with notes and corrections. John Wiley, New York; Toppan Company, Tokyo.

Prigogine, I. (1961). "Introduction to Thermodynamics of Irreversible Processes," 2nd Edn. Interscience, New York.

Truesdell, C. (1962). *J. Chem. Phys.*, **37,** 2336.

Yourgrau, W., Van der Merve, A., and Raw, G. (1966). "Treatise on Irreversible and Statistical Thermophysics." Macmillan, New York.

Chapter 10 Phenomenological Equations For Continuous Multi-component Systems

For simplicity, attention is restricted here to the phenomenological equations which arise from an entropy production of the form of Eqn (9.15).

I. CURIE'S PRINCIPLE

The phenomenological equations of Chapter 7 and Chapter 8 express a linear relationship between scalar flows $\mathscr{I}_i$ and scalar forces $\mathscr{F}_j$.

$$\mathscr{I}_i = \sum_{j=1}^{n} \mathscr{L}_{ij}\mathscr{F}_j \tag{10.1}$$

The form of Eqn (10.1) may be retained for continuous systems if $\mathscr{I}_i$ and $\mathscr{F}_j$ are any of the scalar Cartesian components of the independent thermodynamic flows and forces which appear in the entropy production ϕ_s, but the linear phenomenological equations are now influenced by the spatial symmetry of the continuous system. Anisotropic systems do not necessarily behave in the same way as isotropic systems (De Groot and Mazur, 1962).

In isotropic systems *only*, a great simplification may be made on the basis of a principle which is usually attributed to P. Curie:

"*those terms which correspond to a coupling of entities whose tensorial orders differ by an odd number do not occur*" (Hirschfelder *et al.*, 1964; Fitts, 1962; De Groot and Mazur, 1962).

On this basis there is no coupling between the vectorial flows and the viscous momentum flux or the scalar chemical reaction rate. Very little information appears to be available on the coupling which may occur between the viscous momentum flux and the chemical reaction rate. The coupling between the vectorial flows of mass and energy gives rise to the Soret effect and the Dufour effect (De Groot and Mazur, 1962).

No similar principle holds for anisotropic systems, which must be discussed in the light of their special symmetry characteristics (De Groot and Mazur, 1962). In the remainder of this chapter, attention will be restricted to isotropic, continuous fluid systems.

II. ONSAGER RELATIONS

There is still considerable controversy over the validity of the Onsager Reciprocal Relations in continuous systems because the flows and the forces are in general not of the type discussed in Chapter 7, nor can they be shown unambiguously to be of this type (Coleman and Truesdell, 1960); Yourgrau *et al* , 1966; Wei, 1966).

Considerable ingenuity has been expended in attempts to find flows and forces in continuous systems for which the Onsager theorem is valid (Prigogine, 1961; De Groot and Mazur, 1962; Yourgrau *et al.*, 1966).

Andrews (1967) has concluded that the validity of the Onsager reciprocal relations can be established conclusively only by appeal to a microscopic (e.g. statistical–mechanical) theory or by experiment. There is statistical–mechanical evidence in support of the conclusion that the reciprocal relations are valid for the independent flows and forces which enter the entropy production ϕ_s of Eqn (9.15) (Fitts, 1962; De Groot and Mazur, 1962) and there is also increasing experimental evidence in support of this conclusion (Miller, 1959, 1960, 1965).

We shall therefore *postulate* that, (within the linear approximation), the Onsager reciprocal relations hold for the different sets of independent thermodynamic flows and forces to be obtained from the local entropy production ϕ_s of Eqn (9.15).

III. PHENOMENOLOGICAL EQUATIONS FOR AN ISOTROPIC FLUID MIXTURE

Curie's theorem makes it possible to discuss separately the phenomenological equations which arise for the flow of linear momentum, for the flow of heat and of mass, and for chemical reaction. We shall not examine the possible coupling between chemical reaction and momentum flow (De Groot and Mazur, 1962).

A. The Flow of Linear Momentum

The linear phenomenological equations which relate the components σ_{ij} of the stress tensor $\boldsymbol{\sigma}$ to the components of the thermodynamic force $1/T$ grad $\boldsymbol{u}$, with the exception of the temperature factor $1/T$, lead directly to the Navier Stokes Equation which is now obtained as a logical consequence of the postulates and of the formalism of nonequilibrium thermodynamics (Bird *et al.*, 1955; Fitts, 1962; De Groot and Mazur, 1962).

B. Mechanical Equilibrium

When there are no unbalanced forces within a system, or between a system

1957). We shall consider a system to be in mechanical equilibrium if the acceleration $d\boldsymbol{u}/dt$ of the mass velocity $\boldsymbol{u}$ is everywhere zero.

In this situation the equation of motion takes the form

$$0 = -\operatorname{grad} p + \rho\hat{\boldsymbol{X}}$$

with

$$\rho\hat{\boldsymbol{X}} = \sum_{k=1}^{n} \rho_k \hat{\boldsymbol{X}}_k \tag{10.2}$$

If there is no net volume force then the pressure gradient disappears.

However, the local pressure p is related to the other local intensive state variables by the *Gibbs–Duhem* equation in the form

$$dp = T\sum_{k=1}^{n} \rho_k\, d\left(\frac{\hat{\mu}_k}{T}\right) + \rho\hat{H}\, d(\ln T) \tag{10.3}$$

or, if it is permissible to write Eqn (10.3) in terms of the gradient vectors,

$$\operatorname{grad} p = T\sum_{k=1}^{n} \rho_k \operatorname{grad}\left(\frac{\hat{\mu}_k}{T}\right) + \rho\hat{H}\operatorname{grad}(\ln T) \tag{10.4}$$

so that

$$\operatorname{grad} p - \rho\hat{X} = \sum_{k=1}^{n} \rho_k\left(T\operatorname{grad}\left(\frac{\hat{\mu}_k}{T}\right) - \hat{X}_k + \hat{H}_k \operatorname{grad}(\ln T)\right) \tag{10.5}$$

and therefore when the system is in mechanical equilibrium, the thermodynamic forces $\{T\operatorname{grad}(\hat{\mu}_k/T) - \hat{X}_k + \hat{H}_k\operatorname{grad}(\ln T)\}$ are subject to the restriction

$$\sum_{k=1}^{n} \rho_k\left\{T\operatorname{grad}\left(\frac{\hat{\mu}_k}{T}\right) - \hat{X}_\kappa + \hat{H}_k\operatorname{grad}(\ln T)\right\} = 0 \tag{10.6}$$

and are no longer independent.

If it is permissible to use the thermodynamic identity

$$T\, d\left(\frac{\hat{\mu}_k}{T}\right) = (d\hat{\mu}_k)_T - \hat{H}_k\, d(\ln T) \tag{10.7}$$

in the vectorial form

$$T\operatorname{grad}\left(\frac{\hat{\mu}_k}{T}\right) = (\operatorname{grad}\hat{\mu}_k)_T - \hat{H}_k\operatorname{grad}(\ln T) \tag{10.8}$$

then we find that Eqn (10.6) becomes

$$\sum_{k=1}^{n} \rho_k(\operatorname{grad}\hat{\mu}_k^1)_T = 0 \tag{10.9}$$

A state of mechanical equilibrium is generally considered to be established, at least in simple fluids, well before the attainment of thermodynamic equilibrium. When this is so the discussion of diffusion processes may be simplified (Chapter 11).

C. Heat Flow and Diffusion

Curie's theorem does not forbid a coupling between heat flow and diffusion. These processes contribute the term

$$\boldsymbol{j}_q \cdot \operatorname{grad}\left(\frac{1}{T}\right) - \frac{1}{T}\sum_{k=1}^{n} \boldsymbol{j}_k \cdot (\operatorname{grad} \hat{\mu}_k^1)_T \geqslant 0 \tag{10.10}$$

to the local entropy production ϕ_s, so that the phenomenological equations for heat flow and diffusion are

$$\boldsymbol{j}_q = L_{qq} \operatorname{grad}\left(\frac{1}{T}\right) - \frac{1}{T}\sum_{j=1}^{n} L_{qj} (\operatorname{grad} \hat{\mu}_j^1)_T \tag{10.11}$$

$$\boldsymbol{j}_k = L_{kq} \operatorname{grad}\left(\frac{1}{T}\right) - \frac{1}{T}\sum_{j=1}^{n} L_{kj} (\operatorname{grad} \hat{\mu}_j^1)_T \tag{10.12}$$

The forces $-1/T(\operatorname{grad} \hat{\mu}_j^1)_T$ are independent if the system is *not* in mechanical equilibrium. The restrictions on the $\boldsymbol{j}_k$ leave the reciprocal relations unimpaired and so we may postulate that

$$L_{qk} = L_{kq} \qquad \text{(coupling of heat flow and diffusion)} \tag{10.13}$$

and

$$L_{kj} = L_{jk} \qquad \text{(coupling of diffusion flows)} \tag{10.14}$$

But when a system is in mechanical equilibrium the forces $-1/T\,(\operatorname{grad} \hat{\mu}_{k'}^1)_T$ are no longer independent.

The phenomenological coefficients of Eqns (10.11) and (10.12) are then no longer uniquely defined. The freedom which remains in the definition of these coefficients can generally be used to ensure that the reciprocal relations are satisfied, but it is better to re-write the phenomenological equations in terms of independent flows and forces (Fitts, 1962; De Groot and Mazur, 1962), i.e.

$$\boldsymbol{j}_q = L_{qq} \operatorname{grad}\left(\frac{1}{T}\right) - \frac{1}{T}\sum_{j=1}^{n-1} L_{qj} \{\operatorname{grad} (\hat{\mu}_j^1 - \hat{\mu}_n^1)\}_T \tag{10.15}$$

$$\boldsymbol{j}_k = L_{kq} \operatorname{grad}\left(\frac{1}{T}\right) - \frac{1}{T}\sum_{j=1}^{n-1} L_{kj} \{\operatorname{grad} (\hat{\mu}_j^1 - \hat{\mu}_n^1)\}_T \tag{10.16}$$

The phenomenological coefficients in Eqns (10.11) and (10.12) are the same as those in Eqns (10.15) and (10.16), and the reciprocal relations are postulated to be valid (Fitts, 1962).

The coefficient L_{qq} is related to the thermal conductivity, the coefficients L_{qj} describe the effect of the chemical potential gradient of component j on the transport of heat.

The coefficients L_{kq} represent the effect of a temperature gradient on the diffusion of component k (thermal diffusion). The coefficients L_{kj} represent the influence of the force $-\{\text{grad}\,(\hat{\mu}_j^1 - \hat{\mu}_n^1)\}_T$ on the diffusion of component k.

In a system in mechanical equilibrium, the phenomenological coefficients of Eqns (10.11) and (10.12) are subject to the restrictions (Fitts, 1962)

$$\sum_{j=1}^{n} L_{qj} = 0; \qquad \sum_{j=1}^{n} L_{kj} = 0 \tag{10.17}$$

It is interesting to note that Truesdell (1962) has proposed the following thermodynamic definition of the momentum supplies $\hat{\boldsymbol{p}}_k$ of Chapter 6 for a mixture of perfect fluids

$$\rho\hat{\boldsymbol{p}}_k \equiv \rho_k\left\{\boldsymbol{a}_k + T\,\text{grad}\left(\frac{\hat{\mu}_k}{T}\right) - \hat{\boldsymbol{X}}_k + \hat{\boldsymbol{H}}_k\,\text{grad}\,(\ln T)\right\} \tag{10.18}$$

Neglecting accelerations we have

$$\rho\hat{\boldsymbol{p}}_k \equiv \rho_k\{(\text{grad}\,\hat{\mu}_k^1)_T\} \tag{10.19}$$

so that Eqn (10.9) *becomes equivalent to Eqn* (6.21) *for the conservation of linear momentum in the system.*

Truesdell then demonstrates that the Onsager reciprocal relations for pure diffusion are obtained if, and only if, Stefan's relations hold.

This is equivalent to the requirement that the diffusive interactions be *binary* interactions. The restriction of Truesdell's argument to mixtures of perfect fluids affords an interesting comparison with the use of Curie's theorem to separate the diffusive from the viscous interactions in isotropic systems.

D. Chemical Reaction

The chemical reactions contribute the term

$$\rho\sum_{i=1}^{s}\frac{\hat{A}_i}{T}\cdot\frac{d\lambda_i}{dt} \geqslant 0 \tag{10.20}$$

to the local entropy production. An additional term which represents a coupling with the phenomenon of bulk viscosity is ignored here. The phenomenological equations for chemical reaction take the form

$$\rho \frac{d\lambda_i}{dt} = \frac{1}{T} \sum_{j=1}^{s} \mathscr{L}_{ij} \hat{A}_j \cdots (i = 1, 2, \ldots, s) \tag{10.21}$$

Unfortunately Eqn (10.21) is unsatisfactory as a description of chemical reactions. It is generally concluded that most chemical reactions are too far from equilibrium for the methods of nonequilibrium thermodynamics to be of real value (Prigogine, 1961). This is in marked contrast to the success that is met in describing the transport processes by means of nonequilibrium thermodynamics. Bak (1959); Wei (1962); Hill and Plesner (1964, 1965), have drawn attention to the existence of additional factors which may influence the course of chemical reaction. We may regard Eqn (10.21) as a kinetic law which is applicable only in very restricted circumstances and in a region very near to equilibrium. In this situation one may naturally replace Eqn (10.21) by empirical kinetic equations (Fitts, 1962). The conservation of mass in a system in which both chemical reaction and diffusion may occur is expressed by

$$\rho \frac{dW_k}{dt} = -\operatorname{div} \boldsymbol{j}_k + \rho \sum_{i=1}^{s} \hat{v}_{ki} \frac{d\lambda_i}{dt} \tag{10.22}$$

IV. THE GENERAL TRANSPORT EQUATIONS

A complete statement of the general transport equations for an isotropic continuous medium has been given by Fitts (1962) who derived them on the basis of nonequilibrium thermodynamics. The derivation follows the procedures outlined in the preceding chapters and may be summarised as follows.

By introducing the assumption of local equilibrium it is possible to define the local thermodynamic state of the system as a function of the independent variables $\boldsymbol{u}$, T, p and W_k ($k = 1, 2, \ldots, n$) and their variation with position and time. The local equations of conservation of mass, energy and momentum are used to obtain a balance equation for the entropy [Cf. Eqn (9.9)] which is then rearranged in such a way that an entropy flow ($-\operatorname{div} \boldsymbol{j}_s$) and an entropy production (ϕ_s) can be isolated.

The entropy production ϕ_s is resolved into four distinct contributions from momentum flow, heat flow and diffusion, and from chemical reaction. On this basis the "thermodynamic" flows and forces are identified and the phenomenological equations are constructed, Curie's theorem being used to separate the flows and forces of different tensorial rank.

The general transport equations consist of the equation of conservation of mass (10.22), the phenomenological equations for chemical reaction (10.21), for heat flow and diffusion (10.11 and 10.12), and for the flow of linear momentum (10.23) [Cf. Eqn (5.18)]

$$\rho \boldsymbol{a} - \eta \nabla^2 \boldsymbol{u} - (\tfrac{1}{3}\eta + \vartheta)\,\mathrm{grad}\,(\mathrm{div}\,\boldsymbol{u}) + \mathrm{grad}\,p - \rho\hat{X} = 0 \qquad (10.23)$$

together with the following equations for the temperature and pressure changes in the continuum (Fitts, 1962)

$$\begin{aligned}\rho\alpha\hat{C}_v \frac{dT}{dt} = & -\alpha\boldsymbol{\tau}\colon \mathrm{grad}\,\boldsymbol{u} - \beta T\,\mathrm{div}\,\boldsymbol{u} - \alpha\,\mathrm{div}\,\boldsymbol{j}_{Q_2} \\ & - \rho\sum_{i=1}^{s}\frac{d\lambda_i}{dt}(\alpha\,\Delta\hat{H}_i - \beta T\,\Delta\hat{V}_i) \\ & - \sum_{k=1}^{n}(\alpha\boldsymbol{j}_k\cdot\mathrm{grad}\,\hat{H}'_k + \beta T\hat{V}_k\,\mathrm{div}\,\boldsymbol{j}_k)\end{aligned} \qquad (10.24)$$

$$\begin{aligned}\rho\alpha\hat{C}_v \frac{dp}{dt} = & -\beta\boldsymbol{\tau}\colon \mathrm{grad}\,\boldsymbol{u} - \rho\hat{C}_p\,\mathrm{div}\,\boldsymbol{u} - \beta\,\mathrm{div}\,\boldsymbol{j}_{Q_2} \\ & - \rho\sum_{i=1}^{s}\frac{d\lambda_i}{dt}(\beta\,\Delta\hat{H}_i - \rho\hat{C}_p\,\Delta\hat{V}_i) \\ & - \sum_{k=1}^{n}(\beta\boldsymbol{j}_k\cdot\mathrm{grad}\,\hat{H}_k' + \rho\hat{C}_p\hat{V}_k\,\mathrm{div}\,\boldsymbol{j}_k)\end{aligned} \qquad (10.25)$$

in which $\hat{H}'_k = \hat{\mu}'_k + T\hat{S}_k$ (Fitts, 1962) α is the isothermal compressibility coefficient, β is the thermal expansion coefficient, $\hat{C}_v$ is the specific heat at constant volume, $\hat{C}_p$ is the specific heat at constant pressure, $\Delta\hat{H}_i$ is the enthalpy change for the ith chemical reaction and $\Delta\hat{V}_i$ is the volume change.

A general solution of the transport equations for arbitrary boundary and initial conditions does not exist, and they must generally be simplified before they can be used. This simplification carries with it the danger that some of the physical content of the equations may thereby be lost.

In anisotropic systems the situation is even less amenable to exact analysis.

V. THERMODYNAMIC COUPLING

It may be useful to take the viewpoint that nonequilibrium thermodynamics includes the coupling phenomena in its formalism primarily for the sake of greater generality. The cross-coefficients L_{ij}, $i \neq j$, enter naturally into the phenomenological equations, but it is for experiment (or for microscopic theories) to decide if the reciprocal relations are valid and if the coupling effects are significant.

The success of nonequilibrium thermodynamics in describing multicomponent diffusion, thermal diffusion, ionic transport and the electrokinetic phenomena is not a guarantee that its other applications will be sucessful. Indeed, Koenig *et al.* (1961) have claimed that "Thermodynamic coupling can be invoked by a stroke of the pen. It is neither an essential feature of any special class of systems, dead or alive, nor an explanation of anything." Manes (1963, 1964, 1965) has been equally critical, and has proposed an alternative approach. A balanced review of the situation has been given by Wei (1966).

The formalism of nonequilibrium thermodynamics is very general, it unifies the description of a wide range of physical phenomena in an apparently elegant way, it offers some hope of correlating the kinetic properties of a system with its equilibrium properties, and it acts as some safeguard against the uncritical over-simplification of the analysis of a physical problem.

If sufficient care is exercised, one hopes that the important and measurable (macroscopic) parameters for a system will be well defined within this formalism, so that they will be available for future theoretical analysis should a comprehensive molecular theory of the processes become available. Although the formalism is complex and rather difficult, it has been used for the description of the diffusion of dyes in fibres and films. Such applications of nonequilibrium thermodynamics are still in their infancy (Yedaira, 1960), 1961; Tsuda, 1961; Milicevic, 1962; Sekido and Morita, 1962, Milicevic and McGregor, 1966a, 1966b, 1966c, 1966d). The problems of biophysics are quite closely related to those met in attempts to discuss the diffusion of dyes in polymeric substrates. The methods of nonequilibrium thermodynamics have indeed already been extended to cover biophysical problems (Katchalsky and Curran, 1965). More recent developments in the application of nonequilibrium thermodynamics have been discussed by Knof (1966), and by Donnelly *et al.* (1966).

REFERENCES

Andrews, F. C. (1967). *Ind. Eng. Chem. Fundamentals*, **6**, 48.

Bak, T. A. (1959). "Contributions to the Theory of Chemical Kinetics." Munksgaard, Copenhagen.

Bird, R. B., Curtiss, C. F., and Hirschfelder, J. O. (1955). "Fluid Mechanics and the Transport Phenomena." In "Mass Transfer ··· Transport Properties" (Ed., F. J. Van Antwerpen). (Chemical Engineering Progress Symposium Series No. 16, Vol. 51, p. 69.) American Institute of Chemical Engineers, New York.

Callen, H. B. (1960). "Thermodynamics." John Wiley, New York.

Casimir, H. B. G. (1945). *Revs. mod. Phys.*, **17**, 343.

Cohn, P. M. (1965). "Linear Equations." (Library of Mathematics) (Ed., W. Ledermann). Routledge and Kegan Paul, London.

Coleman, B. D. and Truesdell, C. (1960). *J. Chem. Phys.*, **33,** 28.
Denbigh, K. G. (1951). "The Thermodynamics of the Steady State." Methuen, London.
Donnelly, R. J., Herman, R. and Prigogine, I. (1966). "Nonequilibrium Thermodynamics, Variational Techniques and Stability." University of Chicago Press, Chicago.
Fitts, D. D. (1962). "Nonequilibrium Thermodynamics." McGraw-Hill, New York.
De Groot, S. R. (1951). "Thermodynamics of Irreversible Processes," North-Holland Publishing Company, Amsterdam.
De Groot, S. R. and Mazur, P. (1962). "Nonequilibrium Thermodynamics." North-Holland Publishing Company, Amsterdam.
Haase, R. (1963). "Thermodynamik der irreversiblen Prozesse." Dr. Dietrich Steinkopff Verlag, Darmstadt.
Hill, T. L. and Plesner, I. W. (1964). *J. Chem. Phys.*, **41,** 1359.
Hill, T. L. and Plesner, I. W. (1965). *J. Chem. Phys.*, **43,** 267.
Hirschfelder, J. O., Curtiss, C. F., and Bird, R. B. (1964). "Molecular Theory of Gases and Liquids." Reprint, with notes and corrections. John Wiley, New York.
Katchalsky, A. and Curran, P. F. (1965). "Nonequilibrium Thermodynamics in Biophysics." Harvard University Press, Cambridge, Mass.
Knopf, H. (1966). "Thermodynamics of Irreversible Processes in Liquid Metals." Heywood, London.
Koenig, F. O., Horne, F. H., Mohilner, D. M. (1961). *J. Amer. Chem. Soc.*, **83,** 1029.
Lothe, J. (1966). *J. Chem. Phys.*, **45,** 2678.
Manes, M. (1963). *J. Phys. Chem.*, **67,** 651.
Manes, M. (1964). *J. Phys. Chem.*, **68,** 31.
Manes, M. (1965). *J. Colloid. Sci.*, **20,** 990.
Meixner, J. (1943). *Ann. Physik* (5) **43,** 244.
Meixner, J. and Reik, H. G. (1959). "Thermodynamik der irreversiblen Prozesse." In "Handbuch der Physik", Vol. 3, Part 2. Springer Verlag, Berlin.
Milicevic, B. (1962). *Chimia*, **16,** 29.
Milicevic, B. and McGregor, R. (1966). *Helv. Chim. Acta.*, **49,** (a) 1302; (b) 1319; (c) 2098; (d) 2195.
Miller, D. G. (1959). *J. Phys. Chem.*, **63,** 570.
Miller, D. G. (1960). *Chem. Rev.*, **60,** 15.
Miller, D. G. (1965). *J. Phys. Chem.*, **69,** 3374.
Onsager, L. (1931). *Phys. Rev.* **37,** 405; **38,** 2265.
Prigogine, I. (1961). "Introduction to Thermodynamics of Irreversible Processes," 2nd Edn., Interscience, New York.
Sekido, M. and Morita, Z. (1962). *Bull. Chem. Soc. Japan* **35,** No. 8, 1375.
Truesdell, C. (1962). *J. Chem. Phys.*, **37,** 2336.
Tsuda, K. (1961). *Bull. Textile Res. Inst.* (*Japanese Government*), **58,** 47.
Wei, J. (1962). *J. Chem. Phys.*, **6,** 1578.
Wei, J. (1966). *Ind. Eng. Chem.*, **58,** No. 10, 55.
Yedaira, H. (1960). *Sen-i-Gakkukaishi*, **16,** 403.
Yedaira, H. (1961). *Sen-i-Gakkukaishi*, **17,** 1206.
Yourgrau, W., Van der Merve, A., and Raw, G. (1966). "Treatise on Irreversible and Statistical Thermophysics." Macmillan, New York.
Zemansky, M. W. (1957). "Heat and Thermodynamics," 4th Edn. (International Student Edition). McGraw-Hill, New York; Kogakusha Co. Ltd., Tokyo.

Part III Mass Transport in and between Phases

Chapter 11 Thermodynamic Diffusion Equations

I. MECHANICAL EQUILIBRIUM IN ISOTHERMAL DIFFUSION

A. The Entropy Production and the Reference Frames

The entropy production $(\phi_s)_M$ by diffusion in the mass-fixed reference frame M is

$$(T\phi_s)_M = -\sum_{k=1}^{n} (\boldsymbol{J}_k)_M \cdot (\text{grad } \hat{\mu}_k^1)_{T,p} \tag{11.1}$$

where the notation $(\boldsymbol{J}_k)_M$ is now used for the diffusion flux $\boldsymbol{j}_k$ in the mass-fixed (barycentric) reference frame. The subscripts T, p will for simplicity be dropped in what follows but a restriction to isothermal diffusion in a system in mechanical equilibrium will remain.

$(\boldsymbol{J}_k)_M$ is defined with respect to the velocity $\boldsymbol{u}_{MC}$ $(= \boldsymbol{u})$ of motion of the local centre of mass. $\boldsymbol{u}_{MC}$ itself is defined with respect to a fixed set of external coordinates: the cell-fixed reference frame C. The barycentric velocity or mass-average velocity $\boldsymbol{u}_{MC}$ is but one of several different average velocities of bulk motion which may be defined for a multicomponent fluid. Each choice of average velocity implies a different reference velocity $\boldsymbol{u}_{RC}$ for the diffusion flows.

Let $(\boldsymbol{J}_k)_R$ be the diffusion flux of component k in an arbitrary local reference frame R, i.e. with respect to an arbitrary local reference velocity $\boldsymbol{u}_{RC}$.

$$(\boldsymbol{J}_k)_R = (\boldsymbol{J}_k)_C - \rho_k \boldsymbol{u}_{RC} \tag{11.2}$$

where $(\boldsymbol{J}_k)_C$ is the total mass flux of component k in the cell-fixed reference frame. If $(\boldsymbol{u}_k)_C$ is the average velocity of motion of component k in this reference frame C then

$$(\boldsymbol{J}_k)_R = \rho_k((\boldsymbol{u}_k)_C - \boldsymbol{u}_{RC}) \tag{11.3}$$

If the entropy production $(T\phi_s)_R$ in the new reference frame is defined by analogy with Eqn (11.1) we find

$$(T\phi_s)_R - (T\phi)_M = (\boldsymbol{u}_{RC} - \boldsymbol{u}_{MC}) \sum_{k=1}^{n} \rho_k \cdot \text{grad } \hat{\mu}_k^1 \tag{11.4}$$

The right hand side of Eqn (11.4) vanishes for a system in *mechanical equilibrium* (Eqn 10.9) so that *in this special case* the entropy production in diffusion in an isothermal system is independent of the choice of reference frame for the diffusion flows (Prigogine, 1947).

B. Thermodynamic Diffusion Equations

Phenomenological equations, or *thermodynamic diffusion equations*, can now be written in the general form

$$(\boldsymbol{J}_k)_R = -\sum_{j=1}^{n} (L_{kj})_R \cdot \text{grad}\,\hat{\mu}_j^1 \tag{11.5}$$

where the factor $1/T$ is included in $(L_{kj})_R$.

The reciprocal relations

$$(L_{kj})_R = (L_{jk})_R, \ldots, j, k = 1, 2, \ldots, n \tag{11.6}$$

can unfortunately *not* be assumed to be automatically valid for an arbitrary reference frame R.

There is both theoretical and experimental evidence for the validity of the reciprocal relations

$$(L_{kj})_M = (L_{jk})_M \tag{11.7}$$

for the mass-fixed reference frame M.

Even if all n components are included in Eqn (11.5) it is generally possible so to define the $(L_{kj})_M$ that reciprocal relations hold for them (Kirkwood *et al.*, 1960). We shall postulate that the reciprocal relations (11.7) are valid and examine the consequences this has for other choices of the reference frame R.

II. THE RECIPROCAL RELATIONS AND THE REFERENCE FRAMES

A. The Mass-Fixed Reference Frame

1. Thermodynamic Diffusion Equations

Applying the present notation to the equations of Chapter 6 we have

$$(\boldsymbol{J}_k)_M = (\boldsymbol{J}_k)_C - \rho_k \boldsymbol{u}_{MC} \tag{11.8}$$

$$\sum_{k=1}^{n} (\boldsymbol{J}_k)_M = 0 \tag{11.9}$$

$$\boldsymbol{u}_{MC} = \frac{1}{\rho} \sum_{k=1}^{n} (\boldsymbol{J}_k)_C \tag{11.10}$$

The thermodynamic diffusion equations are identical to Eqns (11.5) except for the subscript M denoting the reference frame, and we assume the reciprocal relations (11.7) to hold for $j, k = 1, 2, \ldots, n$.

Practical diffusion equations are not normally written for this particular reference frame, which is rarely used experimentally.

B. The Component-Fixed Reference Frame

1. Thermodynamic Diffusion Equations

It is often convenient to relate the diffusion flows $(J_k)_n$ to the motion of some component n, which is usually chosen as the solvent ($n = 0$)

$$(\boldsymbol{J}_k)_n = (\boldsymbol{J}_k)_C - \rho_k(\boldsymbol{u}_n)_C \tag{11.11}$$

$$(\boldsymbol{J}_n)_n = 0 \tag{11.12}$$

$$(\boldsymbol{u}_n)_C = \frac{(\boldsymbol{J}_n)_C}{\rho_n}; \qquad (\boldsymbol{u}_n)_R = \frac{(\boldsymbol{J}_n)_R}{\rho_n} \tag{11.13}$$

The thermodynamic diffusion equations

$$(\boldsymbol{J}_k)_n = -\sum_{j=1}^{n} (L_{kj}^1)_n \operatorname{grad} \hat{\mu}_j^1 \tag{11.14}$$

do not lead to reciprocal relations for the $(L_{kj}^1)_n$ when reciprocal relations hold for the $(L_{kj})_M$, i.e. (Kirkwood *et al.*, 1960)

$$(L_{kj}^1)_n = (L_{kj})_M - (\rho_k/\rho_n)(L_{nj})_M \tag{11.15}$$

If, however, we re-write Eqns (11.14) in terms of independent forces by eliminating grad $\hat{\mu}_n^1$

$$(\boldsymbol{J}_k)_n = -\sum_{j=1}^{n-1} (L_{kj})_n \operatorname{grad} \hat{\mu}_j^1 \tag{11.16}$$

where now

$$(L_{kj})_n = (L_{kj}^1)_n - (\rho_j/\rho_n)(L_{kn}^1)_n \tag{11.17}$$

we find that reciprocal relations hold for the $(L_{kj})_n$ if they hold for the $(L_{kj})_M$ (Kirkwood *et al.*, 1960).

2. Practical Diffusion Equations

The *practical diffusion equations* for the solute flows in a nonionic system are a generalisation of Fick's equations

$$(J_k)_n = -\sum_{j=1}^{n-1} (D_{kj})_n \operatorname{grad} \rho_j \tag{11.18}$$

The $(D_{kj})_n$ are the practical diffusion coefficients for the reference frame n and the mass concentrations ρ_j. They do not normally obey reciprocal relations.

There are only $n - 1$ independent components in an n-component system and so (Kirkwood *et al.*, 1960)

$$\text{grad } \hat{\mu}_j = \sum_{i=1}^{n-1} \left(\frac{\partial \hat{\mu}_j}{\partial \rho_i}\right) \text{grad } \rho_i \qquad j = 1, 2 \cdots n - 1 \tag{11.19}$$

Substitution for grad $\hat{\mu}_j$ in Eqn (11.16), when written for a nonionic system, and comparison with Eqn (11.18) gives the result (Kirkwood *et al.*, 1960)

$$(D_{ki})_n = \sum_{j=1}^{n-1} (L_{kj})_n \left(\frac{\partial \hat{\mu}_j}{\partial \rho_i}\right) \tag{11.20}$$

C. The Volume-Fixed Reference Frame

1. Thermodynamic Diffusion Equations

We have

$$(J_k)_V = (J_k)_C - \rho_k \boldsymbol{u}_{VC} \tag{11.21}$$

and

$$\sum_{k=1}^{n} \hat{v}_k (J_k)_V = 0$$

since there must be no net flow of volume across the reference frame. $\hat{v}_k$ is the partial specific volume of component k. We may also use the result

$$\sum_{k=1}^{n} \hat{v}_k \rho_k = 1 \tag{11.22}$$

which follows from the definition of $\hat{v}_k$ as a partial specific volume, in combination with Eqn (11.21) to show that

$$\boldsymbol{u}_{VC} = \sum_{k=1}^{n} \hat{v}_k (J_k)_C \tag{11.23}$$

If thermodynamic diffusion equations for this reference frame are written to include all n components, as in Eqn (11.14), the coefficients $(L_{kj}^1)_V$ do not obey reciprocal relations since (Kirkwood *et al.*, 1960)

$$(L_{kj}^1)_V = (L_{kj})_M - (\rho_k/\rho_n)\{(L_{nj})_M - (L_{nj}^1)_V\} \tag{11.24}$$

Even if the dependent force $-$grad $\hat{\mu}_n$ is eliminated as in Eqn (11.16)

$$(J_k)_V = -\sum_{j=1}^{n-1} (L_{kj})_V \text{ grad } \hat{\mu}_j \tag{11.25}$$

the coefficients $(L_{kj})_V$ still do not obey reciprocal relations. We have

$$(L_{kj})_V = (L_{kj})_n - (\rho_k/\rho_n)(L_{nj})_V \tag{11.26}$$

In order to obtain reciprocal relations for the volume fixed reference frame it appears to be necessary to eliminate the solvent terms and to define new thermodynamic forces which are linear combinations of the $-\text{grad}\, \hat{\mu}_j$ (Miller, 1958, 1959, 1960).

2. Practical Diffusion Equations

The volume fixed reference frame is frequently used in diffusion studies. The practical diffusion equations are (Kirkwood *et al.*, 1960)

$$(J_k)_V = -\sum_{j=1}^{n-1} (D_{kj})_V \,\text{grad}\, \rho_j \tag{11.27}$$

with

$$(D_{ki})_V = \sum_{j=1}^{n-1} (L_{kj})_V \frac{\partial \hat{\mu}_j}{\partial \rho_i} \tag{11.28}$$

and (Kirkwood *et al.*, 1960)

$$(D_{kj})_n = (D_{kj})_V + \frac{\rho_k}{\rho_n \hat{v}_n} \sum_{i=1}^{n-1} \hat{v}_i (D_{ij})_V \tag{11.29}$$

or

$$(D_{kj})_V = (D_{kj})_n - \rho_k \sum_{i=1}^{n-1} \hat{v}_i (D_{ij})_n \tag{11.30}$$

If the ρ_k and the $\hat{v}_k$ are known it is possible to calculate the $(D_{kj})_n$ from the $(D_{kj})_V$, which are experimentally accessible. The $(L_{kj})_n$ may be calculated from the $(D_{kj})_n$ *if* the thermodynamic data $\partial\hat{\mu}_j/\partial\rho_i$ are available and so the reciprocal relations may be tested experimentally (Kirkwood *et al.*, 1960). To date, all experimental tests of this kind have confirmed the reciprocal relations (within the comparatively large experimental error) for correctly defined thermodynamic flows and forces (Miller, 1958, 1959, 1960). These investigations have generally been restricted to binary and ternary systems for obvious reasons.

III. SYSTEMS WITH VOLUME CHANGES ON MIXING

A. The Reference Velocities $\boldsymbol{u}_{MC}$, $\boldsymbol{u}_{VC}$, and $\boldsymbol{u}_{nC}$

In some situations the differences between $\boldsymbol{u}_{VC}$, $\boldsymbol{u}_{MC}$ and $\boldsymbol{u}_{nC}$ will be negligible. If there are no concentration gradients in a system, then $\boldsymbol{u}_{VC}$, $\boldsymbol{u}_{MC}$ and $\boldsymbol{u}_{nC}$ are identical and equal to the bulk velocity of flow of the mixture. If the concentration gradients are sufficiently small then the differences between $\boldsymbol{u}_{MC}$, $\boldsymbol{u}_{VC}$ and $\boldsymbol{u}_{nC}$ may also be small enough to be neglected. These differences can often also be neglected for the diffusion of components present in very low concentrations in an otherwise uniform mixture.

To calculate the diffusion flows from measurements of the total mass flows $(J_k)_C$ will always require information about the bulk velocity of motion of the system (e.g. $\boldsymbol{u}_{MC}$). This becomes very important in problems of *convective diffusion* where a component diffuses in a medium subject to *free convection* or to *forced convection*. Free convection is associated with local density differences such as may arise in a fluid through local temperature differences or through local changes in mass density on mixing of the diffusing components.

If the diffusing components all have identical partial specific volumes $\hat{v}_k = \hat{v}$ then from Eqn (11.22)

$$\sum_{k=1}^{n} \hat{v}_k \rho_k = \hat{v} \sum_{k=1}^{n} \rho_k = \hat{v}\rho = 1 \tag{11.31}$$

and therefore

$$\boldsymbol{u}_{MC} = \boldsymbol{u}_{VC} \tag{11.32}$$

so that the diffusion flows in these two reference frames become equivalent.

If the component have different partial specific volumes then in general $\boldsymbol{u}_{MC} \neq \boldsymbol{u}_{VC}$ and these two reference frames must be discussed separately.

If the components have different partial specific volumes and there are appreciable volume changes on mixing then the condition for mechanical equilibrium $d\boldsymbol{u}/dt = 0$ may no longer be valid. However in most fluid systems the pressure gradients which develop in this way should be quite negligible (De Groot, 1951). Even though the pressure gradients will generally be small, local changes of density will give rise to a hydrodynamic flow of the system. Such an effect is automatically corrected for in the definition of $(J_k)_V$, $(J_k)_M$, and $(J_k)_n$, but in order to calculate these diffusion flows from experimental measurements of the $(J_k)_C$ (the mass flows with respect to the diffusion cell) we must have detailed information about the variation of $\boldsymbol{u}_{VC}$, $\boldsymbol{u}_{MC}$ or $\boldsymbol{u}_{nC}$, respectively, as a function of both position and time.

More explicitly, expressions must be derived to relate the $\boldsymbol{u}_{RC}$ to the partial specific volumes $\hat{v}_k$ and their variation with position, and to the variation of the $(J_k)_R$ with position and time. The expressions obtained will depend on the detailed nature of the specific diffusion problem, e.g. on the initial and boundary conditions and on the geometry and dimensions of the system. For this reason no general solution is available for this type of problem. That bulk flow in a system may have a serious influence on diffusion measurements is clear from the calculations of Szekeley (1965) and others. A practical example concerning diffusion in concentrated polymer solutions has been given for binary systems by Paul (1967).

B. A Simple Experimental Arrangement

A very illuminating but simple experimental situation was examined by Kirkwood *et al.* (1960). They considered free diffusion in a rectangular diffusion cell open at the top and closed at the bottom. The diffusion coordinate x is directed down the diffusion cell. Local changes in volume in the lower regions of the cell (higher values of x) must give rise to a bulk flow of the upper regions by a simple displacement mechanism. The events in one region of the cell influence the mass transfer processes in other regions.

For a simple binary system (component 1 is the solute and component 0 is the solvent) we have (Kirkwood *et al.*, 1960)

$$(J_1)_C = -(1 - \rho_1\hat{v}_1)(D_{11})_0 \frac{\partial \rho_1}{\partial x} - \rho_1 \int_{+\infty}^{x} \left(\frac{\partial \hat{v}_1}{\partial \rho_1}\right)(D_{11})_0 \left(\frac{\partial \rho_1}{\partial x}\right)^2 dx \quad (11.33)$$

and

$$(J_1)_C = -(D_{11})_V \frac{\partial \rho_1}{\partial x} - \rho_1 \int_{+\infty}^{x} \left(\frac{\partial \hat{v}_1}{\partial \rho_1}\right) \frac{(D_{11})_V}{(1 - \rho_1\hat{v}_1)} \left(\frac{\partial \rho_1}{\partial x}\right)^2 dx \quad (11.34)$$

The negative integrals are identical (see Eqn 11.30) and represent the hydrodynamic velocity $\boldsymbol{u}_{VC}$ at position x. If $\hat{v}_1$ is independent of concentration $\boldsymbol{u}_{VC} = 0$ and the bulk flow is zero. (Kirkwood *et al.*, 1960); Hooyman *et al.*, 1953; Onsager, 1945).

If $\hat{v}_1$ is not independent of concentration but nevertheless the concentration gradient $\partial\rho_1/\partial x$ is very small we may again put $\boldsymbol{u}_{VC} \approx 0$ because the integrals are of order $(\partial\rho_1/\partial x)^2$ whereas the diffusion flux is of order $\partial\rho_1/\partial x$.

In either case we have a reduction to the form of *Fick's first equation*

$$(J_1)_C = -(1 - \rho_1\hat{v}_1)(D_{11})_0 \frac{\partial \rho_1}{\partial x} = -(D_{11})_V \frac{\partial \rho_1}{\partial x} \quad (11.35)$$

and a measurement of the diffusion flux $(J_1)_C$ with respect to the cell gives $(D_{11})_V$ directly. $(D_{11})_V$, as will be discussed in more detail later, is the same for both components and is known as the *mutual diffusion coefficient* for this binary diffusion process. $(D_{11})_0$ is the diffusion coefficient for the solute in the solvent fixed reference frame.

IV. IONIC SYSTEMS

In discussing ionic systems we shall refer to the individual ionic species as components, though this terminology is not strictly correct since it is not possible to alter the concentration of a single ionic species completely independently of the concentrations of the other ions in the system. Only certain electrically neutral combinations of ions can be manipulated in this way.

A. Molar Concentration Units

Suppose we have the $(n + 1)$ components $k = 0, 1, 2 \cdots n$ where 0 is the solvent. The diffusion flows $(\mathscr{J}_k)_0$ in the solvent-fixed reference frame in units of moles cm^{-2}.sec^{-1} are

$$(\mathscr{I}_k)_0 \equiv (J_k)_0/M_k \tag{11.36}$$

where M_k is the molar mass of component k. If k is an ionic species, then M_k is the ionic mass and $(\mathscr{I}_k)_0$ is the ion flux in g-ions.cm^{-2}.sec^{-1}.

If the only external force acting is a conservative force associated with an electrical field we may rewrite Eqn (11.5) in the form

$$(\mathscr{I}_k)_0 = -\sum_{j=1}^{n} (\mathscr{L}_{kj})_0 \operatorname{grad} \tilde{\mu}_j \tag{11.37}$$

where $\tilde{\mu}_j$ is the (partial molar) *electrochemical potential* of Chapter 8. Since we have

$$(\mathscr{L}_{kj})_0 = \frac{(L_{kj})_0}{M_k M_j} \tag{11.38}$$

The $(\mathscr{L}_{kj})_0$ are subject to reciprocal relations if these hold for the $(L_{kj})_0$.

For a non-ionic system we have as an analogue of Eqn (11.19) (the solvent is component 0)

$$\operatorname{grad} \mu_j = \sum_{i=1}^{n} \left(\frac{\partial \mu_j}{\partial C_i}\right) \operatorname{grad} C_i \tag{11.39}$$

where μ_j is the (partial molar) chemical potential and C_i is the molar concentration of component i. For such a system we have the practical diffusion equations

$$(\mathscr{I}_k)_0 = -\sum_{j=1}^{n} (\mathscr{D}_{kj})_0 \operatorname{grad} C_j \tag{11.40}$$

with

$$(\mathscr{D}_{kj})_0 = \frac{M_j}{1000 M_k} \cdot (D_{kj})_0 \tag{11.41}$$

and

$$(\mathscr{D}_{ki})_0 = \sum_{j=1}^{n} (\mathscr{L}_{kj})_0 \frac{\partial \mu_j}{\partial C_i} \tag{11.42}$$

The molar concentration units C_k give rise to equations having the same form as those for the mass concentration units ρ_k but the coefficients in the equations are not identical. The reciprocal relations for the solvent-fixed reference frame are however preserved in the molar concentration units. If the concentrations C_i are expressed in moles.cm^{-3}, then the factor 1000 in Eqn (11.41) does not appear.

B. Pure Diffusion in Ionic Systems

If we have n ionic components ($k = 1, 2, \ldots, n$) dissolved in an unionised solvent ($k = 0$) the n ionic concentrations will generally be subject to the *condition of electrical neutrality*

$$\sum_{k=1}^{n} z_k C_k = 0 \tag{11.43}$$

where z_k is the ionic valence (including sign) of component k.

Only $(n - 1)$ of the ionic concentrations are independent, and there is a corresponding restriction on the concentration gradients

$$\sum_{k=1}^{n} z_k \operatorname{grad} C_k = 0 \tag{11.44}$$

The electrical current $\boldsymbol{I}$ in the system is zero for *pure diffusion* (F is the Faraday)

$$\boldsymbol{I} = F \sum_{i=1}^{n} z_i (\mathscr{I}_i)_0 = 0 \tag{11.45}$$

This places an additional restriction on the $(\mathscr{I}_i)_0$ which determines the magnitude of the electrical potential gradient grad φ (the so-called "*diffusion potential*") which is set up during diffusion. For example Eqn (11.37) may be written as

$$(\mathscr{I}_i)_0 = -\sum_{l=1}^{n} (\mathscr{L}_{il})_0 \{\operatorname{grad} \mu_l + z_l F \operatorname{grad} \psi\} \tag{11.46}$$

where F is the Faraday (in coulombs per equivalent) and ψ is the electrical potential (in volts). Substitution for $(\mathscr{I}_i)_0$ in Eqn (11.45) followed by rearrangement leads to the following expression for F grad ψ (Miller, 1967)

$$F \operatorname{grad} \psi = -\frac{\sum_{i=1}^{n} \sum_{l=1}^{n} z_i (\mathscr{L}_{il})_0 \operatorname{grad} \mu_l}{\sum_{i=1}^{n} \sum_{l=1}^{n} z_i (\mathscr{L}_{il})_0 z_l} \tag{11.47}$$

The "diffusion potential" gradient grad ψ generally disappears only when the gradients grad μ_l disappear and it may have any sign. It may therefore reduce or increase the diffusion flux of a given ionic component i, depending on the sign of grad ψ and the sign of z_i.

Because of the term in grad ψ it is not in general possible to reduce Eqn (11.46) directly to the form of the practical diffusion equations (Eqn 11.40). However the terms in grad ψ may be eliminated from the thermodynamic diffusion equations if these are written for the flow of properly selected electrically neutral combinations of ions (Kirkwood *et al.*, 1960; Miller, 1967).

Substitution for F grad ψ in Eqn (11.46) using Eqn (11.47) leads to the result (Miller, 1967)

$$(\mathscr{I}_k)_0 = -\frac{\sum_{j=1}^{n}\sum_{i=1}^{n}\sum_{l=1}^{n}(\mathscr{L}_{kj})_0(\mathscr{L}_{il})_0 z_i[z_l \text{ grad } \mu_j - z_j \text{ grad } \mu_l]}{\sum_{i=1}^{n}\sum_{l=1}^{n} z_i(\mathscr{L}_{il})_0 z_l}$$

$$k = 1, 2 \cdots n \qquad (11.48)$$

The quantity in brackets may be regarded as the gradient grad μ_{lj} of a chemical potential μ_{lj}.

$$\mu_{lj} \equiv (z_l\mu_j - z_j\mu_l) \qquad (11.49)$$

μ_{lj} is formally defined as the chemical potential of a binary ionic combination lj in which z_1 ions of type j are combined with $(-z_j)$ ions of type l. Equation (11.48) includes all the mathematically possible ion combinations but the flux $(\mathscr{I}_k)_0$ can in principle be expressed in terms of the chemical potential gradients of $(n - 1)$ independent electrically neutral combinations of ions so selected that combinations involving two ions of similar charge (e.g. the hypothetical combination of 1 ion of Na^+ *minus* 1 ion of K^+) and combinations which lead to negative concentrations of a neutral combination are not used (Kirkwood *et al.*, 1960). Miller (1967) has shown how Eqn (11.48) may be simplified and used in this way for a ternary system involving two cations and a common anion for example.

If $(\mathscr{I}_{kl})_0$ is the diffusion flux of a neutral combination of ions k and l then

$$(\mathscr{I}_k)_0 = \sum_{l=1}^{n} z_l(\mathscr{I}_{kl})_0 \qquad (11.50)$$

The summation is from $l = 1$ to $l = n$ for generality but in practice only those flows $(\mathscr{I}_{kl})_0$ which correspond to the appropriate $(n - 1)$ neutral ion pairs will be taken as nonzero. The chemical potentials μ_{kl} for the components may be defined as in Eqn (11.49) but in general component k will be selected as a cation $(z_k > 0)$ and component l as an anion $(z_l < 0)$, i.e.

$$\begin{aligned}\mu_{kl} &= -z_l\mu_k + z_k\mu_l \\ &= |z_l|\ \mu_k + |z_k|\ \mu_l \\ &= \nu_l\mu_k + \nu_k\mu_l = \nu_k\mu_l + \nu_l\mu_k = \mu_{lk}\end{aligned} \qquad (11.51)$$

Here we have used the notation of Chapter 8 and μ_{kl} is now the chemical potential of the neutral "salt" $K\nu_lL\nu_k$ and in general

$$\mu_{kl} = \mu_{lk}; \qquad (\mathscr{I}_{kl})_0 = (\mathscr{I}_{lk})_0 \qquad (11.52)$$

For appropriate neutral "salts" as components we can write thermodynamic diffusion equations for the solvent-fixed reference frame in which the phenomenological coefficients obey reciprocal relations and we can also construct corresponding practical diffusion equations. If the $n - 1$ "salt" components are re-numbered as $1, 2 \cdots S$ then Eqns (11.37), (11.40), and (11.42) may be used directly with the upper limit $n = S$ in the summations (Kirkwood *et al.*, 1960; Fitts, 1962; Miller, 1967).

C. Pure Ionic Conduction

In *pure ionic conduction* there are no concentration gradients and no chemical potential gradients. There is however a flow of each ionic component with respect to the solvent and this flow corresponds to a partial ionic current $\boldsymbol{I}_i$ for component i in this reference frame

$$\boldsymbol{I}_i = z_i F(\mathscr{I}_i)_0 = -z_i F\left(\sum_{l=1}^{n} (\mathscr{L}_{il})_0 z_l\right) F \text{ grad } \psi \tag{11.53}$$

Equation (11.53) is analogous to Ohm's Law and for ion i the individual ionic conductance is $z_i F^2 \sum_{l=1}^{n} (\mathscr{L}_{il})_0 z_l$.

The total current $\boldsymbol{I}$ is obtained by summation of the $\boldsymbol{I}_k$. The transference number t_i of ion i is a scalar quantity defined as

$$t_i \equiv \frac{\boldsymbol{I}_i}{\boldsymbol{I}} = \frac{z_i(\mathscr{I}_i)_0}{\sum_{i=1}^{n} z_i(\mathscr{I}_i)_0} \tag{11.54}$$

From Eqn (11.53)

$$t_i = \frac{z_i \sum_{l=1}^{n} z_l(\mathscr{L}_{il})_0}{\sum_{i=1}^{n} \sum_{l=1}^{n} z_i(\mathscr{L}_{il})_0 z_l} \tag{11.55}$$

The specific conductance λ (ohm^{-1} cm^{-1}) is (Miller, 1967)

$$\lambda = F^2 \sum_{i=1}^{n} \sum_{l=1}^{n} z_i(\mathscr{L}_{il})_0 z_l \tag{11.56}$$

and the equivalent conductance Λ (cm^2 ohm^{-1} equiv^{-1}) is

$$\Lambda = \frac{1000F^2}{N} \sum_{i=1}^{n} \sum_{l=1}^{n} z_i(\mathscr{L}_{il})_0 z_l \tag{11.57}$$

where N is the total number of equivalents of electrolyte present per litre.

A detailed procedure for using experimental measurements of conductance, of transference numbers and of diffusion coefficients in order to calculate all of the $(\mathscr{L}_{ij})_0$ for a ternary ionic system has been given by Miller (1967).

An examination of seven different ternary systems showed that the *cross coefficients* $(\mathscr{L}_{ij})_0$ $(i \neq j)$ in the thermodynamic transport equations can not in general be neglected by comparison with the *main coefficients* $(\mathscr{L}_{ij})_0$ $(i = j)$, especially in concentrated solutions. The influence of the cross coefficients should be least in dilute solutions (Miller, 1966).

D. The Nernst–Planck Equations

For very dilute solutions it is possible that the cross coefficients $(\mathscr{L}_{ij})_0$ $(i \neq j)$ may be neglected by comparison with the main coefficients (Miller, 1966, 1967). Let us suppose this is true. Then the thermodynamic diffusion equations take a much simpler form, i.e.

$$(\mathscr{I}_k)_0 = -(\mathscr{L}_{kk})_0\{\text{grad}\ \mu_k + z_k F\ \text{grad}\ \psi\} \qquad k = 1, 2 \cdots n \quad (11.58)$$

Suppose that in addition each ionic species k forms an ideally dilute solution of such a type that we may write each μ_k in the form

$$\mu_k = \mu^0{}_k + RT \ln C_k \quad (11.59)$$

Then

$$\text{grad}\ \mu_k = \frac{RT}{C_k}\ \text{grad}\ C_k \quad (11.60)$$

and Eqn (11.58) becomes

$$(\mathscr{I}_k)_0 = -\frac{(\mathscr{L}_{kk})_0 RT}{C_k}\left\{\text{grad}\ C_k + \frac{z_k C_k F}{RT}\ \text{grad}\ \psi\right\} \quad (11.61)$$

The quantity $((\mathscr{L}_{kk})_0/C_k)$ is the effective *mobility* of component k and the quantity

$$(D_k)_0 \equiv \frac{RT(\mathscr{L}_{kk})_0}{C_k} \quad (11.62)$$

is a diffusion coefficient for component k. We thus obtain the *Nernst-Planck Diffusion Equations* in the form

$$(\mathscr{I}_k)_0 = -(D_k)_0\left\{\text{grad}\ C_k + \frac{z_k C_k F}{RT}\ \text{grad}\ \psi\right\} \qquad k = 1, 2 \cdots n \quad (11.63)$$

These equations are often used in theoretical and experimental studies of ionic diffusion, so that the simplifying assumptions necessary to derive them on the basis of nonequilibrium thermodynamics are of considerable interest. As we have seen in Chapter 8, Eqn (11.59) implies a restriction to very low ionic strengths, or to constant ionic strength if the activity coefficients are included in the $\mu^0{}_k$ (Harned and Owen, 1958).

V. DIFFUSION AND IONIC MOBILITY

Ionic transport can also be discussed on the basis of the *mobilities* l_k of the ions. The mobility l_k of an ion k is defined as the steady velocity of motion which that ion attains in an electric field $\boldsymbol{E} = -\text{grad}\ \psi$ of unit strength. If the solvent is assumed to be stationary, the velocity of motion $(\boldsymbol{u}_k)_0$ with respect to the solvent is then given by

$$(\boldsymbol{u}_k)_0 = l_k(-\text{grad}\ \psi) \tag{11.64}$$

which defines l_k.

The force per g-ion which acts on ions of charge z_k in an electrical field $E = -\text{grad}\ \psi$ is $-z_kF\ \text{grad}\ \psi$. If we introduce a *generalised mobility* μ_k, in the sense of the steady velocity of motion attained under the action of unit driving force per g-ion,

$$(\boldsymbol{u}_k)_0 = \mu_k(-z_kF\ \text{grad}\ \psi) \tag{11.65}$$

which defines μ_k. We have $l_k = z_kF\mu_k$ and a comparison with (11.61) and (11.62) for the absence of concentration gradients shows that

$$(D_k)_0 = RT\mu_k; \qquad (\mathscr{L}_{kk})_0 = C_k\mu_k \tag{11.66}$$

We also have

$$(D_k)_0 = \left(\frac{RT}{z_kF}\right)l_k = \left(\frac{kT}{q}\right)l_k \tag{11.67}$$

in which k is the Boltzmann constant and q is the electrical charge per ion (Nernst, 1888).

Consider for example the pure diffusion in water of an electrically neutral, simple salt CA in which C is a cation of charge z_{C} and A is an anion of charge z_{A}. For the present assumptions the diffusion of each ion can be represented by the equation of the Nernst-Planck type (Eqn 11.63). The zero current condition (Eqn 11.45) gives a relationship between $(J_{\text{C}})_0$ and $(J_{\text{A}})_0$ so that the electrical potential gradient grad ψ can be expressed in terms of z_{A}, z_{C}, $(D_{\text{A}})_0$, $(D_{\text{C}})_0$, C_{A}, C_{C} and the gradients grad C_{A} and grad C_{C}. The electrical neutrality condition (Eqn 11.43) makes it possible to eliminate C_{A} from this expression, and Eqn (11.44) can be used to eliminate grad C_{A}.

One therefore obtains an expression for grad ψ which involves only z_{A}, z_{C}, $(D_{\text{A}})_0$, $(D_{\text{C}})_0$ and grad C_{C} as variables. Substitution for grad ψ in the flux equation (Eqn 11.63) for $(\mathscr{J}_{\text{C}})_0$ gives an expression of the type

$$(\mathscr{J}_{\text{C}})_0 = -(D_{\text{C}}^1)_0\ \text{grad}\ C_{\text{C}} \tag{11.68}$$

in which the apparent diffusion coefficient $(D_{\text{C}}^1)_0$ for the cation C is

$$(D_{\text{C}}^1)_0 = \frac{(|z_{\text{A}}| + |z_{\text{C}}|)(D_A)_0(D_{\text{C}})_0}{(|z_{\text{A}}|\ (D_{\text{A}})_0 + |z_{\text{C}}|\ (D_{\text{C}})_0)} \tag{11.69}$$

so that in view of Eqn (11.67)

$$(D_C^1)_0 = \frac{RT}{F} \cdot \frac{|z_A| + |z_C|}{|z_A|\,|z_C|} \cdot \frac{l_A l_C}{(l_A + l_C)} \tag{11.70}$$

in which $|z_A|$ and $|z_C|$ are the moduli, or the absolute values, of z_A and z_C (Haskell, 1908).

The coupling of the ionic fluxes by the diffusion potential gives an apparent cation diffusion coefficient $(D_C^1)_0$ which is a complex function of the individual ionic mobilities. For a simple 1:1 electrolyte such as NaCl

$$(D_C^1)_0 = \frac{2(D_A)_0(D_C)_0}{(D_A)_0 + (D_C)_0} = \frac{RT}{F} \cdot \frac{2 l_A l_C}{(l_A + l_C)} \tag{11.71}$$

and if the two ions have equal mobilities the diffusion potential disappears ($(D_C^1)_0 = RTl_C/F$). In general the apparent diffusion coefficient $(D_C^1)_0$ will have a value intermediate between the diffusion coefficients of the individual ions. The diffusion potentials equalise the ionic velocities by retarding the faster-diffusing ion. The zero current condition can be used to show that for a simple binary electrolyte CA

$$(\boldsymbol{u}_C)_0 = (\boldsymbol{u}_A)_0 \frac{|z_A|\, C_A}{|z_C|\, C_C} \tag{11.72}$$

When this result is combined with the condition of electrical neutrality we see that $(\boldsymbol{u}_C)_0 = (\boldsymbol{u}_A)_0$ even though both ions carry different charges and have different mobilities.

If we represent the diffusion flux of the neutral salt CA by the symbol $(\mathscr{I})_0$ then since the two types of ions move with identical velocities we have

$$(\mathscr{I})_0 = \frac{(\mathscr{I}_C)_0}{|z_A|} = \frac{(\mathscr{I}_A)_0}{|z_C|} \tag{11.73}$$

because the neutral salt is here assumed to consist of $|z_A|$ ions of type C in combination with $|z_C|$ ions of type A. Similarly, the local concentration C of the salt is

$$C = \frac{C_C}{|z_A|} = \frac{C_A}{|z_C|} \tag{11.74}$$

If the diffusion of the salt CA is represented by the equation

$$(\mathscr{I})_0 = -(D)_0 \operatorname{grad} C \tag{11.75}$$

in which $(D)_0$ is the apparent diffusion coefficient of the salt CA, we find that $(D)_0$ is equal to $(D_C^1)_0$ of Eqns (11.68–11.69). In fact $(D)_0 = (D_C^1)_0 = (D_A^1)_0$ since both ions appear to diffuse with the same diffusion coefficient $(D)_0$.

The Nernst–Planck equations provide a simple description of ionic diffusion, valid in the limit of zero ionic strength. Equations (11.58) include the effects of non-ideality and should be useful up to an ionic strength of about 0.01. Above this ionic strength the cross-terms become important and the full thermodynamic diffusion equations must be used (Miller, 1966, 1967).

A detailed analysis of diffusion in multicomponent systems has been given by De Groot and Mazur (1962) on the basis of matrix methods. Fitts (1962) and Miller (1967) have analysed ternary electrolyte mixtures in some detail. Miller (1966) has examined diffusion of binary electrolytes. These analyses rapidly become very complex as the number of ions increases. Extensive information on the thermodynamic properties of a system is necessary even at the binary level. For this reason, many systems have so far been analysed only on the basis of the simple Nernst–Planck equations.

A discussion of diffusion in electrolytes, which considers molecular details, has been given by Harned and Owen (1958).

VI. MATRIX METHODS AND THE DIFFUSION EQUATIONS

A. Diagonalisation of the Matrix of Phenomenological Coefficients

A set of thermodynamic diffusion equations of the form

$$\begin{aligned} J_1 &= L_{11}X_1 + L_{12}X_2 + L_{13}X_3 \\ J_2 &= L_{21}X_1 + L_{22}X_2 + L_{23}X_3 \\ J_3 &= L_{31}X_1 + L_{32}X_2 + L_{33}X_3 \end{aligned} \tag{11.76}$$

where X_i here represents a generalised thermodynamic force for diffusion, may be represented in a simple matrix notation as follows

$$\begin{bmatrix} J_1 \\ J_2 \\ J_3 \end{bmatrix} = \begin{bmatrix} L_{11} & L_{12} & L_{13} \\ L_{21} & L_{22} & L_{23} \\ L_{31} & L_{32} & L_{33} \end{bmatrix} \begin{bmatrix} X_1 \\ X_2 \\ X_3 \end{bmatrix} \tag{11.77}$$

The set of n^2 ($n = 3$) phenomenological coefficients of Eqn (11.76) form an $n \times n$ (3×3) square matrix in Eqn (11.77). The main coefficients L_{kk} lie on the diagonal. The set of products which forms the right hand sides of the three equations (11.76) is obtained by the multiplication of the square matrix of phenomenological coefficients by the column vector X_1, X_2, X_3 representing the thermodynamic forces, according to the rules of matrix algebra (Frazer *et al.*, 1952).

The matrix of phenomenological coefficients is said to be *symmetric* if $L_{kj} = L_{jk}$. For a symmetric matrix of the expected type it is always possible to define new flows. J_i^1 which are linear combinations of the old flows $\boldsymbol{J}_i$, and to define new forces $\boldsymbol{X}_i^1$ which are linear combinations of the old forces $\boldsymbol{X}_i$, and to do this in such a way that the entropy production is unaltered. At the same time, it is possible so to choose the $\boldsymbol{J}_i^1$ and the $\boldsymbol{X}_i^1$ that the matrix of phenomenological coefficients is *diagonalised*, i.e. Eqn (11.77) becomes

$$\begin{bmatrix} J_1^1 \\ J_2^1 \\ J_3^1 \end{bmatrix} = \begin{bmatrix} L_{11}^1 & 0 & 0 \\ 0 & L_{22}^1 & 0 \\ 0 & 0 & L_{33}^1 \end{bmatrix} \begin{bmatrix} X_1^1 \\ X_2^1 \\ X_3^1 \end{bmatrix} \tag{11.78}$$

and the phenomenological equations reduce to the *uncoupled form*

$$\begin{aligned} \boldsymbol{J}_1^1 &= L_{11}^1 \boldsymbol{X}_1^1 \\ \boldsymbol{J}_2^1 &= L_{22}^1 \boldsymbol{X}_2^1 \\ \boldsymbol{J}_3^1 &= L_{33}^1 \boldsymbol{X}_3^1 \end{aligned} \tag{11.79}$$

Equations (11.79) are much simpler in form than Eqns (11.76) and this procedure may have advantages in the formal manipulation of the thermodynamic diffusion equations for multicomponent systems.

Unfortunately the flows and forces may be transformed in an infinite variety of ways in order to effect this diagonalisation and the specific forms obtained for the fiows and the forces will in general have no real physical significance (De Groot, 1951; Li, 1969; Manes, 1963).

The application of matrix methods to the flux equations of multicomponent diffusion has been discussed in some detail by Toor (1962) and by Cullinan (1965). It appears from this work that multicomponent diffusion problems may be solved using solutions to equivalent binary diffusion problems, but only at the expense of introducing hypothetical "pseudobinary components" into the analysis of the behaviour of the system. De Groot and Mazur (1962) have used the matrix notation extensively in discussing multicomponent diffusion.

VII. MUTUAL DIFFUSION, SELF-DIFFUSION AND THE DIFFUSION OF ISOTOPICALLY LABELLED COMPONENTS

A. Mutual Diffusion

This term usually refers to the interdiffusion of a binary liquid mixture of nonelectrolytes. There are concentration gradients and the activity coefficients are not constant. The "chemical environment" of a molecule is different in different parts of the system. The practical diffusion equations are

$$(\mathscr{J}_1)_V = -(D_{11})_V \operatorname{grad} C_1 \tag{11.80}$$

$$(\mathscr{J}_2)_V = -(D_{22})_V \operatorname{grad} C_2 \tag{11.81}$$

with the restriction

$$\bar{v}_1(\mathscr{I}_1)_V + \bar{v}_2(\mathscr{I}_2)_V = 0 \tag{11.82}$$

where $\bar{v}_1$ and $\bar{v}_2$ are the partial molar volumes.

The Gibbs–Duhem equation places a restriction on the isothermal concentration gradients (in mechanical equilibrium grad $p = 0$)

$$\bar{v}_1 \text{ grad } C_1 + \bar{v}_2 \text{ grad } C_2 = 0 \tag{11.83}$$

Using Eqns (11.82) and (11.83) to write Eqn (11.81) in terms of $(\mathscr{I}_1)_V$ and grad C_1 leads to the result

$$(D_{22})_V = (D_{11})_V = (D)_V \tag{11.84}$$

where $(D)_V$ is the single *mutual diffusion coefficient* which suffices to describe the interdiffusion of the two components.

From Eqn (11.28)

$$(D_{11})_V = (\mathscr{L}_{11})_V(\partial\mu_1/\partial c_1) \tag{11.85}$$

If the chemical potential μ_1 may be written in the form

$$\mu_1 = \mu^0{}_1(T, P) + RT \ln(y_1 C_1) \tag{11.86}$$

where y_1 is a molar activity coefficient, then Eqn (11.85) becomes

$$(D_{11})_V = \frac{RT(\mathscr{L}_{11})_V}{C_1}\left\{1 + \frac{\partial \ln y_1}{\partial \ln C_1}\right\} \tag{11.87}$$

For an ideally dilute solution in which $y_1 \to 1$ and is independent of C_1

$$(D_{11})_V = RT\{(\mathscr{L}_{11})_V/C_1\} \tag{11.88}$$

The constancy of $(D_{11})_V$ in an ideally dilute solution would require $(\mathscr{L}_{11})_V$ to be directly proportional to C_1. The quantity $\{(\mathscr{L}_{11})_V/C_1\}$ may be regarded as the molar mobility of component 1 in the system or as the inverse of a molar friction coefficient for component 1 (Eqn 2.20).

A *friction coefficient formalism* is often used in discussions of mutual diffusion (Tyrrell, 1963). If the momentum supplies of Chapter 6 are defined in accordance with Eqn (10.19) then the *Stefan–Maxwell equations* for diffusion take the form (Onsager, 1945)

$$(\text{grad } \hat{\mu}_k)_{T,p} = -\sum_{j=1}^{n} A_{kj}\rho_j(\boldsymbol{u}_k - \boldsymbol{u}_j) \tag{11.89}$$

If we introduce molar quantities and the appropriate friction coefficients ζ_{kj} we have

$$(\text{grad } \mu_k)_{T,p} = -\sum_{j=1}^{n} \zeta_{kj}C_j(\boldsymbol{u}_k - \boldsymbol{u}_j) \tag{11.90}$$

Since the velocity difference $(\boldsymbol{u}_k - \boldsymbol{u}_j)$ is independent of the choice of reference frame, so are the molar friction coefficients ζ_{kj}. For a two-component system

$$\text{grad}\,\mu_1 = -\zeta_{12}C_2(\boldsymbol{u}_1 - \boldsymbol{u}_2) \qquad (11.91)$$

$$\text{grad}\,\mu_2 = -\zeta_{21}C_1(\boldsymbol{u}_2 - \boldsymbol{u}_1) \qquad (11.92)$$

The condition of mechanical equilibrium leads to the restriction

$$C_1\,\text{grad}\,\mu_1 + C_2\,\text{grad}\,\mu_2 = 0 \qquad (11.93)$$

from which it follows that

$$\zeta_{21} = \zeta_{12} \qquad (11.94)$$

This result may be compared with the symmetry conditions of Chapter 6 which were based on the principle of conservation of linear momentum.

The thermodynamic diffusion equation is

$$(\mathscr{I}_1)_V = -(\mathscr{L}_{11})_V\,\text{grad}\,\mu_1 \qquad (11.95)$$

From the definition of $(\mathscr{I}_k)_V$ and Eqn (11.82) we may rewrite Eqn (11.81) as

$$(\mathscr{I}_1)_V = -\left(\frac{\bar{v}_2 C_1}{\zeta_{12}}\right)\text{grad}\,\mu_1 \qquad (11.96)$$

in deriving which the molar analogue of Eqn (11.22) was used. We have therefore

$$(\mathscr{L}_{11})_V = \frac{\bar{v}_2 C_1}{\zeta_{12}} \qquad (11.97)$$

and for the mutual diffusion coefficient $(D)_V$ (Loflin and McLaughlin, 1969)

$$(D)_V = \frac{\bar{v}_2 RT}{\zeta_{12}}\left(1 + \frac{\partial \ln y_1}{\partial \ln C_1}\right) = \frac{\bar{v}_1 RT}{\zeta_{12}}\left(1 + \frac{\partial \ln y_2}{\partial \ln C_2}\right) \qquad (11.98)$$

B. "Self Diffusion" in Binary Systems

The process of *mutual diffusion* ceases when the chemical potential gradients or concentration gradients disappear and the mixture becomes chemically uniform. The molecular motions of the two components do not however cease and it is still possible to define a *self-diffusion coefficient* D_k for the molecular motions of each component. If $\langle r_k^2 \rangle$ is the mean square displacement of a molecule of component k in time τ then (Chapter 2)

$$D_k \equiv \langle r_k^2 \rangle / 6\tau \qquad (11.99)$$

This type of *self-diffusion coefficient* can be measured for suitable systems by the application of a magnetic field gradient in nmr spin-echo studies. Such measurements have been made by McCall and Douglass (1967) for homogeneous binary mixtures of selected organic liquids. The nmr spin-echo studies give the values of D_1 and D_2, the self diffusion coefficients defined by Eqn (11.99) for each component at the existing composition of the uniform mixture. One would expect $(D)_V$ to be related to D_1 and D_2. A self diffusion coefficient D_k can be related to a corresponding friction coefficient ζ_k

$$D_k = RT/\zeta_k \tag{11.100}$$

There are statistical mechanical considerations which suggest the following expression for ζ_k (Bearman, 1961; Loflin and McLaughlin, 1969)

$$\zeta_k = \sum_{j=1}^{n} C_j \zeta_{kj} \tag{11.101}$$

On this basis, for self diffusion in a binary system

$$\zeta_1 = C_1\zeta_{11} + C_2\zeta_{12} \tag{11.102}$$

$$\zeta_2 = C_1\zeta_{21} + C_2\zeta_{22} \tag{11.103}$$

so that

$$D_1 = \frac{RT}{C_1\zeta_{11} + C_2\zeta_{12}} = \frac{vRT}{(x_1\zeta_{11} + x_2\zeta_{12})} \tag{11.104}$$

and

$$D_2 = \frac{RT}{C_1\zeta_{21} + C_2\zeta_{22}} = \frac{vRT}{(x_1\zeta_{21} + x_2\zeta_{22})} \tag{11.105}$$

The quantities x_1 and x_2 are mole fractions and are related to the concentrations C_1 and C_2 by

$$C_1 = x_1/v \quad \text{and} \quad C_2 = x_2/v, \quad \text{where} \quad v = x_1\bar{v}_1 + x_2\bar{v}_2,$$

The combination of Eqns (11.98), (11.102) and (11.103) gives (Loflin and McLaughlin, 1969)

$$(D)_V = (x_1D_2 + x_2D_1)\left\{\frac{\partial \ln a_1}{\partial \ln x_1}\right\} \times \left\{\frac{x_1\zeta_{12}}{x_1\zeta_{12} + x_2\zeta_{22}} + \frac{x_2\zeta_{12}}{x_2\zeta_{12} + x_1\zeta_{11}}\right\}^{-1} \tag{11.106}$$

which reduces to the simple form

$$(D)_V = (x_1D_2 + x_2D_1)\left\{\frac{\partial \ln a_1}{\partial \ln x_1}\right\} \tag{11.107}$$

only if we have (Tyrrell, 1963; Loflin and McLaughlin, 1969)

$$\zeta_{12} = (\zeta_{11}\zeta_{22})^{\frac{1}{2}} \tag{11.108}$$

Both the simple form (11.107) and Eqn (11.106) reduce to the limiting forms

$$\lim_{x_1 \to 0} (D)_V = D_1 \tag{11.109}$$

$$\lim_{x_2 \to 0} (D)_V = D_2 \tag{11.110}$$

C. The "Self Diffusion" of Isotopically Labelled Molecules

1. Systems of One Chemical Species

From a very restricted but logical point of view the term self-diffusion would be restricted to processes involving only one molecular species. In principle some such technique as the nmr spin-echo technique could be used to measure the mobility of the molecules of a single-component homogeneous fluid and to define a pure self diffusion coefficient for this component. It would not be possible to write macroscopic thermodynamic diffusion equations or practical diffusion equations for this process since there would be no concentration gradients, no activity gradients and indeed no macroscopic diffusion process in the conventional sense. Such a definition of self diffusion seems unnecessarily restrictive.

An approximation to this "pure self diffusion" is obtained when we have only isotopically labelled and unlabelled molecules of the same chemical species. Some authors restrict the term self diffusion to this particular process (Albright and Mills, 1965) which has the following characteristics.

The total concentration $C_{1*} + C_1$ of labelled (C_{1*}) and unlabelled (C_1) molecules remains effectively constant but there are concentration gradients of the labelled and unlabelled molecules which interdiffuse. There are negligible activity coefficient gradients because the chemical environment of a molecule is substantially the same at all points in the system. The close chemical similarity of the labelled and unlabelled molecules is responsible for this.

We have in fact a special type of mutual diffusion in which the two components are chemically almost indistinguishable. We have

$$(\mathscr{I}_{1*})_V = -(D_{1*1*})_V \operatorname{grad} C_{1*} \tag{11.111}$$

and

$$(\mathscr{I}_1)_V = -(D_{11})_V \operatorname{grad} C_1 \tag{11.112}$$

with the isotope mutual diffusion coefficient

$$(D^*)_V = (D_{11})_V = (D_{1*1*})_V = \frac{\bar{v}_1 RT}{\zeta_{1*1}} \tag{11.113}$$

If C_{1*} is very small and if the two components 1* and 1 are so very similar in properties it is a reasonable approximation to suppose that

$$(D^*)_V = \frac{\bar{v}_1 RT}{\zeta_{11}} = \frac{RT}{C_1\zeta_{11}} = \frac{RT}{\zeta_1} \tag{11.114}$$

where (RT/ζ_1) is the *self diffusion coefficient* as defined by Eqn (11.99) for pure component 1. Although there are two distinct components in this system the isotopic diffusion measurements should yield a close approximation to the self diffusion coefficient of the pure unlabelled component.

2. Multicomponent Systems

There is at first sight some inconsistency in the use of the term *self diffusion* for processes in multicomponent systems.

Albright and Mills (1965) proposed the term *intradiffusion* for the diffusion of isotopically labelled molecules of one of the components present in an otherwise homogeneous fluid mixture of two or more distinct chemical components. Although there are concentration gradients of the labelled and unlabelled molecules the diffusion processes occur in a substantially uniform chemical environment: there are no activity coefficient gradients.

Consider a situation in which a homogeneous mixture of n distinct chemical components $k = 1, 2, \ldots, n$ is prepared at uniform temperature and pressure. Suppose that a portion of the mixture is removed and then replaced by an equivalent volume of a mixture of identical temperature, pressure and composition, except for the presence of both labelled and unlabelled molecules of component 1, at the same total concentration as before. There are now concentration gradients of the labelled component 1* and of the unlabelled component 1 but there are no other significant concentration gradients and there are no activity coefficient gradients. Diffusion of the components 1* and 1 will now occur in the system of $(n + 1)$ components $k = 1^*, 1, 2 \cdots n$.

The labelled molecules will often be present in very low concentration and the following conditions should then hold, at least to a very good approximation (Albright and Mills, 1965).

$$\begin{aligned}
&(1)\quad (C_{1^*} + C_1) = \text{const.}\quad (\text{all } x, t)\\
&(2)\quad \text{grad } C_{1^*} + \text{grad } C_1 = 0\quad (\text{all } x, t)\\
&(3)\quad C_k = \text{const.}\qquad k = 2, 3 \cdots n\quad (\text{all } x, t)\\
&(4)\quad \text{grad } C_k = 0\quad \text{for}\quad k = 2, 3 \cdots n\quad (\text{all } x, t)\\
&(5)\quad (\mathscr{I}_k)_V = 0\quad \text{for}\quad k = 2, 3 \cdots n\quad (\text{all } x, t)\\
&(6)\quad \boldsymbol{u}_{VC} = \boldsymbol{u}_{MC} = \boldsymbol{u}_{nC} = 0\quad \text{for}\quad k = 2, 3 \cdots n\quad (\text{all } x, t)\\
&(7)\quad (\boldsymbol{u}_k)_V = (\boldsymbol{u}_k)_M = (\boldsymbol{u}_k)_C = 0\quad \text{for}\quad k = 2, 3 \cdots n\quad (\text{all } x, t)
\end{aligned} \tag{11.115}$$

The practical diffusion equations are

$$(\mathscr{I}_{1*})_V = -(D_{1*1})_V \text{ grad } C_1 - (D_{1*1*})_V \text{ grad } C_{1*} \tag{11.116}$$

$$(\mathscr{I}_1)_V = -(D_{11})_V \text{ grad } C_1 - (D_{11*})_V \text{ grad } C_{1*} \tag{11.117}$$

Using condition 2 we find (Albright and Mills, 1965)

$$(\mathscr{I}_{1*})_V = -((D_{1*1*})_V - (D_{1*1})_V) \text{ grad } C_{1*} \tag{11.118}$$

$$(\mathscr{I}_1)_V = -((D_{11})_V - (D_{11*})_V) \text{ grad } C_1 \tag{11.119}$$

so that we have a pseudo-binary system in which the diffusion processes can be described by a single *intradiffusion coefficient* $(D^+)_V$

$$(D^+)_V = (D_{11})_V - (D_{11*})_V = (D_{1*1*})_V - (D_{1*1})_V \tag{11.120}$$

The derivation of Eqn (11.120) makes use of conditions (1) to (5) together with the Gibbs–Duhem Equation and the derived relationship

$$\sum_{k=1*,1}^{n} \bar{v}_k \text{ grad } C_k = 0 \tag{11.121}$$

but it should be noted that conditions 1 to 7 can be reconciled with Eqn (11.111) only for $\bar{v}_{1*} = \bar{v}_1$, which is at least a plausible restriction.

Equations (11.118, 11.119 and 11.120) should be valid for the diffusion of isotopically labelled molecules of component 1 (1*) in a system of an arbitrary number of components n so long as the conditions of (11.115) hold. Unfortunately these equations do not make explicit the fact that the intradiffusion coefficient $(D^+)_V$ may be influenced by the presence of any or all of the other components $k = 2, \ldots, n$. This dependence becomes clearer for equations written in a friction coefficient formalism.

The application of Eqns (11.90) to this system leads to the following results

$$(D^+)_V = \left(\frac{RT}{\zeta_{11*}(C_{1*} + C_1) + \sum_{j=2}^{n} \zeta_{1j} C_j} \right) = \left(\frac{RT}{\zeta_{1*1}(C_1 + C_{1*}) + \sum_{j=2}^{n} \zeta_{1*j} C_j} \right) \tag{11.122}$$

Symmetry considerations however lead one to expect (Bearman 1961)

$$\zeta_{1*1} = \zeta_{11*} \tag{11.123}$$

so that Eqn (11.122) is consistent with the more general requirement that

$$\zeta_{1*j} = \zeta_{1j} \qquad j = 1*, 1, 2, \ldots, n \tag{11.124}$$

on the basis of which we find

$$(D^+)_V = \frac{RT}{\zeta_1} = D_1 = \frac{RT}{\zeta_{1*}} = D_{1*} \tag{11.125}$$

so that $(D^+)_V$ is at least approximately equal to the "self-diffusion coefficient" D_1 of component 1, defined according to Eqns (11.99–11.101) *for the existing composition of the mixture*.

On this basis, intradiffusion measurements should give the same diffusion coefficient as is obtained by the nmr spin echo technique. This has been shown to be true for the benzene-cyclohexane system (McCall and Douglass, 1967) and there is therefore some justification for retaining the term "self-diffusion" to describe the behaviour of a labelled species in a multicomponent system.

For the special case of the diffusion of trace amounts of 1* in a binary mixture of 1 and 2 the previous assumptions lead to the result

$$\frac{(D)_V}{(D^+)_V} = \bar{v}_2\left(\frac{\zeta_{11}C_1 + \zeta_{12}C_2}{\zeta_{12}}\right)\left(1 + \frac{\partial \ln y_1}{\partial \ln C_1}\right) \tag{11.126}$$

where $(D)_V$ is the conventional mutual diffusion coefficient for the binary mixture and $(D^+)_V$ is the intradiffusion coefficient or self diffusion coefficient for the diffusion of the labelled molecules 1* in the mixture 1* + 1 + 2. We note that

$$\lim_{C_1 \to 0} \frac{(D)_V}{(D^+)_V} = 1 \tag{11.127}$$

as observed experimentally by Tilley and Mills (1967) for the sucrose–water system.

The preceding equation must be modified if the properties of the component 1 differ significantly from those of the labelled molecules 1* in such a way that conditions 1 to 7 are no longer satisfied.

REFERENCES

Albright, J. G. and Mills, R. (1965). *J. Phys. Chem.*, **69,** 3120.
Bearman, R. J. (1961). *J. Phys. Chem.*, **65,** 1961.
Cullinan, H. T. Jr. (1965). *Ind. Engng. Chem. Fund.*, **4,** 133.
De Groot, S. R. (1951). "Thermodynamics of Irreversible Processes." North Holland Publishing Co., Amsterdam.
De Groot, S. R. and Mazur, P. (1962). "Nonequilibrium Thermodynamics." North Holland Publishing Co., Amsterdam.
Dudd, J. L. and Vrentas, J. S. (1965). *Ind. Engng. Fund.*, **4,** 301.
Fitts, D. D. (1962). "Nonequilibrium Thermodynamics." McGraw-Hill, New York.
Frazer, R. A., Duncan, W. J., and Collar, A. R. (1952). "Elementary Matrices." Cambridge University Press, Cambridge.

Harned, H. S. and Owen, B. B. (1958). "The Physical Chemistry of Electrolytic Solutions," 3rd Edn. Reinhold, New York.
Hartley, G. S. (1931). *Phil. Mag.* (8) **12,** 487.
Hartley, G. S. and Runnicles, D. F. (1938). *Proc. Roy. Soc.* (London). *A 168*, 401.
Haskell, R. (1908). *Phys. Rev.*, **27,** 145.
Hooyman, G. J., Holtan, H. Jr., Mazur, P., and De Groot, S. R. (1953). *Physica*, **19,** 1095.
Kirkwood, J. G., Baldwin, R. L., Dunlop, P. J., Gosting, L. J., and Kegeles, G. (1960). *J. Chem. Phys.*, **33,** 1505.
Li, J. C. M. (1969). *J. Phys. Chem.*, **73,** 186.
Loflin, T. and McLaughlin, E. (1969). *J. Phys. Chem.*, **73,** 186.
McCall, D. W. and Douglass, D. C. (1967). *J. Phys. Chem.*, **71,** 987.
Manes, M. (1963). *J. Colloid Sci.*, **20,** 900.
Miller, D. G. (1958). *J. Phys. Chem.*, **62,** 767.
Miller, D. G. (1959). *J. Phys. Chem.*, **63,** 570.
Miller, D. G. (1960). *Chem. Revs.*, **60,** 15.
Miller, D. G. (1966). *J. Phys. Chem.*, **70,** 2639.
Miller, D. G. (1967). *J. Phys. Chem.*, **71,** 616.
Mills, R. (1965). *J. Phys. Chem.*, **71,** 616.
Mills, R. (1965). *J. Phys. Chem.*, **69,** 3116.
Mills, R. (1965). *J. Phys. Chem.*, **69,** 3116.
Nernst, W. (1888). *Z. physik. Chem.*, **2,** 613.
Onsager, L. (1945). *Ann. N.Y. Acad. Sci.*, **46,** 241.
Paul, D. R. (1967). *Ind. Engng. Chem. Fund.*, **6,** 217.
Prigogine, I. (1947). "Etude Thermodynamique des Phenomenes Irreversible." Desoer, Liege.
Szekeley, J. (1965). *Trans. Faraday Soc.*, **61,** 2679.
Tilley, J. F. and Mills, R. (1967). *J. Phys. Chem.*, **71,** 2756.
Toor, H. L. (1962). *A.I.Ch. Engng. J.*, **10,** 460.
Tyrrell, H. J. V. (1961). "Diffusion and Heat Flow in Liquids." Butterworths, London.
Tyrrell, H. J. V. (1963). *J. Chem. Soc.*, **300,** 1599.

Chapter 12 Systems of Two Uniformly Accessible Phases

I. MASS TRANSFER BETWEEN THE TWO PHASES

A. The Kinetic Behaviour of a Simple Discontinuous System

Suppose we have a discontinuous system in which isotopically labelled molecules (1*) and unlabelled molecules (1) of a single nonionic chemical component are present in two sub-systems ϕ and σ. The system is isothermal and the only irreversible process is the transport of the labelled molecules from sub-system σ to sub-system ϕ. The phenomenological equation is (Chapter 8)

$$\frac{dN_{1*}^{\phi}}{dt} = V^{\phi}\frac{dC_{1*}^{\phi}}{dt} = -\frac{1}{T}L_{1*1*}\,\Delta\mu_{1*} \tag{12.1}$$

and the labelled molecules form an ideally dilute solution in each sub-system

$$\mu_{1*}^{\phi} = \mu_{1*}^{0\phi} + RT\ln C_{1*}^{\phi} \tag{12.2}$$

$$\mu_{1*}^{\sigma} = \mu_{1*}^{0\sigma} + RT\ln C_{1*}^{\sigma} \tag{12.3}$$

Since $\Delta\mu_{1*} = \mu_{1*}^{\phi} - \mu_{1*}^{\sigma}$ it is possible to write Eqn (12.1) in the form

$$V^{\phi}\frac{dC_{1*}^{\phi}}{dt} = -\frac{L_{1*1*}}{T}(\Delta\mu_{1*}^{0} + RT\ln C_{1*}^{\phi}/C_{1*}^{\sigma}) \tag{12.4}$$

At equilibrium the affinity $-\Delta\mu_{1*}$ is zero and the concentrations in the two sub-systems are $(C_{1*}^{\phi})_{\infty}$ and $(C_{1*}^{\sigma})_{\infty}$. These concentrations are related by the equilibrium partition coefficient K_{1*}, $(t = \infty)$,

$$(C_{1*}^{\phi})_{\infty} = K_{1*}(C_{1*}^{\sigma})_{\infty} \tag{12.5}$$

In this particular example we expect $K_{1*} = 1$ but this will not be true in general. If we introduce a *relative concentration* c_{1*} for sub-system ϕ

$$c_{1*} = C_{1*}^{\phi}/(C_{1*}^{\phi})_{\infty} \tag{12.7}$$

we can now rearrange Eqn (12.4) to give the kinetic equation (Milicevic and McGregor, 1966)

$$\frac{dc_{1*}}{dt} = -B\ln\{(c_{1*})((C_{1*}^{\sigma})_{\infty}/C_{1*}^{\sigma})\} \tag{12.8}$$

with the rate parameter B

$$B = \frac{L_{1^*1^*}R}{V^{\phi}(C_{1^*}^{\phi})_{\infty}} \tag{12.9}$$

V^{σ} and V^{ϕ} are different but constant, and their ratio is

$$a = V^{\sigma}/V^{\phi} \tag{12.10}$$

The total number of moles N_{1^*} remains constant at all times so that

$$\frac{C_{1^*}^{\sigma}}{(C_{1^*}^{\sigma})_{\infty}} = 1 + \frac{K_{1^*}}{a}(1 - c_{1^*}) \tag{12.11}$$

and now

$$\frac{dc_{1^*}}{dt} = -B \ln\left(\frac{c_{1^*}}{1 + \dfrac{K_{1^*}}{a}(1 - c_{1^*})}\right) \tag{12.12}$$

The ratio (K_{1^*}/a) characterises the effects of the volume relationships on the kinetics but an alternative parameter can be based on the *equilibrium exhaustion* (E_{∞}) of sub-system σ.

$$E_{\infty} = \frac{(C_{1^*}^{\sigma})_0 - (C_{1^*}^{\sigma})_{\infty}}{(C_{1^*}^{\sigma})_0} = \frac{1}{1 + a/K} \tag{12.13}$$

$(C_{1^*}^{\sigma})_0$ is the initial concentration in phase σ $(t = 0)$.

It is assumed that initially all the labelled molecules are in sub-system σ, in deriving Eqn (12.13). In this situation the parameter E_{∞} is a useful alternative to the ratio a/K.

When the kinetic equation (12.12) is integrated from $t = 0$ to $t = t$ we find

$$\int_0^{(c_{1^*})_t} \frac{dc_{1^*}}{\ln\left[\dfrac{c_{1^*}}{K/a(1 - c_{1^*}) + 1}\right]} = -Bt \tag{12.14}$$

The integral can be expressed only as an infinite series. A simpler form is obtained if phase σ is infinite in extent (a so-called infinite solution or infinite dyebath). Now E_{∞} approaches zero and K/a approaches zero so that Eqn (12.14) becomes

$$\int_0^{(c_{1^*})_t} \frac{dc_{1^*}}{\ln c_{1^*}} = -Bt \tag{12.15}$$

This integral also can be expressed only as an infinite series and represents *mass transfer from a sub-system of constant concentration*, i.e.

$$\lim_{\substack{K/a \to 0 \\ E_{\infty} \to 0}} (C_{1^*}^{\sigma})_{\infty} = (C_{1^*}^{\sigma})_t = (C_{1^*}^{\sigma})_0 \tag{12.16}$$

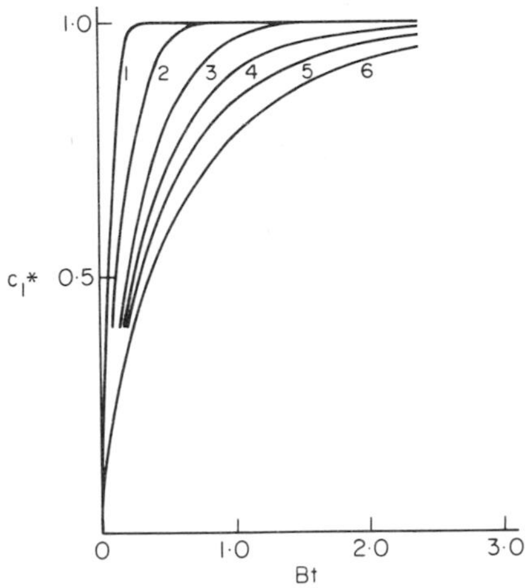

Fig. 8. *The Variation of the Relative Concentration* c_{1*} *with the Dimensionless Time Variable Bt (Reproduced with permission from Milicevic and McGregor, 1966).*
The numbers on the curves refer to the different values of $E_\infty(\mathscr{L})$: 1. 99%, 2. 90%, 3. 70%, 4. 50%, 5. 30%, and 6. 0% ("ixffnite solution").

In Fig. 8 we have graphical solutions of Eqn (12.14) for various values of E_∞ (Milicevic and McGregor, 1966). These kinetic curves have been derived by thermodynamic means and they show the asymptotic approach to equilibrium characteristic of most mass transfer processes. They show an *irreversible progression in time* (Chapters 1 and 2).

For a system which is near to equilibrium ($c_{1*} \rightarrow 1$) we can use the approximation

$$\ln c_{1*} \approx (c_{1*} - 1) \tag{12.17}$$

and now Eqn (12.15) is easily integrated to give a simple exponential kinetic equation

$$c_{1*} = 1 - \exp(-Bt) \tag{12.18}$$

or in differential form:

$$\frac{dC_{1*}^{\phi}}{dt} = B((C_{1*}^{\phi})_\infty - (C_{1*}^{\phi})_t) \tag{12.19}$$

Equations (12.18) and (12.19) are very commonly used in simple analyses of mass transfer between phases, even in complex multicomponent systems (Gordon and Sherwood, 1954). This usage is often empirical and the equations themselves may then be regarded as providing a definition of the rate parameter B which characterises the mass transfer process.

The discontinuous model requires the entropy production to occur *at the interface* between the two sub-systems or *in some thin but finite interfacial region* (De Groot and Mazur, 1962). The parameter B of the discontinuous model does not characterise any processes occurring within either sub-system, except when it is used in a purely formal, empirical sense to describe a real process such as dyeing or the washing of textiles (Parish, 1962). Some of the theoretical difficulties in the use of mass transfer coefficients of this type have been examined by Friedly (1970).

B. The Kinetic Behaviour of a Simple Continuous System

The phenomenological equation for the isothermal diffusion of species 1* in the system of labelled and unlabelled molecules is

$$j_{1*} = -L_{1*1*} \operatorname{grad} \hat{\mu}_{1*} \tag{12.20}$$

and the general properties of the system are such that Fick's Laws should be obeyed, with a constant diffusion coefficient (Chapter 11), in the form

$$j_{1*} = -D_{1*} \operatorname{grad} \rho_{1*} \tag{12.21}$$

and

$$\frac{\partial \rho_{1*}}{\partial t} = D_{1*} \nabla^2 \rho_{1*} \tag{12.22}$$

Since Eqn (12.22) applies only locally within the system, the behaviour of the system as a whole can not be determined unless Eqn (12.22) can be integrated over the volume of the system and for the time of the mass transfer process. To carry out this integration the spatial configuration of the system must be specified, together with the necessary *initial conditions* and *boundary conditions*. At this point purely thermodynamic methods prove inadequate and extra-thermodynamic information or assumptions are needed to complete the model. This is in marked contrast to the discontinuous model system. The main problem proves to be the establishment of the boundary conditions at the interfaces between sub-systems. Consider a simple composite system of two sub-systems σ and ϕ. Sub-system ϕ is in the form of a so-called "infinite slab" of thickness $2l$ in the direction of the x-axis (Fig. 9). The slab is of such great area in proportion to its thickness that we do not need to consider diffusion in through the edges.

The slab ϕ is immersed in sub-system σ which is a liquid mixture of non-ionic components 1 and 1*, and which is maintained at constant concentration by virtue of its great extent and by the provision of thorough stirring or agitation (convective mass transfer). Initially the slab ϕ is in equilibrium with the liquid component 1 and contains no labelled molecules, whereas labelled molecules are present at a constant concentration in sub-system σ.

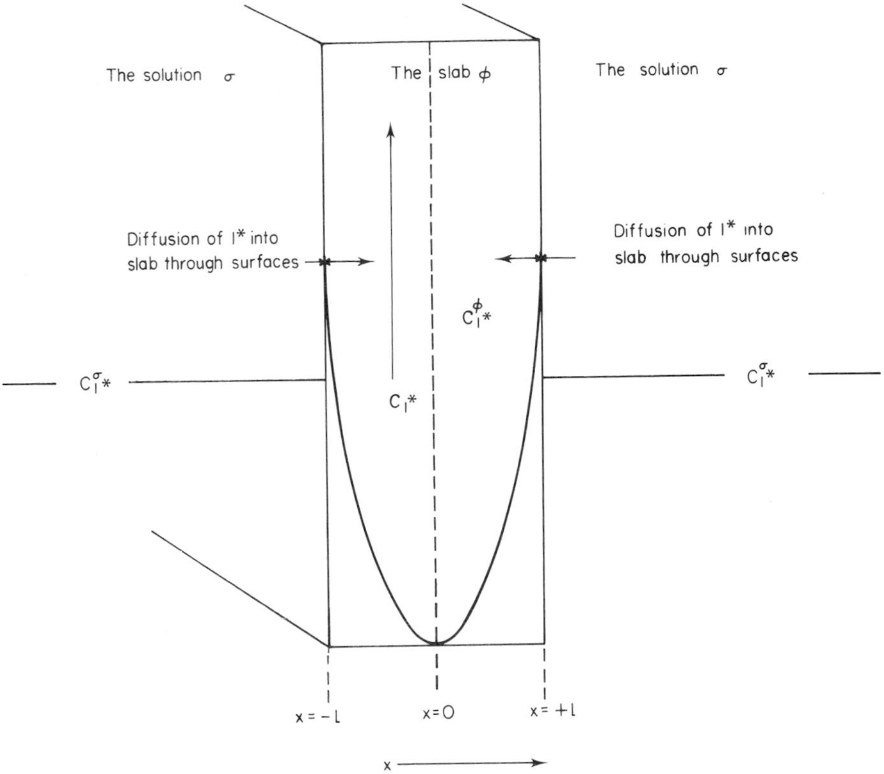

Fig. 9. *A Simple Continuous System.*
The diffusing molecules penetrate through the surfaces of the slab ϕ and diffusion occurs along the x-axis only, but in both directions.

At $t = 0$ we have the *initial condition*

$$C_{1*}^{\phi} = 0 \quad \text{in} \quad -l < x < l \quad \text{at} \quad t = 0 \tag{12.23}$$

The diffusion of labelled molecules into the slab is assumed to be subject to the *boundary conditions*.

$$C_{1*}^{\phi} = (C_{1*}^{\phi})_{\infty} \quad \text{at} \quad x = \pm l \quad \text{for} \quad t \geqslant 0 \tag{12.24}$$

which represent the instantaneous establishment of *a constant surface concentration* equal to the final equilibrium concentration of labelled molecules in phase ϕ.

The diffusion of labelled molecules into phase ϕ is governed by the unidimensional equation (cf. 12.22)

$$\frac{\partial C_{1*}^{\phi}}{\partial t} = D_{1*} \frac{\partial^2 C_{1*}}{\partial x^2} \tag{12.25}$$

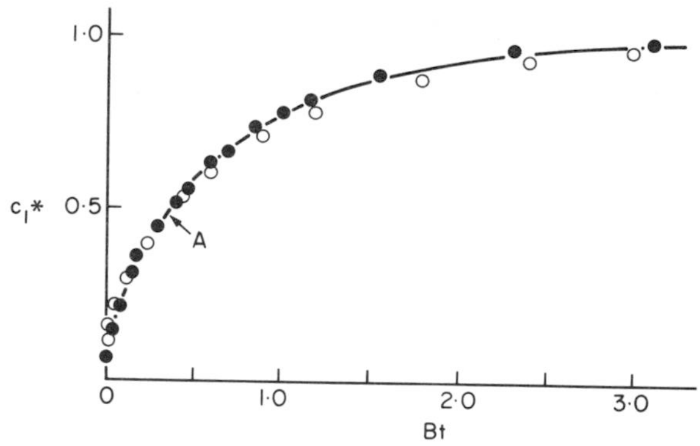

Fig. 10. *The Variation of the Relative Concentration c_{1*} with the Dimensionless Time Variable Bt (Reproduced with permission from Milicevic and McGregor, 1966).*
The curve is calculated for the discontinuous model with $E_\infty = 0$. The solid circles ● are calculated for diffusion from a constant surface concentration into a so-called "infinite slab" of infinite surface area and finite thickness. The open circles were computed for diffusion under the same constant surface concentration into an infinitely long cylinder of finite radius. The three curves were made to coincide at point A for this comparison.

The mathematical solution of this problem is well known (Crank, 1956) and is shown graphically in Fig. 10, where it is compared with the predictions of the discontinuous model. The similarity in form is very striking, as is the observation that an approximate solution to the diffusion Eqns (12.23–12.25) for long times can be written in the form (Anderson *et al.*, 1965; Crank, 1956)

$$c_{1*} = 1 - b \exp(-B^1 t) \tag{12.26}$$

which closely resembles Eqn (12.18).

Essentially the same kinetic curves have been given by two quite dissimilar kinetic models, which illustrates the unfortunate fact that integral kinetic data of this type are not a sensitive guide to the underlying kinetic mechanisms. The *concentration distributions* within the sub-systems are however much more informative (Fig. 11). A more detailed comparison of the thermodynamic differences between the two types of system has been given elsewhere, together with an analysis of the nature of the Liapunov Function for the discontinuous system (Milicevic and McGregor, 1966; La Salle and Lefschetz, 1961; Wei, 1962).

C. A System with Intermediate Kinetics

Imagine the slab ϕ to be bounded on each surface by an interfacial region which offers some resistance to the passage of the labelled molecules in either direction through the interface.

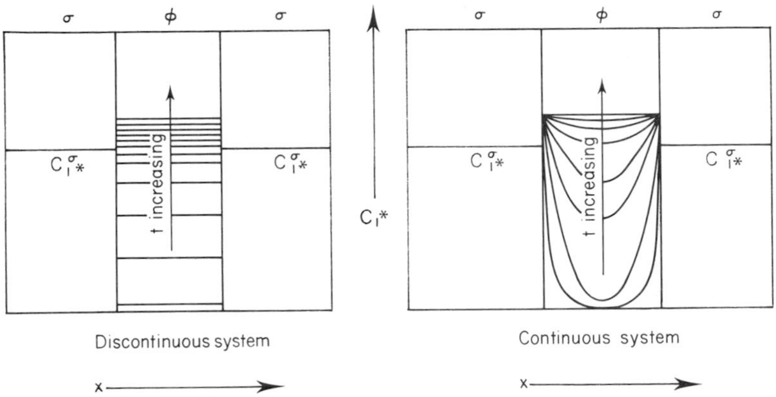

Fig. 11. *A Comparison of the Concentration Distributions in the Continuous and Discontinuous Model Systems During Mass Transfer* (*Schematic*).
For this comparison the "solution phase" was assumed to have a constant concentration ($E_\infty = 0$). For the continuous system diffusion occurred into phase ϕ from a constant surface concentration, and the distributions are shown for different times t.

The net rate of transport in the x-direction through the interface at $x = -l$ is formally described by (compare Fig. 18, p. 188)

$$(\mathscr{I}_{1*})_{x=-l} = k_1^0(C_{1*}^{\sigma})_{x=-l} - k_2^0(C_{1*}^{\phi})_{x=-l} \tag{12.27}$$

and at equilibrium across the interface

$$k_1^0(C_{1*}^{\sigma})_\infty = k_2^0(C_{1*}^{\phi})_\infty \tag{12.28}$$

k_1^0 is a velocity constant for the transfer of molecules from phase σ to phase ϕ through the interface; k_2^0 characterises the reverse process. Both k_1^0 and k_2^0 are taken as constants.

Since we assume $(C_{1*}^{\sigma})_{x=-l}$ to be constant and equal to $(C_{1*}^{\sigma})_\infty$ we can rewrite Eqn (12.27) as

$$(\mathscr{I}_{1*})_{x=-l} = k_2^0((C_{1*}^{\phi})_\infty - (C_{1*}^{\phi})_{x=-l}) \tag{12.29}$$

which may be compared with Eqn (12.19).

The rate of diffusion of component 1* from the interface into phase ϕ is

$$(\mathscr{I}_{1*})_{x=-l} = -D_{1*}\left(\frac{\partial C_{1*}^{\phi}}{\partial x}\right)_{x=-l} \tag{12.30}$$

The conservation of mass requires the fluxes in Eqns (12.29) and (12.30) to be equal, if accumulation at the interface is to be avoided, and so we find

$$\left(\frac{\partial C_{1*}^{\phi}}{\partial x}\right)_{x=-l} + \left(\frac{k_2^0}{D_{1*}}\right)((C_{1*}^{\phi})_\infty - (C_{1*}^{\phi})_{x=-l}) = 0 \tag{12.31}$$

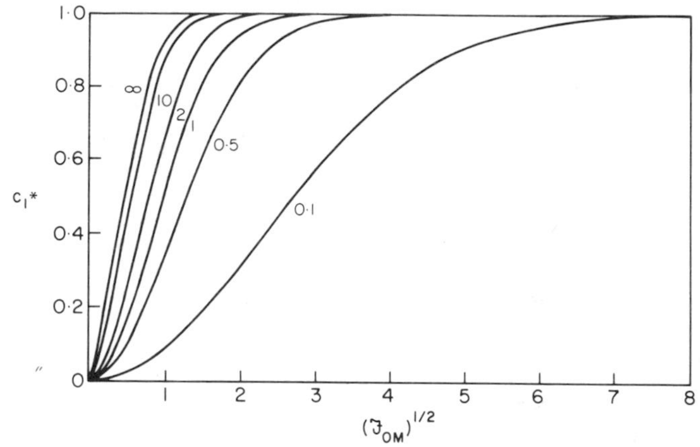

Fig. 12. *The Relative Sorption c_{1*} as a Function of the Dimensionless Boundary Variable L and the Fourier Number $\mathscr{F}_{OM} = D_{1*}t/l^2$.*
(Adapted with permission from Crank, 1956). In the limit as $L \to \infty$ the behaviour corresponds to diffusion from a constant surface concentration. In the limit as $L \to 0$ the behaviour conforms to that of a discontinuous system. The numbers adjacent to the curves are the values of L.

Equation (12.31) is the new *boundary condition* at $x = -l$ and a similar equation applies at $x = +l$.

The kinetic behaviour is determined by the ratio (k_2^0/D_{1*}) which enters the problem as part of the *dimensionless boundary variable* $(k_2^0 l/D_{1*})$.

The mathematical solution of Eqns (12.23) and (12.25) subject to the boundary conditions (12.31) at each interface is shown in Fig. 12. The behaviour of c_{1*}^{ϕ} is determined by the two *dimensionless groups* $(k_2^0 l/D_{1*})$ and $(D_{1*}t/l_2)$. Equation (12.31) is a *radiation boundary condition* of a type frequently encountered in heat transfer studies (Carslaw and Jaeger, 1947; Crank, 1956).

D. The Simple Model Systems as Limiting Forms of Behaviour

Behaviour characteristic of a discontinuous system is obtained only *in the limit* as $(k_2^0 l/D_{1*}) \to 0$. For any finite nonzero value of $k_2^0 l/D_{1*}$ the behaviour will deviate from that of a perfectly discontinuous system. In the limit the kinetics is governed by Eqn (12.18) with the rate parameter

$$B = \frac{A^{\phi} k_2^0}{V^{\phi}} \tag{12.32}$$

where A^{ϕ} is the surface area of phase ϕ and V^{ϕ} is its volume.

Only *in the limit* as $k_2^0 l/D_{1*} \to \infty$ do we obtain behaviour characteristic of the simple continuous model of diffusion from a constant surface concentration. In general we can expect this simple model to hold in approximation only.

II. MASS TRANSFER AND CHEMICAL REACTION

A. A Single Uniformly Accessible Phase

Whenever we have simultaneous mass transfer and chemical reaction these two types of process will interact via the equations of conservation of mass even though nonequilibrium thermodynamics does not admit the possibility of a direct thermodynamic coupling between these processes in isotropic systems.

A general discussion of this type of problem rapidly becomes very complicated (De Groot and Mazur, 1962; Ulanowicz and Frazier, 1968). We shall consider initially the simple special case of a single chemical reaction in an isothermal continuum in which the concentrations of the nonionic component k are so small that the cross-coefficients in the thermodynamic diffusion equations can be neglected (Friedlander and Keller, 1965; McGregor and Milicevic, 1966), i.e. if we include the factor $1/T$ in L_{kk}

$$\boldsymbol{j}_k = -L_{kk} \operatorname{grad} \hat{\mu}_k \qquad k = 1, \ldots, n \tag{12.33}$$

The equation of conservation of mass becomes

$$\rho \frac{dW_k}{dt} = -\operatorname{div} \boldsymbol{j}_k + \rho \hat{v}_k \frac{d\lambda}{dt} \tag{12.34}$$

If the mass density ρ remains constant and there is no convective mass transport, and if the system is in a *stationary state* Eqn (12.34) becomes

$$\frac{\partial \rho_k}{\partial t} = -\operatorname{div} \boldsymbol{j}_k + \hat{v}_k J_R = 0 \tag{12.35}$$

where $J_R \equiv \rho\, d\lambda/dt$ is defined as the scalar chemical reaction rate. The phenomenological equation for chemical reaction has the form

$$J_R = L_R \hat{A} \tag{12.36}$$

if the temperature factor $(1/T)$ is included in the phenomenological coefficient L_R for chemical reaction. The specific chemical affinity $\hat{A}$ is defined in Chapter 8.

If L_{kk} is taken to be constant then it follows from Eqns (12.33), (12.35), and (12.36) that

$$\hat{v}_k L_R \hat{A} = L_{kk} \nabla^2 \hat{\mu}_k \tag{12.37}$$

Multiplication by $\hat{v}_k$ and summation over all components k reduces Eqn (12.37) to the form (Friedlander and Keller, 1965)

$$\lambda_R^2 \nabla^2 \hat{A} = \hat{A} \tag{12.38}$$

where λ_R is defined by

$$\lambda_R \equiv \sqrt{\frac{1}{L_R} \sum_{k=1}^{n} \frac{L_{kk}}{\hat{v}_k^2}} \tag{12.39}$$

and is known as the *characteristic diffusion reaction length*. The significance of λ_R becomes clearer on consideration of a unidimensional problem involving the x-coordinate only. The general solution of Eqn (12.38) has the form

$$\hat{A} = \hat{A}_1 \exp(x/\lambda_R) + \hat{A}_2 \exp(-x/\lambda_R) \tag{12.40}$$

so that two distinct limiting cases may be established, one for $x/\lambda_R \gg 1$ and one for $x/\lambda_R \ll 1$.

The situation $x/\lambda_R \ll 1$ corresponds to very small distances, very high rates of diffusion and low rates of chemical reaction ($\lambda_R \gg 0$). In these situations the chemical reaction rates are not diffusion limited and

$$\hat{A} \approx \hat{A}_1 + \hat{A}_2 = \text{const.} \tag{12.41}$$

The situation $x/\lambda_R \gg 1$ corresponds to very large distances, very low rates of diffusion, and very high rates of chemical reaction. In such situations the chemical reaction rates become diffusion limited and the affinity $\hat{A}$ is no longer constant

$$\hat{A} \approx \hat{A}_1 \exp(x/\lambda_R) \tag{12.42}$$

The dimensionless ratio x/λ_R characterises the relative rates of diffusion and chemical reaction in the system.

It is important to note that this single phase can be treated as one of the sub-systems of a discontinuous model system *only* when $x/\lambda_R \ll 1$ and the phase tends towards homogeneity of the component concentrations. In any other situation it is necessary to use the equations for continuous sub-systems and it is not possible to define a scalar affinity for a mass transfer process between the sub-systems, except in a local sense.

We note that in general the rate of mass transport in a single phase, and between different phases, will be influenced by the existence of chemical reactions.

The special case of an "instantaneous equilibrium" of the chemical reactions corresponds to the limit when the chemical reaction rates are extremely high ($L_R \to \infty$, $\lambda_R \to 0$, $x/\lambda_R \to \infty$). If we do not use the steady-state assumption of Eqn (12.35) but introduce the equilibrium condition for chemical reaction

$$\hat{A} = -\sum_{k=1}^{n} \hat{v}_k \hat{\mu}_k = 0 \tag{12.43}$$

we note that the rate of chemical reaction is zero ($J_R = 0$) and that the equations of continuity for the components have the form for diffusion unaccompanied by chemical reaction. There is however a significant difference in that the system now contains an equilibrium mixture of reactants and products, both of which may take part in the mass transfer processes.

If the chemical reactions involve the dimerisation or aggregation of the components, or the formation of complexes between the components, then these dimers, aggregates and complexes are the reaction products and separate diffusion equations may be written for them.

If the chemical reactions involve the local adsorption or immobilisation of the diffusing components by a molecular network through which the components diffuse, then the adsorbed components are the reaction products and their diffusion coefficients may well be vanishingly small. In this way the formalism of nonequilibrium thermodynamics includes the phenomenon of diffusion accompanied by an immobilising chemical reaction (Willis, *et al.*, 1945; Crank, 1956).

In all cases, if the chemical reactions take place at a rate comparable with that of the mass transfer processes then the detailed behaviour will depend on the relative rates of diffusion and chemical reaction as represented by the ratio x/λ_R. The significance of the ratio x/λ_R is not limited to systems in a steady state of diffusion and chemical reaction, but the solution of problems of diffusion and chemical reaction can not be made using purely thermodynamic methods. Additional extra-thermodynamic information is needed concerning the ratio x/λ_R or related parameters.

B. Interphase Mass Transfer and Chemical Reaction

The chemical reactions are coupled with the interphase mass transfer primarily through the equations of conservation of mass. For very rapid and strongly exothermic or endothermic reactions it may be necessary to consider the temperature gradients in the system (Eqn 10.24) and even the pressure gradients (Eqn 10.25).

In some situations the existence of chemical reaction may alter the rate of mass transfer but leave the general form of the dependence of the mass transfer rates on the thermodynamic affinities unchanged. Simple examples related to dyeing have been given by Milicevic and McGregor (1966).

Ulanowicz and Frazier (1968) have examined reaction–diffusion coupling in steady-state interphase mass transfer in multicomponent, multireaction, two-phase systems. The presence of nonequilibrium chemical reaction generally increased the mass transfer rates, but the maximum augmentation occurred when the chemical reactions were in "instantaneous reaction equilibrium." They also found that nonequilibrium reaction may exist near the interface even when reaction equilibrium exists in the bulk phases.

III. THE EQUILIBRIUM STATE

If there are no restrictions on the freedom of distribution of any species between the phases then the equilibrium distributions are subject to Eqn (8.126) for example. To generalise this equation to cover sub-systems which are only incompletely accessible to a given species we may introduce structure factors χ_k. Suppose that sub-system ϕ is not completely accessible to component k, as might arise if ϕ were polymeric or of nonuniform crystallinity or order. Then Eqn (8.126) could be written as (McGregor and Harris, 1970)

$$\frac{C_k^{\phi}}{C_k^{\sigma}} = \exp\left\{-\frac{(\Delta\mu^0{}_k)_C + \bar{v}_k^{\phi}\,\Delta\rho + z_k F\,\Delta\psi + RT\ln y_k^{\phi}/y_k^{\sigma} + RT\ln\chi_k}{RT}\right\} \tag{12.44}$$

in which the structure factor χ_k^{ϕ} characterises the "accessibility" of phase ϕ to component k, in a formal sense.

By introducing an "*apparent standard affinity*" $-\overline{\Delta\mu_k^0}$ defined by

$$\overline{\Delta\mu_k^0} = [(\Delta\mu_k^0)_C + \bar{v}_k^{\phi}\,\Delta p + RT\ln y_k^{\phi}/y_k^{\sigma} + RT\ln\chi_k^{\phi}] \tag{12.45}$$

and a *distribution coefficient* K_k defined by

$$K_k = \exp\{-\overline{\Delta\mu_k^0}/RT\} \tag{12.46}$$

the introduction of a *Donnan coefficient* λ

$$\lambda = \exp\{-F\,\Delta\psi/RT\} \tag{12.47}$$

makes it possible to write Eqn (12.44) in the simpler form

$$C_k^{\phi} = \lambda^{z_k}K_k C_k^{\sigma} \tag{12.48}$$

where K_k is not in general constant but depends on the parameters of Eqn (12.45). However, K_k will have a finite value in a given experimental situation.

Equation (12.48) can be applied to a computational analysis of the distribution of ions between two phases (McGregor and Harris, 1970) if *the conditions of electrical neutrality* in sub-systems σ and ϕ can be used to compute the equilibrium value of λ.

For electrical neutrality in phase σ, if this is supposed to be a normal homogeneous solution,

$$\sum_{k=1}^{n} z_k C_k^{\sigma} = 0 \tag{12.49}$$

For electrical neutrality in phase ϕ, if this is supposed to contain immobilised ionic groupings such as charged groups on a polymer network, the electrical neutrality condition is

$$\sum_{k=1}^{n} z_k C_k^{\sigma} + C^{\oplus} = 0 \tag{12.50}$$

where $C^{\oplus}$ is the net charge on the polymer matrix (i.e. on sub-system ϕ) by the ionisation of these groups.

If the sub-system ϕ contains basic groups B_i which dissociate according to the equation

$$\begin{array}{ccc} \phi - B_i^{\oplus}H & \overset{K_{B_i}}{\rightleftharpoons} & \phi - B_i + H^+ \\ (1-\beta_i)B_i & & \beta_i B_i \quad C_1^{\phi} \end{array} \tag{12.51}$$

then the concentration B_i^+ of charged basic groups of type i is

$$B_i^{\oplus} = \frac{C_1^{\phi} B_i}{C_1^{\phi} + K_{B_i}} \tag{12.52}$$

If sub-system ϕ contains acidic groups A_j which dissociate as follows

$$\begin{array}{ccc} \phi - A_jH & \overset{K_{A_j}}{\rightleftharpoons} & \phi - A_j^{\ominus} + H^+ \\ (1-\alpha_j)A_j & & \alpha_j A_j \quad C_1^{\phi} \end{array} \tag{12.53}$$

then the concentration of acidic groups of type j which are ionised is

$$A_j^{\ominus} = \frac{K_{A_j} A_j}{K_{A_j} + C_1^{\phi}} \tag{12.54}$$

The electrical neutrality condition (12.50) now becomes

$$F(\lambda_D) = \sum_{k=1}^{n} z_k \lambda_D^{z_k} K_k C_k^{\sigma} + \sum_j \frac{\lambda_D K_1 C_1^{\sigma} B_i}{\lambda_D K_1 C_1^{\sigma} + K_{B_i}} - \sum_j \frac{K_{A_j} A_j}{K_{A_j} + \lambda_D K_1 C_1^{\sigma}} = 0 \tag{12.55}$$

If Eqn (12.55) can be solved for λ_D by iterative techniques, for example, then the concentrations C_k^{ϕ} in system ϕ at equilibrium can be calculated from the values of K_k and C_k^{σ}. This procedure has been used in studies of the mechanism of sorption of acid dyes by polyamides (McGregor and Harris, 1969, 1970) and on the sorption of cationic dyes by acrylic polymer fibers.

This analysis is based on Eqn (8.126) which was derived for a discontinuous system on the basis of nonequilibrium thermodynamics. The same equation can be derived by more conventional thermodynamic approaches, as might be expected (Guggenheim, 1959). The use of the electrical neutrality conditions (Guggenheim, 1959) and of the postulated dissociation equilibria provides a simple model for the effect of the ionisable groups in a substrate on the equilibrium partition of ions. This model can be made more complex to account for specific interactions in the system, for example.

Some special features arise when certain components are unable to pass freely from one phase to the other, as in the case of the ionisable groups in the previous example. This is examined in more detail in Chapter 13.

Guggenheim (1959) has emphasised the experimental difficulties associated with the measurement of the electrical potential difference $\Delta\psi$ of Eqn (12.47), and hence also with the absolute measurement of λ and the coefficients K_k.

It seems appropriate to regard λ and the single-ion distribution coefficients K_k as *purely formal parameters* which serve to describe the behaviour of a real system, or to establish the behaviour of a simple mathematical model of the real system. In most systems it is impossible to separate the "chemical" effects from the electrical effects in any absolute sense (Guggenheim, 1959) but this does not necessarily imply that the use of λ and the K_k is without value (Helfferich, 1962).

The *ionic distribution equations* (12.48) can be combined in two distinct ways to eliminate λ and to obtain expressions involving measurable quantities only.

If we consider two ions A and C then

$$C_A^\phi = \lambda^{z_A} K_A C_A^\sigma \tag{12.56}$$

and

$$C_C^\phi = \lambda^{z_C} K_C C_C^\sigma \tag{12.57}$$

so that

$$\frac{(C_A^\phi)^{z_C}}{(C_C^\phi)^{z_A}} = \frac{(K_A)^{z_C}(C_A^\sigma)^{z_C}}{(K_C)^{z_A}(C_C^\sigma)^{z_A}} \tag{12.58}$$

or

$$\left(\frac{C_A^\phi}{C_A^\sigma}\right)^{z_C}\left(\frac{C_C^\sigma}{C_C^\phi}\right)^{z_A} = \frac{(K_A)^{z_C}}{(K_C)^{z_A}} \tag{12.59}$$

If z_A and z_C are both positive we obtain a formal *cation exchange equation*

$$\left(\frac{C_A^\phi}{C_A^\sigma}\right)^{|z_C|}\left(\frac{C_C^\sigma}{C_C^\phi}\right)^{|z_A|} = \frac{(K_A)^{|z_C|}}{(K_C)^{|z_A|}} = K_C^A \tag{12.60}$$

in which K_C^A is the *selectivity coefficient*, or the equilibrium coefficient for the formal exchange reaction

$$|z_A|\, C_C^\phi + |z_C|\, C_A^\sigma \overset{K_C^A}{\rightleftharpoons} |z_C|\, C_A^\phi + |z_A|\, C_C^\sigma \tag{12.61}$$

in which ion A displaces ion C from phase ϕ; K_C^A is a measure of the preference which phase ϕ appears to show for ion A as opposed to ion C.

The selectivity coefficient K_C^A can be measured if C_A^ϕ, C_C^ϕ, C_A^σ and C_C^σ can be measured. The relationship of K_C^A to K_A and to K_C is purely formal, but can be useful.

An apparent standard affinity $(\bar{A}^0)_C^A$ can be defined for this ion exchange process

$$(\bar{A}^0)_C^A \equiv RT \ln K_C^A \tag{12.62}$$

and we note the formal relationship

$$(\bar{A}^0)_C^A = |z_C|\, \bar{A}_A^0 - |z_A|\, \bar{A}_C^0 \tag{12.63}$$

where $\bar{A}_A^0$ and $\bar{A}_C^0$ are the apparent single ion affinities (Eqn 12.46).

If z_A and z_C are both negative we obtain a formal *anion exchange equation* which is the same as Eqn (12.60). The selectivity coefficient K_C^A now refers to a formal anion-exchange process of the type shown in Eqn (12.61), and equations (12.62) and (12.63) are valid for this anion exchange process too.

Suppose instead that we choose to consider a pair of ions of *opposite* charges, in which ion C is a cation and ion A is an anion. Then since $z_C > 0$ and $z_A < 0$ we obtain directly from Eqn (12.59) the result

$$\left(\frac{C_C^\phi}{C_C^\sigma}\right)^{|z_A|}\left(\frac{C_A{}^\phi}{C_A{}^\sigma}\right)^{|z_C|} = (K_C)^{|z_A|} \cdot (K_A)^{|z_C|} = K_{CA} \tag{12.64}$$

in which K_{CA} can be measured if C_C^ϕ, C_A^ϕ, C_C^σ and C_A^σ can be measured. The relationship of K_{CA} to K_C and to K_A is purely formal but can be useful. K_{CA} is the equilibrium coefficient for the formal distribution process

$$|z_A|\, C_C{}^\sigma + |z_C|\, C_A{}^\sigma \overset{K_{CA}}{\rightleftharpoons} |z_A|\, C_C^\phi + |z_C|\, C_A^\phi \tag{12.65}$$

in which the electrically-neutral "salt" $C_{|z_A|}A_{|z_C|}$ distributes itself between phases ϕ and σ. K_{CA} is a measure of the extent to which this neutral "salt" appears to prefer to concentrate in phase ϕ as opposed to phase σ.

A corresponding apparent standard affinity $(\bar{A}^0)_{CA}$ can be defined for this process

$$(\bar{A}^0)_{CA} = RT \ln K_{CA} \tag{12.66}$$

and we note the formal relationship

$$(\bar{A}^0)_{CA} = |z_A|\, \bar{A}_C^0 + |z_C|\, \bar{A}_A^0 \tag{12.67}$$

Equations (12.60) and (12.64) represent two alternative ways of discussing sorption equilibria in ionic systems without the explicit use of λ and the ionic distribution coefficients K_k. It should be noted that these two equations are derived from the same basic equations, and do not necessarily correspond to different theories of the sorption processes. The ion-exchange equations (12.60) can still be used, for example, even when there is no electrical neutrality condition of the type

$$|z_A|\, C_A{}^\phi + |z_C|\, C_C{}^\phi = \text{const.} \tag{12.68}$$

which commonly appears in simple ion-exchange theories (Helfferich, 1962).

REFERENCES

Anderson, R. B., Bayer, J., and Hofer, L. J. E. (1965). *Ind Engng Chem. Process Design Dev.*, **4**, 167.

Carslaw, H. S. and Jaeger, J. C. (1947). "Conduction of Heat in Solids." Oxford University Press, Oxford.

Crank, J. (1956). "The Mathematics of Diffusion." Clarendon Press, Oxford.
De Groot, S. R. and Mazur, P. (1962). "Nonequilibrium Thermodynamics." North Holland Publishing Co., Amsterdam.
Fitts, D. D. (1962). "Nonequilibrium Thermodynamics." McGraw-Hill, New York.
Friedlander, S. K. and Keller, K. H. (1965). *Chem. Engng. Sci.*, **20,** 121.
Friedly, J. C. (1970). *Chem. Engng. Sci.*, **25,** 119.
Gordon, K. F. and Sherwood, T. K. (1954). "Mass Transfer Between Two Liquid Phases." In "Collected Research Papers," Spring Meeting, American Institute of Chemical Engineering, Toronto.
Guggenheim, E. A. (1959). "Thermodynamics." North Holland Publishing Co., Amsterdam.
Helfferich, F. (1962). "Ion Exchange." McGraw-Hill, New York.
La Salle, B. J. and Lefschetz, S. (1961). "Stability by Liapunov's Direct Method." Academic Press, New York and London.
McGregor, R. and Harris, P. W. (1969). "A Chemical Engineering Approach to Dyeing Problems: The Sorption of Acid Dyes by Polyamides." Research Monograph M20, Allied Chemical Corporation Fibers Division, Petersburg.
McGregor, R. and Harris, P. W. (1970). *J. Applied Polymer Sci.*, **14,** 513.
Milicevic, B. and McGregor, R. (1966). *Helv. Chim. Acta.*, **49,** 1302.
Parish, G. J. (1962). *J. Soc. Dyers Col.*, **78,** 109.
Ulanowicz, R. E. and Frazier, G. C. Jr. (1968). *Chem. Engng. Sci.*, **23,** 1335.
Wei, J. (1962). *J. Phys. Chem.*, **6,** 1578.
Willis, H. F., Warwicker, J. O., Urquhart, A. R. and Standing, H. A. (1945). *Trans. Faraday Soc.*, **21,** 506.

Chapter 13 Membrane Processes

I. THE CONTINUOUS AND DISCONTINUOUS FORMALISMS

The equations of Chapter 8 can be used to describe membrane processes. The phenomenological equations are written in terms of the differences in composition, pressure and temperature between the solutions on either side of the membrane. The membrane does not enter explicitly into the equations and is characterised only indirectly by the values obtained for the phenomenological coefficients.

An alternative approach is to regard the membrane as an intermediate, continuous third phase of the composite system. The continuous formalism describes the local behaviour in the membrane. The local phenomenological equations are integrated over the membrane to determine the average flows and forces for the membrane, and the adjacent solutions are important only insofar as they determine the boundary conditions at the membrane-solution interfaces. In this way it is possible to construct hypothetical model membranes and to obtain expressions for the dependence of the phenomenological coefficients of the discontinuous formalism on the detailed properties of the membrane.

It should be emphasised that this procedure leads to concepts which do not arise naturally from a direct application of the discontinuous formalism of Chapter 8.

II. THE MEMBRANE AS A CHOICE OF REFERENCE FRAME

We shall assume that the transport processes of importance occur exclusively *within* the membrane, so that we do not need to consider for example convective diffusion in the adjacent solutions (cf. Chapter 14) or interfacial resistances to mass transfer (cf. Chapter 12). A generalisation to include these effects will be given in Chapter 14.

All the concentration gradients and all the dissipative processes take place within the membrane, i.e. in the region $0 < x < l$ where the x-coordinate is in the flow direction and is oriented normal to the flat surfaces of the membrane (of area A).

The surface area A of the membrane is very large by comparison with l so that edge effects and lateral mass transfer within the membrane may be neglected (Barrer *et al.*, 1962). The membrane is isotropic and uniform in its properties at all points on an arbitrary reference-plane constructed normal to the transport axis (x) within the membrane.

Mikulecky and Caplan (1966) have shown quite generally for isotropic membranes, and with some restrictions for anisotropic membranes, that the membrane itself is a legitimate choice of frame of reference for a steady state membrane process. This is true even when a state of mechanical equilibrium does not exist and viscous flow occurs, provided that the mean density of the membrane, over a lateral reference plane, is constant in the direction of flow. The local dissipation function must be averaged over such a reference plane at each depth x within the membrane and the flows must be averages of this type, as indeed they usually are experimentally. The forces conjugate to the membrane-centred flows are the gradients of electrochemical potential of the permeating species.

In the discussion of the different reference frames for diffusion in Chapter 11 it became clear that the reciprocal relations for the mass-fixed frame of reference implied corresponding reciprocal relations for the component-fixed reference frame when the system was in mechanical equilibrium and the gradient grad $\hat{\mu}_n^1$ of the reference component was eliminated from the diffusion equations. Reciprocal relations could not however be guaranteed for other choices of frame of reference, such as the cell-fixed reference frame.

De Groot and Mazur (1962) considered a typical membrane process as taking place in a three-phase system and showed that the phenomenological coefficients which characterise the resistance offered by the membrane in the discontinuous formalism obey Onsager symmetry when the gradients across the membrane are all linear. The flows in this instance are defined with respect to the interface between the membrane and phase ϕ, for example.

Schlögl (1956) claimed that in the case of a membrane having a distinct pore structure through which mass transport occurs, the pore walls may provide a local reference frame in which the Onsager reciprocal relations for diffusion are preserved. However, it is necessary that the pores are small enough to ensure that the fluid in them is homogeneous over the pore cross section, and the electrical space charge per unit volume of fluid must also be uniform over the pore cross section.

Where the pores have a diameter which is very large with respect to the thickness of the electrical double layer, the argument offered by Schlögl is inapplicable, but a correct averaging procedure can still give mean local flows which are defined with respect to the membrane and which may be postulated to give reciprocal relations for the phenomenological coefficients (Mikulecky and Caplan, 1966).

III. THE INFLUENCE OF MEMBRANE STRUCTURE

The structure of a solid phase may have a very pronounced effect on mass transfer processes. This will be discussed in some detail in later chapters. For the present we consider membrane structure only insofar as it may influence the formulation of a treatment based on nonequilibrium thermodynamics, and we consider only ideal membranes of stable and reproducible "fine structure." These restrictions will be removed in later chapters. Mikulecky and Caplan (1966) distinguish between two types of situations.

(a) "The membrane pores are smaller than, of the same magnitude as, or not very much larger than the mean free path of the permeating molecules." It is possible to treat such a membrane as a continuous phase.
(b) The membrane pores are very much larger than the mean free path of the diffusing molecules. This type of membrane may be regarded as a two-phase system. The membrane constitutes a more or less rigid matrix and the entropy production takes place only in the "internal solution" phase. There is no entropy production within the actual membrane matrix.

The concept of a "mean free path" does not seem particularly appropriate in condensed phases, and might better be replaced by the term "average jump distance" for diffusion.

Situation (b) is found in mass transfer through the type of sintered glass filter which has very large pores by comparison with molecular dimensions and in which the pore system has a random but definite "microscopic geometry."

It is also found in permeation through porous assemblies such as textile yarns and fabrics.

Situation (a) is one in which the molecular network constituting the membrane takes part at the molecular level in frictional interactions with all of the permeating components. The membrane molecules represent a true component of the system and must be included in the thermodynamic equations. In situation (b) the membrane matrix represents little more than a solid "container" within which the dissipative processes occur. In this case the membrane does not enter as a component of the system but only as a second phase which defines the geometry of the permeation channels. The permeating fluid is taken to be stationary at the internal interfaces between the two phases in the membrane. The entropy production is calculated only within the fluid phase.

Intermediate types of behaviour are possible, as is the simultaneous occurrence of both types of permeation process within the same membrane. In some types of membrane it may even be necessary to consider the phenomenon of surface transport—along the internal interfaces (Cleland, 1965; Barrer, 1968; Eberly and Vohsberg, 1965).

IV. "LARGE-PORE" MEMBRANES

Here we restrict attention primarily to the two-phase type of membrane in which the pore system has a characteristic dimension much greater than the thickness of the electrical double layer. The term "membrane" here includes porous assemblies of particles and of fibers.

An indirect measure of the thickness of the electrical double layer is given by the *Debye length* $1/x$ where x is defined as

$$x = \left(\frac{4\pi e^2}{\varepsilon kT}\sum_i n_i z_i^{\,2}\right)^{\frac{1}{2}} \tag{13.1}$$

e is the electronic charge, n_i is the number of ions of charge $z_i e$ per unit volume of solution, ε is the dielectric constant, k is the Boltzmann constant and T is the absolute temperature. Suppose that the pore system can be allotted a characteristic radius r which represents some kind of average dimension for a pore. Then the corresponding *electrokinetic radius* (rx) is a measure of the extent to which the radius r exceeds the thickness of the electrical double layer. Table II shows representative values of rx for capillaries containing an aqueous solution of a 1:1 electrolyte at 25°C.

TABLE II. Typical Values of the Electrokinetic Radius rx in Capillary Systems at 25°C Containing an Aqueous Solution of a 1:1 Electrolyte

Molar Concentration of 1:1 electrolyte	$1/x$ (cm)	Electrokinetic Radius rx $r = 10^{-5}$ cm	$r = 10^{-4}$ cm	Radius of a Capillary for which $rx = 20$ (in cm)
2.0	2.1×10^{-8}	476.0	4760.0	4.0×10^{-7}
1.0	3.0×10^{-8}	333.0	3330.0	6.0×10^{-7}
1.0×10^{-1}	9.5×10^{-8}	105.2	1052.0	1.9×10^{-6}
1.0×10^{-2}	3.0×10^{-7}	33.3	333.0	6.0×10^{-6}
1.0×10^{-3}	9.5×10^{-7}	10.5	105.0	1.9×10^{-5}
1.0×10^{-4}	3.0×10^{-6}	3.33	33.3	6.0×10^{-5}
1.0×10^{-5}	9.6×10^{-6}	1.04	10.4	1.9×10^{-4}
Equilibrium water	2.1×10^{-5}	0.47	4.7	4.3×10^{-4}

A. The Electrokinetic Phenomena

1. Experimental Observations

(a) *The Streaming Current*
Experience has shown that when a steady volume flow J_v of a poorly-conducting liquid is induced through a capillary or a porous membrane by a pressure difference ΔP, there is a simultaneous flow of electricity I. This *streaming current* may be measured by a sensitive ammeter of very low resistance connected to electrodes in contact with each face of the membrane, for example (Davies and Rideal, 1961). The electrical potential difference $\Delta\psi$ across the electrodes approaches zero and one finds experimentally that

$$I \propto \Delta P \qquad (\text{Lim } \Delta\psi \to 0) \tag{13.2}$$

(b) *Electro-osmosis*
Suppose that an electrical potential difference $\Delta\psi$ is applied across the electrodes and that a steady flow of electricity (I) results. This flow of electricity is in general accompanied by a flow of liquid (J_v) even in the absence of a significant pressure difference ΔP across the membrane. This fluid flow is known as the electro-osmotic flow, and experimentally

$$J_v \propto \Delta\psi \qquad (\text{Lim } \Delta P \to 0) \tag{13.3}$$

(c) *The Electro-Osmotic Pressure*
If the electro-osmotic flow is prevented, a pressure difference (ΔP) develops across the membrane as a consequence of a steady flow of electricity I. This is the *electro-osmotic pressure* and

$$\Delta P \propto \Delta\psi \qquad (\text{Lim } J_v \to 0) \tag{13.4}$$

(d) *The Streaming Potential*
Suppose a steady volume flow J_v of liquid is induced by a pressure difference ΔP and there is no conducting path to support the streaming current I in its passage from one boundary of the membrane to the other via any external "circuit." Then a *streaming potential* $\Delta\psi$ develops across the membrane

$$\Delta\psi \propto \Delta P \qquad (\text{Lim } I \to 0) \tag{13.5}$$

(e) *Darcy's Law*
If the fluid flow is laminar and there is no streaming potential when a pressure difference ΔP is applied we find that *Darcy's Law* is generally obeyed, i.e.

$$J_v \propto \Delta P \qquad (\text{Lim } \Delta\psi \to 0) \tag{13.6}$$

(f) *Ohm's Law*

When there is no pressure difference ΔP, the conduction of electricity through the membrane obeys *Ohm's Law*, i.e.

$$I \propto \Delta\psi \qquad (\text{Lim } \Delta P \to 0) \tag{13.7}$$

2. The Application of Nonequilibrium Thermodynamics to the Electrokinetic Phenomena

(a) *Phenomenological Equations*

The electrokinetic phenomena at the simplest level take place in the absence of any chemical potential gradients of the chemical components of the fluid. It follows from Eqn (8.46) that the phenomenological equations are (Prigogine, 1961)

$$\left.\begin{aligned} J_v &= L_{vv}\,\Delta P + L_{vc}\,\Delta\psi \\ I &= L_{cv}\,\Delta P + L_{cc}\,\Delta\psi \end{aligned}\right\} \tag{13.8}$$

in which the flows J_v and I are now defined to be positive when ΔP and $\Delta\psi$ are positive, respectively, and the factor $1/T$ is included in the phenomenological coefficients.

The Onsager Relations

$$L_{vc} = L_{cv} \tag{13.9}$$

are postulated to hold and we can relate the experimental observations to Eqns (13.8)

(i) Streaming Current

$$I = L_{cv}\,\Delta P \qquad (\Delta\psi = 0) \tag{13.10}$$

(ii) Ohm's Law

$$I = L_{cc}\,\Delta\psi \qquad (\Delta P = 0) \tag{13.11}$$

(iii) Electro-Osmosis

$$J_v = L_{vc}\,\Delta\psi \qquad (\Delta P = 0) \tag{13.12}$$

(iv) Darcy's Law

$$J_v = L_{vv}\,\Delta P \qquad (\Delta\psi = 0) \tag{13.13}$$

In addition, two distinct types of *stationary state* are possible and these give rise to the other electrokinetic effects, which involve the "forces" rather than the "flows," i.e.

(v) The Electro-Osmotic Pressure

For $I \neq 0$ and $J_v = 0$ we have a stationary nonequilibrium state in which the rate of production of entropy is not zero and in which

$$\left(\frac{\Delta P}{\Delta \psi}\right)_{J_v=0} = -\frac{L_{vc}}{L_{vv}} \tag{13.14}$$

(vi) The Streaming Potential

For $J_v \neq 0$ and $I = 0$ we have a stationary nonequilibrium state in which

$$\left(\frac{\Delta \psi}{\Delta P}\right)_{I=0} = -\frac{L_{cv}}{L_{cc}} \tag{13.15}$$

The *symmetry condition* $L_{vc} = L_{cv}$ implies the identical proportionality factors in the equations for the *streaming current* and for *electro-osmosis* as indeed is observed experimentally, and leads also to *Saxen's relations* (Prigogine, 1961)

(vii) Saxen's Relations

$$\left(\frac{\Delta \psi}{\Delta P}\right)_{I=0} = -\left(\frac{J_v}{I}\right)_{\Delta P=0} \tag{13.16}$$

and

$$\left(\frac{\Delta P}{\Delta \psi}\right)_{J_v=0} = -\left(\frac{I}{J_v}\right)_{\Delta E=0} \tag{13.17}$$

Nonequilibrium thermodynamics leads quite generally to the above results, which are not dependent on the detailed nature of the membrane since they are derived for a discontinuous system.

The phenomenological coefficient L_{vv} characterises the *Darcy's Law permeability* of the membrane and the coefficient L_{cc} characterises its *Ohm's Law conductivity*.

The phenomenological coefficient L_{cv} ($= L_{vc}$) characterises the *electrokinetic interactions* in the membrane.

(b) *The Electroviscous Effect*

In the stationary state in which there is no current flow ($I = 0$) and in which a streaming potential ($\Delta\psi$) develops, there may still be adherence to Darcy's Law but the *permeability* is modified. We find that

$$J_v = L_{vv}\left(1 - \frac{L_{vc}^2}{L_{vv}L_{cc}}\right)\Delta P \tag{13.18}$$

Since the main coefficients L_{vv} and L_{cc} are never negative and the coefficient L_{vc} occurs as L_{vc}^2, the *permeability is always decreased by the electrokinetic effects*. The fluid viscosity η usually enters Darcy's Law in the form

$$J_v = \frac{\text{const.}}{\eta}\,\Delta P \qquad (\Delta\psi = 0) \tag{13.19}$$

The streaming potential causes a decrease in permeability which may be attributed to a higher apparent viscosity η_a of the permeating fluid

$$\eta/\eta_a = \left(1 - \frac{L_{vc}^{\;2}}{L_{vv}L_{cc}}\right) \tag{13.20}$$

or

$$\eta_a \geqslant \eta \tag{13.21}$$

3. Expressions for the Phenomenological Coefficients in Simple Model Membranes

The phenomenological equations do not provide any basis for the prediction of the magnitude of the phenomenological coefficients. They do however provide a minimum set of well-defined phenomenological coefficients for the description of the experimental phenomena and they imply the existence of useful reciprocal relations between these coefficients. Further details can come only from the integration of the local phenomenological equations over the membrane (De Groot and Mazur, 1962; Mikulecky and Caplan, 1966) or from molecular theories. The solution of the local transport equations is possible only for especially simple systems of very simple geometry. The behaviour of well-defined *model systems* of this type is however very useful in interpreting the behaviour of real systems.

The phenomenological equations can provide little insight into the mechanistic details of the transport processes, but they are very general and provide a concise summary of the effects to be anticipated in a given situation.

(a) *Electrokinetic Effects in a Straight Circular Capillary*

When the Navier Stokes Equation is solved for the laminar flow of an isothermal fluid of constant density and constant shear viscosity η through a straight circular capillary of radius r and length l, *Poiseuille's equation* is obtained (Davies and Rideal, 1961)

$$J_v = \frac{\pi r^4}{8\eta l}\,\frac{\Delta P}{l} \tag{13.22}$$

and so

$$L_{vv} = \frac{\pi r^4}{8\eta l} = \left(\frac{\pi r^2}{l}\right)\frac{r^2}{8\eta} \tag{13.23}$$

When the liquid in the capillary tube is stationary and Ohm's Law is obeyed we have

$$I = \frac{1}{R}\,\Delta\psi \tag{13.24}$$

where R is the total resistance of the liquid and its capillary tube container. If the material of the capillary is a good insulator we need consider only conduction through the fluid and along the internal surface of the capillary.

If the specific conductivity of the liquid is K_l and the surface conductivity of the capillary is K_s then

$$\frac{1}{R_l} = K_l \frac{\pi r^2}{l} \tag{13.25}$$

where R_l is the resistance of the liquid and

$$\frac{1}{R_s} = K_s \frac{2\pi r}{l} \tag{13.26}$$

where R_s is the resistance of the surface.

The total resistance R is

$$\frac{1}{R} = \frac{1}{R_s} + \frac{1}{R_l} \tag{13.27}$$

and so (Davies and Rideal, 1961)

$$I = \frac{\pi r^2}{l} K_l \left(1 + \frac{2K_s}{rK_l}\right) \tag{13.28}$$

and

$$L_{cc} = \frac{\pi r^2}{l} K_l \left(1 + \frac{2K_s}{rK_l}\right) \tag{13.29}$$

The existence of the electrokinetic phenomena is explained by the theories of the *ionic double layer* (Davies and Rideal, 1961). At some point near a solid–liquid interface, the fluid is stationary with respect to the solid surface. This point is generally considered to lie somewhere near the inner boundary of the diffuse part of the ionic double layer and this "plane of shear" within the double layer is generally at some electrostatic potential ζ with respect to the bulk of the fluid phase. This *Zeta Potential* ζ can be related to an effective surface charge density σ_s of electrostatic charge on the stationary boundary of the plane of shear. This surface charge influences the distribution of ions in the moving liquid boundary layer near the plane of shear, with the result that the moving fluid carries a net electrostatic charge and a flow of fluid is associated with a flow of electricity. This effect is large only if the diffuse layer is extensive and the Zeta Potential is high, for example in a fluid of low conductivity such as distilled water. The presence of high concentrations of electrolyte decreases the thickness of the ionic double layer and decreases the influence of the surface charge: the Zeta Potential ζ disappears.

To calculate the magnitude of the electrokinetic effects, the local transport equations must be integrated over the volume of fluid in the membrane, and appropriate electrostatic terms must be included to take account of local departures from electrical neutrality in the fluid. The mathematical solution of this problem is complex even for simple geometries and for the additional, simplifying assumptions that are often made.

A simple theory of the electrical double layer leads to the following results for a straight circular capillary *of large electrokinetic radius* ($rx > 100$; Davies and Rideal, 1961)

$$I = -\frac{\varepsilon\zeta}{4\pi\eta} \cdot \frac{\pi r^2}{l} \Delta P \tag{13.30}$$

Consequently,

$$L_{cv} = -\frac{\pi r^2 \varepsilon\zeta}{4\pi\eta l} \tag{13.31}$$

and the electrokinetic effects disappear when the Zeta Potential $\zeta = 0$. For the electroviscous effect we find

$$\frac{\eta}{\eta a} = 1 - \frac{\varepsilon^2\zeta^2}{2\pi^2 r^2 \eta K_l\left(1 + \dfrac{2K_s}{rK_l}\right)} \tag{13.32}$$

An estimate of the electroviscous effect can be made for the following typical experimental conditions (Davies and Rideal, 1961) for a 10^{-4} M KCl solution.

$$\varepsilon = 80; \quad \zeta = -70 \text{ mV}; \quad \eta = 10^{-2} \text{ poise}$$
$$r = 1.5 \times 10^{-5} \text{ cm}; \quad K_l(1 + 2K_s/rK_l) = 10^{-4} \text{ ohm}^{-1} \text{ cm}^{-1}$$

We find $\eta_a = 1.10 \times 10^{-2}$ poise so that the apparent viscosity of 10^{-4} M KCl should be about 10% higher than normal in a capillary of radius 1.5×10^{-5} cm. This is in rough agreement with experiment but unfortunately the parameters given imply that the electrokinetic radius is too small for Eqn (13.32) to be valid.

The effects can be much greater in systems of very small electro-kinetic radius, although these systems then have a much greater internal surface area and the surface conductivity may tend to reduce the observed effects significantly.

According to Rice and Whitehead (1965) we should expect to find (the surface conductivity is ignored),

$$L_{cv} = -\frac{\pi r^2}{l} \cdot \frac{\varepsilon\zeta}{4\pi\eta} \cdot f(rx) \tag{13.33}$$

in which the function $f(rx)$ approaches unity for large values of rx and takes smaller values as rx decreases. The apparent Zeta Potential ζ_a obtained experimentally deviates from the true value as follows

$$\zeta_a = \zeta \cdot f(rx) < \zeta \tag{13.34}$$

so that one tends to find too low a value for ζ in systems of low electrokinetic radius.

The electroviscous effect for large electrokinetic radii is given by (Rice and Whitehead, 1965)

$$\eta/\eta_a = 1 - 8\beta/(rx)^2 \qquad (rx \gg 1) \tag{13.35}$$

and the parameter β is

$$\beta = \frac{\varepsilon^2 \zeta^2 x^2}{16\pi^2 \eta K_l} \tag{13.36}$$

Equations (13.32) and (13.35) are identical if the surface conductivity is ignored. The surface conductivity *reduces* the electrokinetic effects. Equations (13.32) and (13.35) should be valid for $rx > 100$, but in this region of electrokinetic radius the electroviscous effects should be negligible. These equations tend to overestimate the effects.

More detailed analyses of this problem have been given by De Groot and Mazur (1962), Burgreen and Nakache (1964), Mikulecky and Caplan (1966). Electrokinetic flow in fine capillary channels has been examined in detail by Hildreth (1970), with particular attention to the "surface conductivity."

(b) *A Simple Capillary Analogy for Porous Media*

The simplest model for a porous medium is an assembly of straight circular capillary tubes in which all the capillaries are parallel and of equal length l. The capillary radii are all equal. The capillaries are embedded in an impermeable matrix in such a way that fluid flow takes place through the capillaries only. Suppose that the total cross sectional area of the assembly normal to the flow direction is A, and that the capillaries together form a fraction ε of this cross sectional area. Then from Eqns (13.23), (13.29) and (13.31)

$$L_{vv} = \frac{\varepsilon A}{l} \cdot \frac{r^2}{8\eta} \tag{13.37}$$

$$L_{cc} = \frac{\varepsilon A}{l} \cdot K_l \left(1 + \frac{2K_s}{rK_l}\right) \tag{13.38}$$

$$L_{cv} = -\frac{\varepsilon A}{l} \cdot \frac{\varepsilon \zeta}{4\pi\eta_0} \tag{13.39}$$

In a porous medium we can expect to have a porosity such that flow is possible in more than one direction. If a medium is not too "highly structured" (Chapter 15) and if the following conditions are satisfied

$$r \ll d \ll l$$

where d is a characteristic dimension of the "averaging volume" over which our measurements characterise the system, and l is the macroscopic external dimension of the solid, then the *cross-sectional "void area" fraction* ε becomes equivalent to the *volume "void fraction"* ε.

In such a situation, and for an *arbitrary* flow direction in the porous solid, the area of void open to fluid flow is given by εA where ε is the *porosity* of the porous medium (cf. Chapter 14)

$$\varepsilon \equiv \frac{\text{void volume}}{\text{total volume}} \tag{13.40}$$

A characteristic length for a porous medium, and one which is often used to replace the radius r, is the *mean hydraulic radius m*

$$m \equiv \frac{\text{volume of void open to flow}}{\text{surface area exposed to flow}} \tag{13.41}$$

For a straight circular capillary

$$m = r/2 \tag{13.42}$$

If the capillaries are not straight, an empirical "tortuosity factor" τ_v can be introduced which relates the effective length l of the capillary to the thickness L of the membrane in the flow direction

$$l = \tau_v L \tag{13.43}$$

The constant in Eqn (13.37) reflects the particular geometry of a straight circular capillary. For capillaries of more general cross sectional shape we might introduce an empirical shape factor k_v and replace Eqn (13.37) by the equation

$$L_{vv} = \frac{\varepsilon A}{\tau_v L} \frac{m^2}{k_v \eta_0} \tag{13.44}$$

To carry the capillary analogy further, for membranes consisting of porous assemblies of solid particles such as fibers, it is necessary to express m in terms of parameters which characterise the solid particles and their mode of packing. The simplest and most convenient parameter is *the specific surface area* S_0 of the particles.

$$S_0 \equiv \frac{\text{surface area of the solid particles}}{\text{volume of the solid particles}} \tag{13.45}$$

we find

$$m = \frac{\varepsilon}{S_0(1 - \varepsilon)} \tag{13.46}$$

so that the phenomenological coefficient is

$$L_{vv} = \frac{1}{K_v S_0{}^2} \frac{\varepsilon^3}{(1 - \varepsilon)^2} \frac{A}{L} \tag{13.47}$$

where the new parameter $K_v \equiv k_v \tau_v$ is commonly known as the *Kozeny Constant* and the permeability equation

$$J_v = \frac{1}{K_v S_0{}^2} \frac{\varepsilon^3}{(1 - \varepsilon)^2} \frac{A}{L} \Delta P \tag{13.48}$$

is the *Kozeny Carman Equation*. K_v is best regarded as an empirical parameter chosen to give agreement with experiment over the porosity range, and for the geometry, of the system examined.

There are difficulties in the consistent extension of the capillary analogy to include the conduction of electricity and the electrokinetic effects.

In a capillary the internal surface is continuous along each flow channel. Assemblies of particles have a very different surface topology so that the conductive pathways along the surfaces and through the liquid may differ from each other in a different manner from that characteristic of a capillary. It is unlikely that the geometrical factors τ_v and k_v will have the same values and the factor $1/m$ may not correctly represent the relative importance of the surface and bulk conduction in the equation

$$L_{cc} = \frac{\varepsilon_A}{\tau_I L} K_l \left(1 + \frac{K_s}{m K_l}\right) \tag{13.49}$$

in which τ_I is a tortuosity factor for the bulk flow of electricity in the fluid. Therefore we should replace m in Eqn (13.49) by αm, in which α is a correction factor for this effect.

Similarly we may write

$$L_{cv} = -\frac{\varepsilon_A}{\tau_E L} \cdot \frac{\varepsilon \zeta}{k_E 4\pi\eta} \tag{13.50}$$

in which τ_E is a tortuosity factor for the electrokinetic effects and k_E may deviate from unity.

Since it is not possible to make a rigorous correction for these effects in assemblies of particles such as fibers it is not possible to derive absolute values of the Zeta Potentials from the phenomenological coefficients L_{cv}. At best one can derive values of the apparent Zeta Potentials ζ_a

$$\zeta_a = (\zeta/\tau_E k_E) \times f(rx, \beta) \tag{13.51}$$

which include the indeterminate quantities τ_E and k_E.

These difficulties have been recognised by many workers (Overbeck and Wijga, 1946; Overbeck, 1952; Biefer and Mason, 1959; Davies and Rideal, 1961; Milicevic and McGregor, 1967).

Biefer and Mason (1959) have shown the difficulties that exist with porous assemblies of fibers. A useful review of fluid flow in porous media has been given by Scheidegger (1957). More recent developments are examined by Greenkorn and Kessler (1969) and by Whitaker (1969).

An alternative approach to studies of the permeability of assemblies of particles is to derive expressions for L_{vv} by summing the resistances which the individual particles offer to the fluid flow. The resistances are calculated from the so-called "drag theories" (Scheidegger, 1957). This type of approach becomes more useful as the porosity of the assembly increases. Applications to fluid flow through textiles have been discussed by McGregor (1965).

B. Permeation through "Large-Pore" Membranes

This problem is usually discussed by integrating the local transport equations for the fluid component of the membrane, with the inclusion of the electrokinetic effects arising from surface charges on the internal surfaces of the membrane, but of course this is possible only for very simple geometries (De Groot and Mazur, 1962; Burgreen and Nakache, 1964; Rice and Whitehead, 1965; Mikulecky and Caplan, 1966) and generally the surface conductivity is ignored.

For diffusion or permeation measurements with complex large-pore membranes such as sintered glass discs this approach is no longer so useful (Kamal and McLaughlin, 1966). Often the local phenomenological equations for a homogeneous fluid are used as if they refer to the whole membrane (Bennion and Rhee, 1969), though empirical corrections for the porosity of the membrane and for the tortuosity of the flow channels may be used to derive "true" values of the diffusion coefficients in the membranes.

The significance of experimental data obtained with "large-pore" membranes is very dependent on the design of the experimental apparatus, because of the complications which may be caused by the bulk flow of the fluid through the membrane, by the electrokinetic effects and by the diffusion potentials (Scattergood and Lightfoot, 1968; Helfferich, 1952; Schlögl, 1953; Helfferich and Ocker, 1957; Schlögl and Stein, 1958; Meares, 1958; Mackie and Meares, 1955a, 1956; Manecke and Heller, 1956; McHardy, 1962; Thain, 1964; Rastogi and Jha, 1966; Talen and Staverman, 1966; Cleland, 1965).

A possible criterion for the correctness of a "large-pore" model in interpreting experimental data is provided by the effect of temperature on the rates of permeation. If the temperature dependence of the permeation rates corresponds to the temperature dependence of $1/\eta$, where η is the shear viscosity of the liquid postulated to be present in the pore system, then this is evidence in support of the "large-pore" model. If the temperature-dependence of the permeation rates is very different from this, then either the "large-pore" model is inapplicable or additional processes have not been taken into account, such as adsorptive interactions between the permeating species and the pore walls (Staverman *et al.*, 1966; Standing *et al.*, 1947; Cleland, 1965) or temperature-dependent interactions between the diffusing molecules, such as dimerisation or aggregation.

V. "SMALL-PORE" MEMBRANES

We shall include in the class of "small-pore" membranes all those membranes with pores of low electrokinetic radius. The ionic concentration tends to uniformity across the pore cross-sections, but the average concentrations may differ in pores of different diameters (Schmid, 1950).

Macroscopically homogeneous polymer membranes are included though here the "pores" may consist of more or less continuous pathways through the less ordered regions of the polymer and their dimensions may be subject to local thermal fluctuations. These "pores" may be regarded as pathways through a more or less dense and disordered polymer matrix or polymer "gel", which may have none of the properties of the liquid phases bounding the polymer membrane (cf. Chapter 15).

Only a comparatively small fraction of the volume of a "small-pore" membrane may be accessible to permeating molecules, and these molecules will generally follow a very tortuous pathway through the membrane. Whether such a membrane can be said to possess a well defined pore structure will depend on the definition adopted for the term "pore," and the characteristics of the pore system can often be defined only empirically.

If the membrane molecules behave as a thermodynamic component of the system, then we have a "molecular membrane" in which the membrane molecules take part in intimate molecular or diffusive frictional interactions with the permeating species. Here the concept of a pore may be inappropriate, except as a clearly recognised simplification of the real situation.

A. Permeation through "Small-Pore" Membranes

Capillary models are used to describe permeation through "small-pore" membranes and to interpret the phenomenological equations obtained from the discontinuous formalism (Rastogi and Singh, 1966; Kedem and Katchalsky, 1958, 1961, 1963; Staverman, 1952; Cleland *et al.*, 1964; Cleland, 1965; Talen and Staverman, 1966; Staverman *et al.*, 1966).

The use of capillary models for systems having pores with apparent radii of the order of 10 Å to 50 Å is not too easy to justify, except perhaps in ordered solids such as the Zeolites. The membrane component will probably take part in intimate molecular interactions with the permeating components and these interactions may be very selective in nature.

Indeed the application of a pressure gradient to force a fluid mixture through such "*micropore membranes*" can result in at least a partial separation of the components of the fluid. This is the phenomenon of *ultrafiltration* (Cleland, 1965; Talen and Staverman, 1966) and it may be caused by selective molecular interactions or by geometrical "obstruction effects" in the membrane which selectively hinder the permeation of molecules of different shapes and sizes.

Often it becomes a matter of taste whether one prefers to think in terms of a discrete pore structure or of permeation through a homogeneous "molecular gel." In other situations however this difference of viewpoints may have a real physical basis. The effect of temperature can be particularly significant here, as can the molecular size of the permeating species. When a polymer membrane is well above its glass transition temperature the polymer molecules in the accessible regions through which permeation occurs may participate intimately in frictional interactions with the diffusing species. In this case the homogeneous "gel" model, with appropriate but empirical corrections for tortuosity and porosity, will be appropriate and the temperature dependence of the permeation rates is likely to reflect the temperature dependence of the motions of the polymer segments in the accessible regions: i.e. the polymer viscosity is important rather than that of a permeating fluid. When such a membrane is well below its glass transition temperature however the polymer molecules will be effectively "frozen," and permeation through the membrane will be much more difficult. Very small molecules may however still permeate through any "frozen-in" system of voids or pores which exists in the membrane and the "small-pore" model may then have some physical justification even for a "homogeneous" polymer membrane (Frisch, 1965; Meares, 1966).

The electrokinetic effects in "large-pore" membranes were related in the previous section to the presence of a surface charge on the stationary liquid phase adhering to the capillary walls, this surface charge being responsible for the existence of the Zeta Potential ζ and for the electrokinetic effects. In some "small-pore" membranes the *ionisable groupings* which are present on the molecular matrix of the membrane may play a role rather similar to that of the surface charge in "large-pore" membranes. Molecules which themselves carry ionisable groups and which become firmly adsorbed on the membrane matrix may have the same kind of effect. Highly swollen membranes may perhaps be regarded as permeated by a continuous internal solution, and this internal solution of ions may have a net space charge opposite in sign to that on the membrane matrix. When permeation takes place through the membrane, from an ionic solution of one concentration to an ionic solution of lower concentration, diffusion potentials will be set up within the membrane because of the coupling of the ionic fluxes (Chapter 11). The integration of the local diffusion equations across the membrane of thickness l, (Kirkwood, 1954), for the steady state of permeation, gives an expression for the net diffusion potential $\Delta\psi$ across the membrane. Ignoring for the present the boundary potentials at each membrane interface (Schlögl, 1954) we see that such an electrical potential difference $\Delta\psi$ may give rise to *electro-osmosis* of the internal solution. This electro-osmosis may occur in any direction, depending on the particular experimental situation.

When a membrane separates two non-ionic solutions of different concentrations an *osmotic flow* of the solvent and solution tends to occur through the membrane, and this flow always proceeds from the more dilute to the more concentrated solution.

When the electro-osmotic flow reinforces the osmotic flow and the net flow takes place from the more dilute to the more concentrated solution we have the phenomenon of *positive anomalous osmosis*. When the electro-osmotic effect predominates and the net flow is from the more concentrated to the more dilute solution we have *negative anomalous osmosis* (Schlögl, 1955). The osmotic effects can have a large influence on the rates of permeation through a membrane, and on the concentration distributions within the membrane, especially in highly swollen and highly charged membranes (Meares, 1968). These effects are important in water desalination processes (Meares, 1966; Bennion and Rhee, 1969).

A friction coefficient formalism based on generalised Maxwell–Stefan equations has been developed for the analysis of membrane processes (Lightfoot *et al.*, 1962; Scattergood and Lightfoot, 1968). Friction coefficient formalisms more closely related to nonequilibrium thermodynamics have been introduced by Spiegler (1958) and by Laity (1959a, b) and have been used or further modified by several workers (Kedem and Katchalsky, 1958, 1961, 1963; Mackay and Meares, 1959; Caramazza *et al.*, 1963; Kressman *et al.*, 1963; Cleland, 1965; Spiegler and Kedem, 1966; Bennion and Rhee, 1969; Wills and Lightfoot, 1966).

Approximate matrix methods of analysis for multicomponent mass transport in membranes have been discussed by Wills (1967).

The effect of membrane adsorption on anomalous osmosis has been discussed by Staverman *et al.* (1966). The implications of membrane permeability for osmotic measurements of molecular weight have received attention (Talen and Staverman, 1966).

A general solution of the Nernst–Planck equations for permeation through a membrane in which no osmotic effects (or bulk flows) occur, and in which interfacial rate effects can be neglected, has been given by Schlögl (1954) who presents very interesting calculations of the steady-state distributions of the ions and of the electrical potential ψ in the membrane. The computations are for a model system which provides a very useful reference system for the behaviour of real systems. Further calculations by Schlögl and Schödel (1955) have shown the modifying effect which bulk flow may have on the concentration distributions in a membrane in the steady-state (Schlögl, 1964). Other authors who have included the osmotic effects in analyses of permeation through membranes are Mackie and Meares (1955b), Mackay and Meares (1960, 1961), Helfferich (1962a, b; 1963a, b), Helfferich and Plesset (1958), Toyoshima *et al.* (1967) and Scattergood and Lightfoot (1968).

Useful review articles have been written by Bergsma and Kruissink (1961), Helfferich (1962a), Schlögl (1964), and Meares (1968) amongst others.

Although we have classified membranes into two main types on the basis of pore sizes, this does not exclude the possibility that a real membrane may possess a wide distribution of pore sizes spanning both pore types, and that mass transport may occur through the membrane matrix itself at the same time as it takes place through the pores in the membrane (Meares, 1966).

VI. MEMBRANE SELECTIVITY AND MEMBRANE EQUILIBRIA

A. Membrane Selectivity

For simplicity we shall consider the permeation of an isothermal binary mixture of a nonionic solute (1) and a nonionic solvent (0) through a membrane which separates the mixture ϕ of components (1) and (0) from the mixture σ of components (1) and (0).

The entropy production in terms of the "mass flows" $\mathscr{J}_k$ is, based on the discontinuous formalism,

$$\begin{aligned} T\frac{d_I S}{dt} &= -\sum_{k=0}^{1} (\Delta\mu_k)_T \cdot \mathscr{J}_k \\ &= -\sum_{k=0}^{1} (\Delta\mu_k)_{T,p}\mathscr{J}_k - \mathscr{J}_v\,\Delta P \\ &= -\sum_{k=0}^{1} \left(\frac{(\Delta\mu_k)_{T,p}}{\bar{v}_k^{\,\phi}}\right)(\mathscr{J}_k)_v - \mathscr{J}_v\,\Delta P \end{aligned} \tag{13.52}$$

$\mathscr{J}_v \equiv \sum_{k=0}^{1} \bar{v}_k^{\,\phi} \cdot \mathscr{J}_k$ is the total volume flow of the two components to phase ϕ and $(\mathscr{J}_k)_v \equiv \bar{v}_k^{\,\phi} \cdot \mathscr{J}_k$ is the corresponding partial volume flow of component k.

The flows and forces of Eqn (13.52) are not independently variable. It is not possible to vary $(\Delta\mu_1)_{T,p}$, by varying the concentration of component 1 in phase ϕ for example, without also changing $(\Delta\mu_0)_{T,p}$. It is usual to suppose that $(\Delta\mu_0)_{T,p}$ and $(\Delta\mu_1)_{T,p}$ are related by the Gibbs-Duhem equation in the form

$$C_0^{\phi}(\Delta\mu_0)_{T,p} + C_1^{\phi}(\Delta\mu_1)_{T,p} = 0 \tag{13.53}$$

and that the term in $(\Delta\mu_0)_{T,p}$ can therefore be eliminated from Eqn (13.52) to give

$$T\frac{d_I S}{dt} = -\left(\frac{(\Delta\mu_1)_{T,p}}{\bar{v}_1^{\phi}}\right)\cdot(\mathscr{I}_1^{\,1})_v - \mathscr{I}_v\,\Delta P \tag{13.54}$$

where the new volume flow $(\mathscr{I}_1^{\,1})_v$ is defined by

$$\begin{aligned}(\mathscr{I}_1^{\,1})_v &\equiv (\mathscr{I}_1)_v - \frac{\bar{v}_1^{\phi}C_1^{\phi}}{\bar{v}_0^{\phi}C_0^{\phi}}\cdot(\mathscr{I}_0)_v \\ &= \frac{(\mathscr{I}_1)_v - \bar{v}_1^{\phi}C_1^{\phi}\mathscr{I}_v}{\bar{v}_0^{\phi}C_0^{\phi}}\end{aligned} \tag{13.55}$$

and is a rather complex relative flow of component 1 with respect to the total volume flow $\mathscr{I}_v$. In analyses which treat the membrane as an intervening third phase, the flow $(\mathscr{I}_1^{\,1})_v$ appears as a particular kind of "diffusion flow" of component 1 with respect to the total volume flow $\mathscr{I}_v$ (Cleland, 1965).

The thermodynamic flows and forces of Eqn (13.54) may now be treated as independent and therefore

$$-(\mathscr{I}_1^{\,1})_v = L_{11}\frac{(\Delta\mu_1)_{T,p}}{\bar{v}_1^{\phi}} + L_{1V}\,\Delta P \tag{13.56}$$

$$-(\mathscr{I}\,)_v = L_{V1}\frac{(\Delta\mu_1)_{T,p}}{\bar{v}_1^{\phi}} + L_{VV}\,\Delta P \tag{13.57}$$

An *osmotic flow* $\mathscr{I}_v$ may occur when there is no pressure difference ΔP if the chemical potential difference $(\Delta\mu_1)_{T,p}$ is not zero.

The application of a pressure difference ΔP to a system in which $(\Delta\mu_1)_{T,p}$ is zero may give rise to a relative flow $(\mathscr{I}_1^{\,1})_v$ which corresponds to some degree of selective permeation or separation of the two components (1) and (0). This is *ultrafiltration* and is important for water desalination processes.

In some analyses (Kedem and Katchalsky, 1958; Cleland, 1965; Staverman, 1952) the *osmotic pressure* $\Delta\pi$ corresponding to the chemical potential difference $(\Delta\mu_1)_{T,p}$ is introduced into the phenomenological equations, i.e.

$$\Delta\pi \equiv \frac{(\Delta\mu_1)_{T,p}}{\bar{v}_1^{\phi}} \tag{13.58}$$

so that

$$-(\mathscr{I}_1{}^1)_v = L_{11}\,\Delta\pi + L_{1V}\,\Delta P \tag{13.59}$$

$$-(\mathscr{I})_v = L_{V1}\,\Delta\pi + L_{VV}\,\Delta P \tag{13.60}$$

If the membrane is slightly permeable to the solute (1) an *apparent* equilibrium state can often be reached in which the *osmotic flow* $(\mathscr{I})_v$ effectively ceases on application of an opposing pressure difference ΔP, i.e.

$$0 = L_{V1}\,\Delta\pi + L_{VV}\,\Delta P \tag{13.61}$$

The *apparent osmotic pressure* ΔP is related to the true osmotic pressure $\Delta\pi$ as follows (Kedem and Katchalsky, 1958)

$$\Delta P = -\frac{L_{V1}}{L_{VV}}\,\Delta\pi \tag{13.62}$$

where the quantity $-L_{V1}/L_{VV}$ is Staverman's reflection coefficient σ (Staverman, 1952).

Generally $\sigma \to 1$ and $\Delta P \to \Delta\pi$ as the membrane becomes completely impermeable to the solute. If the membrane is not completely impermeable to the solute then $\sigma < 1$ and $\Delta P < \Delta\pi$: the apparent osmotic pressure is less than the true osmotic presure. This apparent equilibrium state is one in which the osmotic flow $(\mathscr{I})_v$ vanishes but in which $(\mathscr{I}_1{}^1)_v$ is not zero because the membrane is not completely impermeable to the solute. Since however $(\mathscr{I}^1)_v$ is generally rather small its effects become apparent primarily through the ratio $\Delta P/\Delta\pi$ and the reflection coefficient σ. This situation is important when osmometry is used to determine the molecular weight of a dissolved substance.

B. Membrane Equilibrium

If all components can pass freely from one solution (σ) to the other (ϕ) through an intervening membrane then the equilibrium distributions of the components are given by Eqns (12.44) to (12.48) with $\chi_k = 0$ in each homogeneous solution

The electrical neutrality conditions are

$$\sum_{k=1}^{n} z_k C_k^{\sigma} = \sum_{k=1}^{n} z_k C_k^{\sigma} = 0 \tag{13.63}$$

1. A Simple Donnan Membrane Distribution

Let solutions ϕ and σ both be normal aqueous solutions at the same pressure, and suppose that all activity coefficients are equal to unity. Since $K_k = 1$ in this situation,

$$C_k{}^{\phi} = \lambda^{Z_k} C_k{}^{\sigma} \tag{13.64}$$

and if all components have free passage through the membrane Eqn (13.63) becomes

$$\sum_{k=1}^{n} z_k C_k^{\phi} = \sum_{k=1}^{n} z_k \lambda^{z_k} C_k^{\sigma} = \sum_{k=1}^{n} z_k C_k^{\sigma} = 0 \qquad (13.65)$$

One solution of Eqn (13.65) requires that $\lambda = 1$, in which case we would find $\Delta\psi = 0$. It is found experimentally that there is no electrical potential difference $\Delta\psi$ between the two solutions in this situation, and their compositions are identical at equilibrium.

If the membrane *prevents* a certain component j from passing through, and if this component is present only in solution ϕ then now

$$\sum_{\substack{k=1\\k\neq j}}^{n} z_k C_k^{\phi} + z_j C_j^{\phi} = \sum_{\substack{k=1\\k\neq j}}^{n} z_k \lambda^{z_k} C_k^{\sigma} + z_j C_j^{\phi} = \sum_{\substack{k=1\\k\neq j}}^{n} z_k C_k^{\sigma} = 0 \quad (13.66)$$

It follows that $\lambda \neq 1$ if $C_j^{\phi} \neq 0$.

The unequal distribution of species j has given rise to a *Donnan Membrane Potential* $\Delta\psi$ across the membrane and the distributions of the unconstrained components are correspondingly modified. The effect is greater the higher the value of the product $z_j C_j^{\phi}$. Ions of multiple charge have their equilibrium distributions altered much more than ions of single charge (cf. Eqn 13.64). The result of the presence of species j is a *Donnan Membrane Distribution* of ions which differs from that to be expected in the absence of a Donnan Membrane Potential.

As an example suppose two aqueous solutions of sodium chloride are separated by a membrane and that one solution (ϕ) contains the sodium salt $\mathrm{Na}_{z_D}D$ of a dye. The dye anion is unable to pass through the membrane into solution σ. The electrical neutrality conditions are

$$C_{\mathrm{Na}}^{\sigma} - C_{\mathrm{Cl}}^{\sigma} = C_{\mathrm{Na}}^{\phi} - C_{\mathrm{Cl}}^{\phi} - z_D C_D^{\phi} = 0 \qquad (13.67)$$

If there is no pressure difference and the activity coefficients are equal to unity

$$\begin{aligned} C_{\mathrm{Na}}^{\phi} &= \lambda C_{\mathrm{Na}}^{\sigma} \\ C_{\mathrm{Cl}}^{\phi} &= (1/\lambda) C_{\mathrm{Cl}}^{\sigma} \end{aligned} \qquad (13.68)$$

Eqn (13.66) becomes

$$\lambda C_{\mathrm{Na}}^{\sigma} - (1/\lambda) C_{\mathrm{Cl}}^{\sigma} - z_D C_D^{\phi} = 0 \qquad (13.69)$$

or, multiplying by λ and using Eqn (13.67)

$$\lambda^2 C_{\mathrm{Na}}^{\sigma} - \lambda (z_D C_D^{\phi}) - C_{\mathrm{Cl}}^{\sigma} = 0 \qquad (13.70)$$

When no dye is present, $\lambda = 1$ and $C_{Na}{}^{\phi} = C_{Na}{}^{\sigma}$, $C_{Cl}{}^{\sigma} = C_{Cl}{}^{\phi}$. If dye is present then $\lambda \neq 0$ and

$$C_{Na}{}^{\phi}/C_{Na}{}^{\sigma} = \lambda = C_{Cl}{}^{\sigma}/C_{Cl}{}^{\phi} \tag{13.71}$$

Although the distribution of ions is modified, we still find that

$$C_{Na}^{\sigma} \times C_{Cl}^{\sigma} = C_{Na}{}^{\phi} \times C_{Cl}{}^{\phi} \tag{13.72}$$

i.e. the *product* of the "free" ion concentrations on each side of the membrane is the same. This arises from the requirement that the chemical potential of sodium chloride be the same at equilibrium in each solution. Similar results are obtained if the dye is present in unequal concentrations in each solution.

VII. SELECTIVITY AND THE SORPTION OF IONS

We have seen how selective *permeability* can influence both the kinetics and the equilibria in membrane systems. This is a convenient point to emphasise the importance of selectivity in the *sorption* of ions by a fiber, or in the *distribution* of ions between two phases. A simplex example related to polyamide dyeing will suffice to illustrate this point (Milicevic and McGregor, 1967).

Suppose a solid polyamide in fiber or film form is immersed in an aqueous solution containing hydrochloric acid and the free acid of an anionic dye HD at low pH. The solution pH is kept constant at a suitably low value so that the electrical neutrality condition in the solution is

$$C_{Cl}^{\sigma} + C_{D}^{\sigma} = C_{H}^{\sigma} = \text{const.} \tag{13.73}$$

The electrical neutrality condition in the fiber phase is

$$C_{Cl}^{\phi} + C_{D}^{\phi} = B^{+} = \text{const.} \tag{13.74}$$

because we assume that there are no free hydrogen ions in the fiber and that all of the amine end groups are protonated, giving a total concentration B^{+} of charged groups in the fiber.

The distribution of the dye anions and the chloride anions between the two phases is written as an *anion-exchange process* (Helfferich, 1962a)

$$(Cl^{-})^{\phi} + (D^{-})^{\sigma} \rightleftharpoons (Cl^{-})^{\sigma} + (D^{-})^{\phi} \tag{13.75}$$

The equilibrium coefficient K_{Cl}^{D}

$$K_{Cl}^{D} = \frac{C_{Cl}{}^{\sigma} \cdot C_{D}{}^{\phi}}{C_{Cl}^{\phi} \cdot C_{D}{}^{\sigma}} \tag{13.76}$$

is a measure of the tendency of the fiber to sorb the dye anion in preference to the chloride anion and is therefore known as the *selectivity coefficient*.

In fact

$$K_{\text{Cl}}^{\text{D}} = K_{\text{D}}/K_{\text{Cl}} \tag{13.77}$$

where K_{D} and K_{Cl} are the effective or apparent distribution coefficients for the individual ions, defined in accordance with Eqns (12.45) and (12.46). K_{Cl}^{D} is unlikely to be constant, but will be treated here as if it were. In this case we may convert Eqn (13.76) to the form of a *sorption isotherm* relating the *relative dye sorption* θ_{D}

$$\theta_{\text{D}} = C_{\text{D}}^{\phi}/B^{+} \tag{13.78}$$

to the "dye anion mole fraction" x_{D}^{σ}

$$x_{\text{D}}^{\sigma} = \frac{C_{\text{D}}^{\sigma}}{C_{\text{D}}^{\sigma} + C_{\text{Cl}}^{\sigma}} \tag{13.79}$$

We obtain the result (Helfferich, 1962a; Milicevic and McGregor, 1967)

$$\frac{\theta_{\text{D}}}{1 - \theta_{\text{D}}} = K_{\text{Cl}}^{\text{D}} \frac{x_{\text{D}}^{\sigma}}{1 - x_{\text{D}}^{\sigma}} \tag{13.80}$$

in which the shape of the sorption isotherm at a constant pH is dependent on the value of the selectivity coefficient K_{Cl}^{D}.

For $K_{\text{Cl}}^{\text{D}} = 1$ the isotherm relating θ_{D} to x_{D}^{σ} is *linear*. As K_{Cl}^{D} increases, the curvature of the sorption isotherm increases and it becomes '*Langmuir*' in shape. This observation is very important for the interpretation of equilibrium sorption isotherms (Helfferich, 1962a).

When calculations are made for a much more general system the same basic principle holds: the isotherm shape depends on the value of K_{D} relative to the K_i values of the other anions in the system (McGregor and Harris, 1969, 1970).

It is perhaps worth pointing out that a similar effect can occur in non-ionic systems if lattice requirements place restrictions on the total concentrations of the components in each phase (Everett, 1964; Milicevic and McGregor, 1967).

An undue emphasis on the behaviour of the dye molecule or dye ion, to the exclusion of the other molecules or ions in the system, can lead to an incorrect interpretation of the equilibrium sorption behaviour.

REFERENCES

Barrer, R. M., Barries, J. A. and Rogers, M. G. (1962). *Trans. Faraday Soc.*, **58,** 2473.

Barrer, R. M. (1968). "Diffusion and Permeation in Heterogeneous Media." *In* "Diffusion in Polymers," (Eds. Crank, J. and Park, G. S.). Academic Press, New York and London.

Bennion, D. N. and Rhee, B. W. (1969). *Ind. Engng. Chem. Fundamentals*, **8,** 36.
Bergsma, F. and Kruissink, C. A. (1961). *Fortschr. Hochpolym Forsch.* **2,** 307.
Biefer, G. J. and Mason, S. G. (1959). *Trans. Faraday Soc.*, **55,** 1239.
Burgreen, D. and Nakache, F. R. (1964). *J. Phys. Chem.*, **68,** 1084.
Caramazza, R. A., Dorst, W., Hoeve, A. J. C. and Staverman, A. J. (1963). *Trans. Faraday Soc.*, **59,** 2415.
Carman, P. C. (1948). *Discuss. Faraday Soc.*, **3,** 72.
Cleland, R. L. (1965). *Trans. Faraday Soc.*, **61,** 336.
Davies, J. T. and Rideal, E. K. (1961). "Interfacial Phenomena." Academic Press, New York and London.
De Groot, S. R. and Mazur, P. (1962). "Nonequilibrium Thermodynamics." North-Holland Publishing Co., Amsterdam.
Eberly, P. E. Jr. and Vohsberg, D. B. (1965). *Trans. Faraday Soc.*, **61,** 2724.
Everett, D. H. (1964). *Trans. Faraday Soc.*, **60,** 1803.
Frisch, H. L. (1965). *Polymer Letters*, **3,** 13.
Greenkorn, R. A. and Kessler, D. R. (1969). *Ind. Engng. Chem.*, **61,** 14.
Helfferich, F. (1952). *Z. Electrochem.* **56,** 947.
Helfferich, F. (1962a). "Ion Exchange." McGraw-Hill, New York.
Helfferich, F. (1962b). *J. Phys. Chem.*, **66,** 39.
Helfferich, F. (1963a). *J. Phys. Chem.*, **67,** 1157.
Helfferich, F. (1963b). *J. Chem. Phys.*, **38,** 1688.
Helfferich, F. and Ocker, H. D. (1957). *Z. phys. Chem. Frankf. Ausg.* **10,** 214.
Helfferich, F. and Plesset, M. S. (1958). *J. Chem. Phys.* **28,** 418.
Hildreth, D. (1970). *J. Phys. Chem.*, **74,** 2006.
Kamal, I. and McLaughlin, E. (1966). *Trans. Faraday Soc.*, **62,** 1762.
Kedem, O. and Katchalsky, A. (1958). *Biochim. Biophys. Acta.*, **27,** 227.
Kedem, O. and Katchalsky, A. (1961). *J. Gen. Physiol.*, **45,** 143.
Kedem, O. and Katchalsky, A. (1963). *Trans. Faraday Soc.*, **59,** 1918.
Kozeny, J. (1927). *Sber. Akad. Wiss. Wien. Mathnaturiv. Kl. Abt. IIa*, **136,** 271.
Kressman, T. R. E., Stanbridge, P. A., and Tye, F. L. (1963). *Trans. Faraday Soc.*, **59,** 2139.
Laity, R. W. (1959a). *J. Chem. Phys.*, **30,** 682.
Laity, R. W. (1959b). *J. Phys. Chem.*, **63,** 80.
Lightfoot, E. N., Cussler, E. L. Jr., and Rettig, R. L. (1961). *Amer. Inst. Chem. Engng. J.*, **8,** 708.
McGregor, R. (1965). *J. Soc. Dyers. Colourists.*, **81,** 429.
McGregor, R. and Harris, P. W. (1969). "A Chemical Engineering Approach to Dyeing Problems: The Sorption of Acid Dyes by Polyamides" Research Monograph M. 20. Fibers Division, Allied Chemical Corporation, Petersburg.
McGregor, R. and Harris, P. W. (1970). *J. Applied Polym. Sci.* **14,** 513.
McHardy, W. J. (1962). Ph.D. Thesis, Aberdeen University.
Mackay, D. and Meares, P. (1959). *Kolloidzeitschr.*, **167,** 31.
Mackay, D. and Meares, P. (1960). *Kolloidzeitschr.*, **171,** 139.
Mackay, D. and Meares, P. (1961). *Kolloidzeitschr.*, **176,** 23.
Mackie, J. S. and Meares, P. (1955a). *Proc. Roy. Soc.*, **A232,** 510.
Mackie, J. S. and Meares, P. (1955b). *Proc. Roy. Soc.*, **A232,** 498.
Mackie, J. S. and Meares, P. (1956). *Discuss. Faraday Soc.*, **21,** 111.
Manecke, G. and Heller, H. (1956). *Discuss, Faraday Soc.*, **21,** 101.
Meares, P. (1958). *J. Chim. phys.*, **55,** 273.

Meares, P. (1966). *European Polymer J.*, **2,** 241.
Meares, P. (1968). "Transport in Ion-Exchange Polymers." *In* "Diffusion in Polymers" (Eds., J. Crank and G. S. Park). Academic Press, London and New York.
Mikulecky, D. C. and Caplan, S. R. (1966). *J. Phys. Chem.*, **70,** 3049.
Milicevic, B. and McGregor, R. (1967). *Textilveredlung*, **2,** 120.
Overbeck, J. Th. G. and Wijga, P. W. O. (1946). *Rec. Trav. Chim. Pays-Bas*, **65,** 556.
Overbeck, J. Th. G. (1952). "Electrokinetic Phenomena." *In* "Colloid Science," Vol. 1 (Ed., H. R. Kruyt). Elsevier, New York.
Prigogine, I. (1961). "Introduction to Thermodynamics of Irreversible Processes," 2nd Edn. Interscience, New York.
Rastogi, R. P. and Jha, K. M. (1966). *Trans. Faraday Soc.*, **62,** 585.
Rastogi, R. P. and Singh, K. (1966). *Trans. Faraday Soc.*, **62,** 1754.
Rice, C. L. and Whitehead, R. (1965). *J. Phys. Chem.*, **69,** 4017.
Scattergood, E. M. and Lightfoot, E. N. (1968). *Trans. Faraday Soc.*, **64,** 1135.
Scheidegger, A. E. (1957). "The Physics of Flow in Porous Media." University of Toronto Press, Toronto.
Schlögl, R. (1953). *Z. Elektrochem.*, **57,** 195.
Schlögl, R. (1954). *Z. Elektrochem.*, **58,** 672.
Schlögl, R. (1955). *Z. Physik. Chem.*, **3,** 73.
Schlögl, R. (1956). *Discuss. Faraday Soc.*, **21,** 46.
Schlögl, R. (1964). "Stofftransport durch Membranen." Steinkopff Verlag, Darmstadt.
Schlögl, R. and Schödel, U. (1955). *Z. phys. Chem. Frankf. Ausg.* **5,** 372.
Schlögl, R. and Stein, B. (1958). *Z. Elektrochem.*, **62,** 340.
Schmid, G. (1950). *Z. Elektrochem.*, **54,** 424.
Spiegler, K. S. (1958). *Trans. Faraday Soc.*, **54,** 1408.
Spiegler, K. S. and Kedem, L. (1966). *Desalination*, **1(4),** 311.
Standing, H. A., Warwicker, J. O., and Willis, H. F. (1947). *J. Textile Inst.*, **38,** T 335.
Staverman, A. J. (1952). *Trans. Faraday Soc.*, **48,** 176.
Staverman, A. J., Kruissink, C. A., and Pals, D. T. F. (1966). *Trans. Faraday Soc.*, **62,** 2805.
Talen, J. L. and Staverman, A. J. (1966). *Trans. Faraday Soc.*, **62,** 2794.
Thain, J. F. (1964). Ph.D. Thesis. Aberdeen University.
Toyoshima, Y., Kobatake, Y., and Fujita, H. (1967). *Trans. Faraday Soc.*, **63,** 2828.
Whitaker, S. (1969). *Ind. Engng. Chem.*, **61,** 14.
Wills, G. B. and Lightfoot, E. N. (1966). *Ind. Engng Chem. Fundamentals*, **5,** 114.
Wills, G. B. (1967). *Trans. Faraday Soc.*, **63,** 579.

Chapter 14 Convective Diffusion to a Solid Surface

I. BASIC EQUATIONS

The transfer of chemical components to or from a solid surface immersed in a solution takes place both by convection with the flow of the solution and by diffusion in the solution. This combination of mass transfer processes is known as *convective diffusion*.

Since even pure diffusion in liquids can be an extremely complex process (Chapter 11), we shall for simplicity consider in this chapter only a very dilute solution of a single nonionic solute.

The solution behaves as an incompressible Newtonian fluid of constant density ρ and constant shear viscosity η. The flow velocities are low and are in the laminar region to which the Navier–Stokes equation can be applied. The solute forms an ideally dilute solution in the solvent component.

In real systems complications may arise from the presence of other components, from diffusion potentials, from local variations in density and from frame of reference effects. Care is necessary in extending the results of this chapter to more complex systems.

The equation of conservation for the solute for the assumptions stated is

$$\frac{\partial c}{\partial t} = D\,\nabla^2 c - \boldsymbol{u}\cdot\text{grad}\,c \tag{14.1}$$

because the solute can be assumed to obey Fick's first law, i.e.

$$\boldsymbol{j} = -D\,\text{grad}\,c \tag{14.2}$$

and the solution is so dilute that frame of reference effects are negligible, i.e.

$$\boldsymbol{j} = (J)_M = (J)_C = (J)_V \cdots \text{for } \boldsymbol{u} = 0 \cdots \tag{14.3}$$

Equation (14.1) is the *convective diffusion equation* for the mass transfer of the solute. In Cartesian coordinates it becomes

$$\frac{\partial c}{\partial t} = D\left\{\frac{\partial^2 c}{\partial x^2} + \frac{\partial^2 c}{\partial y^2} + \frac{\partial^2 c}{\partial z^2}\right\} - \left\{u_x\frac{\partial c}{\partial x} + u_y\frac{\partial c}{\partial y} + u_z\frac{\partial c}{\partial z}\right\} \tag{14.4}$$

A problem in convective diffusion can not be solved without information about the velocity $\boldsymbol{u}$ as a function of position and time. The Navier–Stokes equation when written in terms of the partial time derivative $\partial\boldsymbol{u}/\partial t$ takes the form

$$\frac{\partial \boldsymbol{u}}{\partial t} + \boldsymbol{u} \cdot \operatorname{grad} \boldsymbol{u} + \operatorname{grad}(p/\rho) - \nu \nabla^2 \boldsymbol{u} - \boldsymbol{g} = 0 \tag{14.5}$$

which is equivalent to the following set of equations in Cartesian Coordinates

$$\left.\begin{aligned}
\frac{\partial u_x}{\partial t} + u_x \frac{\partial u_x}{\partial x} + u_y \frac{\partial u_x}{\partial y} + u_z \frac{\partial u_x}{\partial z} &= -\frac{1}{\rho}\frac{\partial p}{\partial x} + \nu \nabla^2 u_x + g_x \\
\frac{\partial u_y}{\partial t} + u_x \frac{\partial u_y}{\partial x} + u_y \frac{\partial u_y}{\partial y} + u_z \frac{\partial u_y}{\partial z} &= -\frac{1}{\rho}\frac{\partial p}{\partial y} + \nu \nabla^2 u_y + g_y \\
\frac{\partial u_z}{\partial t} + u_x \frac{\partial u_z}{\partial x} + u_y \frac{\partial u_z}{\partial y} + u_z \frac{\partial u_z}{\partial z} &= -\frac{1}{\rho}\frac{\partial p}{\partial z} + \nu \nabla^2 u_z + g_z
\end{aligned}\right\} \tag{14.6}$$

The conservation of mass for the solution as a whole requires

$$\frac{\partial u_x}{\partial x} + \frac{\partial u_y}{\partial y} + \frac{\partial u_z}{\partial z} = 0 \tag{14.7}$$

Equations (14.6) and (14.7) can not be solved for u_x, u_y, u_z until the problem is specified in more detail. The *boundary conditions* will be determined by the shape, size, and location of any solid objects in the fluid, by the shape and dimensions of the boundaries of the fluid, and by the velocity of the fluid at given reference points in the system. The *initial conditions* will specify for example the initial velocities and pressures at certain points in the system.

The simplest situations occur when the fluid flow is *steady*, i.e. when $\partial\boldsymbol{u}/\partial t = 0$ at all points in the fluid, but even then mathematical solutions of equations (14.6) and (14.7) are extremely difficult to obtain for even the simplest three-dimensional systems. A reduction of the problem to one of flow in two dimensions does not always make a solution attainable, even for two-dimensional flow past obstacles of very simple geometrical shape.

The more important features of convective diffusion can fortunately be revealed by the analysis of certain very simple two-dimensional problems as outlined in the useful monograph by Levich (1962).

II. CONVECTIVE DIFFUSION TO AN "INSTANTANEOUSLY ADSORBING" SURFACE

A flat plate is immersed in the solution, which flows with a steady mainstream velocity u_0 parallel to the surfaces of the plate as in Fig. 13. The x-axis coincides with the flow direction and the origin of the x-axis is at the leading

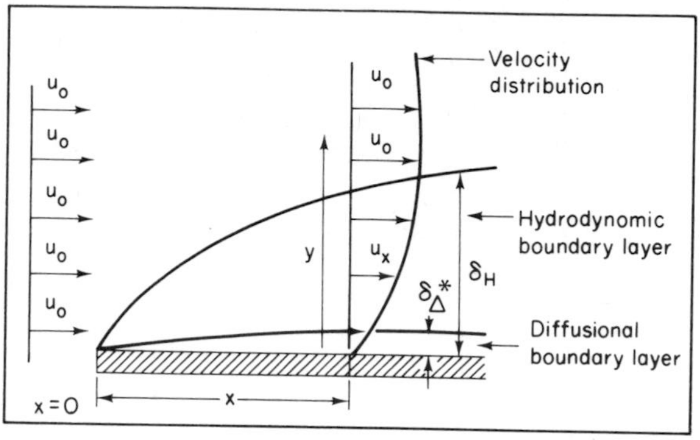

Fig. 13. *A Simple Problem in Convective Diffusion to a Flat Plate.* (Reproduced by permission from Levich, 1962). The horizontal arrows represent the fluid velocity μ_x in magnitude and direction, at the point of origin of the arrows. μ_0 is the main stream velocity and the fluid is in steady flow. The diffusional boundary layer σ_D is about one tenth the thickness of the hydrodynamic boundary layer σ_H in water, but both are parabolic in shape.

edge of the plate. The y-axis is normal to this direction and extends into the solution above the plate.

The solute molecules are instantaneously sorbed by the solid on contact with its surfaces: we have an "*instantaneously adsorbing*" *surface*. This gives the following boundary condition in the layer of liquid at $y = 0$, adjacent to the surface

$$c = 0 \quad \text{at} \quad y = 0 \quad \text{for all } t \tag{14.8}$$

As one moves away from the surface in the y-direction the solute concentration increases to that of the bulk of the solution

$$c \to c^0 \quad \text{as} \quad y \to \infty \quad \text{for all } t \tag{14.9}$$

We shall consider only a *steady state* of convective diffusion (Levich, 1962) for which Eqn (14.4) becomes

$$D\frac{\partial^2 c}{\partial y^2} = u_x\frac{\partial c}{\partial x} + u_y\frac{\partial c}{\partial y} \tag{14.10}$$

It has been assumed that diffusion occurs predominantly in the y-direction. To calculate the convective diffusion flux to the surface we must solve Eqn (14.10) for c as a function of the coordinates x and y, or for $(\partial c/\partial y)_{y=0}$ for different values of x

$$\begin{array}{l}\text{Convective Diffusion Flux}\\ \text{at point } x \text{ on Surface}\end{array} = D\left[\left(\frac{\partial c}{\partial y}\right)_{y=0}\right]_x \tag{14.11}$$

To do this the Navier–Stokes equation must be solved for the steady state flow, under the specified boundary conditions.

Levich (1962) assumes that external forces are negligible, and that $\partial^2 u_x/\partial y^2 \gg \partial^2 u_x/\partial x^2$, i.e. the changes in the second derivative of the x-component of the fluid velocity occur primarily normal to the surface.

The first Eqn of the set (14.6) becomes, for example

$$u_x \frac{\partial u_x}{\partial x} + u_y \frac{\partial u_y}{\partial x} = -\frac{1}{\rho}\frac{\partial p}{\partial x} + \nu \frac{\partial^2 u_x}{\partial y^2} \tag{14.12}$$

The fluid layer adjacent to the solid is assumed to be stationary with respect to the solid, so that the boundary conditions on the plate are

$$u_x = u_y = 0 \quad \text{at} \quad y = 0 \quad \text{for } x \geqslant 0 \tag{14.13}$$

$$u_x \to u^0 \quad \text{as} \quad y \to \infty \quad \text{for } x \geqslant 0 \tag{14.14}$$

We shall not discuss here the mathematical details of the solution of these equations, which leads to expressions for the variation of u_x and c with the x- and y-coordinates. The results are shown schematically in Fig. 14 (Levich, 1962).

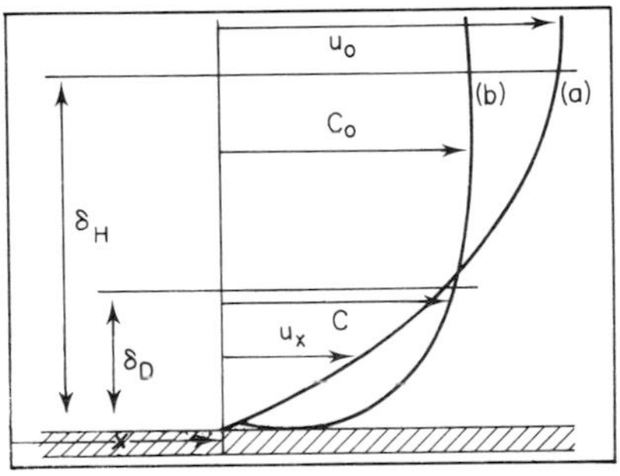

Fig. 14. *The Velocity and Concentration Distributions Near the Surface of the Plate.* (Reproduced by permission from Levich, 1962). Curve (b) shows the variation of solute concentration C, and curve (a) shows the variation of fluid velocity μ_x, with distance y above the surface of the plate at the point x. The curves apply to the steady state of convective, diffusion to an "instantaneously adsorbing" surface.

We may identify two distinct regions in the vicinity of the solid surface. The *hydrodynamic boundary layer* may be defined in several ways but we shall define it as that region of fluid (adjacent to the surface) in which the fluid velocity rises from zero at the solid surface to, say, 99% of the main stream velocity u^0. The thickness of this layer above any point on the surface is δ_H^*. The fluid velocity decreases within the layer as the surface is approached and so a point is eventually reached at which diffusion begins to play an important part in supplying solute to the solid surface.

At this point concentration gradients begin to appear in the fluid and the local concentration of solute c begins to fall below the mainstream concentration c^0. We enter the *diffusional boundary layer* of thickness δ_D^* within

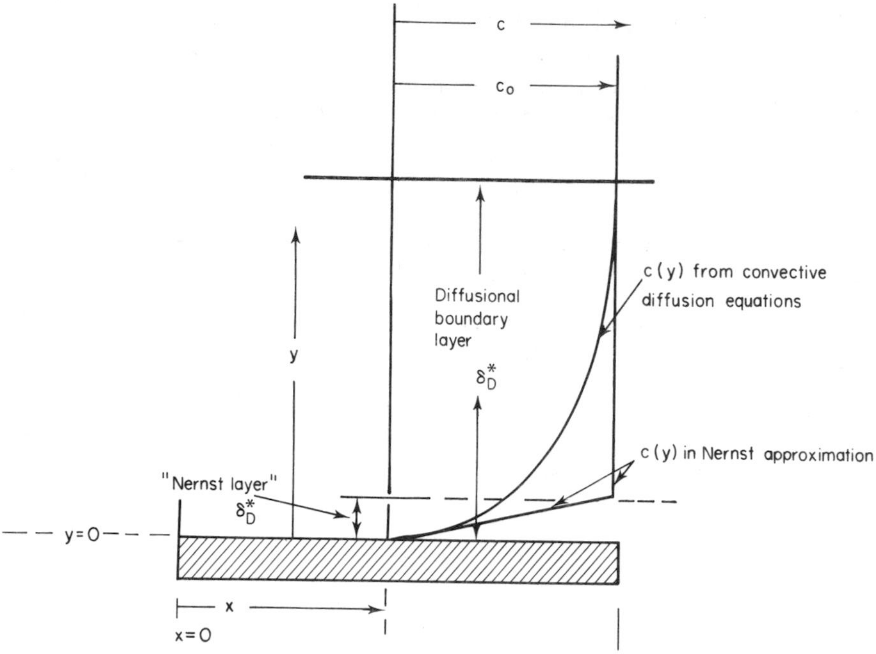

Fig. 15. *The Apparent Thickness* δ_D *of the Nernst Diffusional Boundary Layer* (*Schematic*). The smooth curve $c(y)$ represents the true concentration distribution above the plate. The Nernst model replaces this by the linear approximation in the "Nernst Layer."

which solute transport occurs both by convection and by diffusion. Except at the solid surface the liquid in the diffusional boundary layer will *not* normally be stationary. The diffusional boundary layer thickness δ_D^* will be defined here as the layer of fluid within which the concentration of solute rises to 99% of the main stream concentration c_0 as one moves away from the surface along the y-axis. δ_D^* will be found to be related to δ_H^*.

In Nernst's original approach to this problem (Nernst, 1904) the liquid within the diffusional boundary layer was assumed to be stationary and the supply of solute to the surface was represented as taking place by a quasi-steady-state diffusion process across this boundary layer of thickness δ_D, i.e. (Fig. 15)

$$\frac{\partial c}{\partial t} = D\frac{\partial^2 c}{\partial y^2} = 0 \quad \text{in} \quad 0 < y < \delta_D \tag{14.15}$$

with

$$c = 0 \quad \text{at} \quad y = 0 \qquad x \geqslant 0 \quad \text{all } t \tag{14.16}$$

and

$$c = c_0 \quad \text{at} \quad y = \delta_D \qquad x \geqslant 0 \quad \text{all } t \tag{14.17}$$

The solution of Eqn (14.15) for these boundary conditions is (Crank, 1956)

$$c = (y/\delta_D)c_0 \qquad 0 \leqslant y \leqslant \delta_D \tag{14.18}$$

and the convective diffusion flux to the surface is

$$-(J_y) = D\frac{c_0}{\delta_D} \qquad x \geqslant 0, \tag{14.19}$$

i.e. in this model the surface is treated as if it were *uniformly* accessible to the solute. The total flux to the surface of area A is simply $-A(J_y)$.

This model is convenient but unrealistic because the surface is not in fact uniformly accessible to the solute, and the concentration gradient in the diffusional boundary layer is rarely linear.

We may however retain Eqn (14.19) because it is conveniently simple in form, and regard it as a definition of the *apparent thickness* δ_D of the diffusional boundary layer.

If the convective diffusion flux $-(J)_y$ is correctly calculated from the convective diffusion equations then δ_D can be calculated from Eqn (14.19) and the nature of the deviations from Nernst's simple model will become

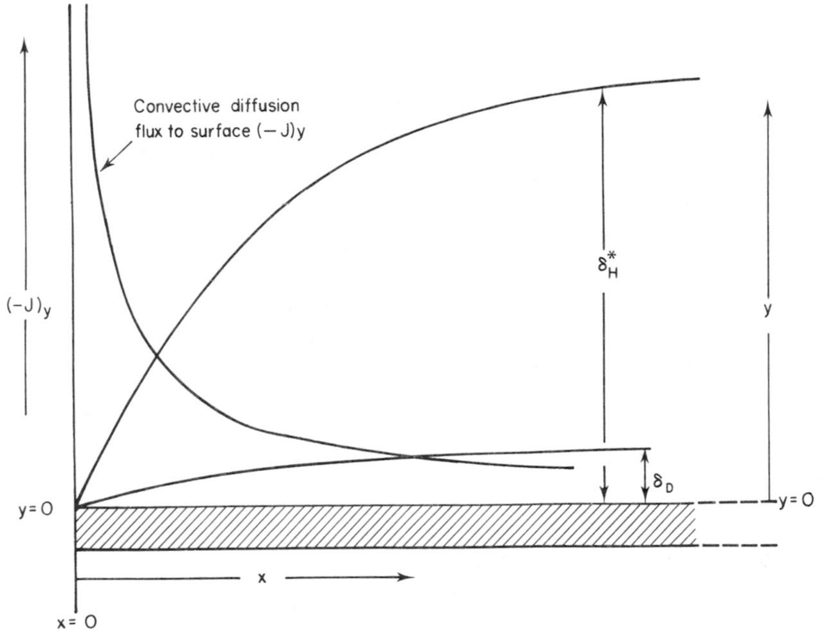

Fig. 16. *The Hydrodynamic and Diffusional Boundary Layers on a Flat Plate, and the Local Convective Diffusion Flux (Schematic).*
(Adapted with permission from Levich, 1962). The convective diffusion flux $(-J)y$ approaches infinity in the limit as $x \to 0$ and $\delta_D \to 0$.

clear. We shall use these apparent values of δ_D from the Nernst model in the rest of this chapter, without by this implying that the boundary layer is assumed to be static except of course at $y = 0$ on the surface.

For the flat plate in the present problem Levich (1962) obtains the result

$$\delta_D \approx 3\left(\frac{D}{\nu}\right)^{\frac{1}{3}}\left(\frac{\nu x}{u_0}\right)^{\frac{1}{2}} \approx 0.6\left(\frac{D}{\nu}\right)^{\frac{1}{3}}\delta_H^* \tag{14.20}$$

As shown in Fig. 16, the surface is *not* uniformly accessible to the solute: δ_D and hence also $-(J_y)$ take different values at different points on the surface. The calculated dependence of δ_D upon D clearly shows the limitations of the Nernst model.

The hydrodynamic and diffusional boundary layers are parabolic in shape and increase in thickness as x increases. The convective diffusion flux varies very markedly with x for small values of x, and at any point on the solid is found to vary as $(u_0)^{\frac{1}{2}}$.

The computations for an instantaneously adsorbing surface represent the *maximum possible* rate of supply of solute to a surface attainable by convective diffusion under the specified conditions.

III. DIMENSIONLESS GROUPS FROM THE CONVECTIVE DIFFUSION EQUATIONS

A. The Form of the Mathematical Solutions

Levich's monograph (1962) contains solutions to two-dimensional problems in convective diffusion for a variety of flow geometries and we shall use some of these results in later chapters.

A noticeable feature of the mathematical solutions is that certain combinations of key variables frequently occur. Consider Eqn (14.20). The fluid properties are indicated by the *dimensionless group* (D/ν) where both the diffusion coefficient D and the kinematic viscosity ν have the same dimensions $[L]^2[T]^{-1}$. This group characterises the solution for convective diffusion and when written as its inverse is known as the *Schmidt Number Sc*

$$Sc = \nu/D = \eta/\rho D \tag{14.21}$$

Suppose we wished to relate δ_D to a characteristic dimension of the flat plate, such as its length L. Then the dimensionless group (δ_D/L) would enter the problem and Eqn (14.20) could be written as

$$\left(\frac{\delta_D}{L}\right) = 3\left(\frac{D}{\nu}\right)^{\frac{1}{3}}\left(\frac{x}{L}\right)^{\frac{1}{2}}\left(\frac{\nu}{u_0 L}\right)^{\frac{1}{2}} \tag{14.22}$$

in which the additional dimensionless groups (x/L) and (ν/u_0L) appear. The group (ν/u^0L) characterises the fluid flow regime and its inverse is known as the *Reynolds Number*, *Re*

$$Re = \frac{u_0 L}{\nu} = \frac{\rho u_0 L}{\eta} \tag{14.23}$$

Equation (14.19) gives the convective diffusion flux across a Nernst layer of thickness δ_D. We can relate this to the flux that would be expected across a Nernst layer of thickness L

$$\frac{-(J_y)_{\delta_D}}{-(J_y)_L} = \frac{Dc_0}{\delta_D} \times \frac{L}{Dc_0} = \frac{L}{\delta_D} \tag{14.24}$$

This ratio characterises the efficiency of the mass transfer process and is known as the *Nusselt Number*, *Nu*

$$Nu = L/\delta_D \tag{14.25}$$

Equation (14.22) now becomes

$$Nu^{-1} = 3Sc^{-\frac{1}{3}} \cdot Re^{\frac{1}{2}}(x/L)^{\frac{1}{2}} \tag{14.26}$$

or, more generally, we have

$$Nu = Nu(Sc, Re, x/L) \tag{14.27}$$

This equation expresses a common feature of even the most complex convective diffusion processes. The convective diffusion flux, in the dimensionless form *Nu*, can be expressed as a function of the Schmidt and Reynolds numbers.

This could have been deduced by "inspectional analysis" of the underlying differential equations and boundary conditions.

B. "Inspectional Analysis" of the Differential Equations and Boundary Conditions

We introduce a characteristic length L, a characteristic time τ, a characteristic velocity u_0 and a characteristic concentration c_0, so as to write the equations in terms of the following dimensionless variables

$$\bar{x} = x/L; \quad \bar{u}_x = u_x/u_0$$

$$\bar{y} = y/L; \quad \bar{u}_y = u_y/u_0 \tag{14.28}$$

$$\bar{z} = z/L; \quad \bar{u}_z = u_z/u_0$$

$$\bar{t} = t/\tau; \quad \bar{c} = c/c_0 \tag{14.29}$$

In terms of these variables the convective diffusion equation becomes

$$\frac{\partial c}{\partial t} = \left(\frac{D\tau}{L^2}\right)\left\{\frac{\partial^2 \bar{c}}{\partial \bar{x}^2} + \frac{\partial^2 \bar{c}}{\partial \bar{y}^2} + \frac{\partial^2 \bar{c}}{\partial \bar{z}^2}\right\} - \left(\frac{u_0\tau}{L}\right)\left(\bar{u}_x \cdot \frac{\partial \bar{c}}{\partial \bar{x}} + \bar{u}_y \frac{\partial \bar{c}}{\partial \bar{y}} + \bar{u}_2 \frac{\partial \bar{c}}{\partial \bar{z}}\right) \quad (14.30)$$

Equation (14.30) has been obtained from Eqn (14.4) by a *transformation of variables* which has preserved the essential features of Eqn (14.4). This type of transformation is known as a *similarity transformation* and the dimensionless groups $(D\tau/L^2)$ and $(u_0\tau/L)$ in Eqn (14.30) are particular *similarity parameters* (Birkhoff, 1955; Ames, 1965). Systems of similar geometry will behave in a similar way only if these similarity groups or parameters have the same value in each system. The theories of modelling systems, or of scaling them up or down in size, are based on this principle. It is for this reason that dimensionless groups can be so useful. (Langhaar, 1951; Catchpole and Fulford, 1966).

In the absence of convection ($u_0 = 0$) we have pure diffusion determined by the *Fourier* number $\mathscr{F}o_M$ for diffusive mass transfer

$$\mathscr{F}o_M = \frac{D\tau}{L^2} \quad (14.31)$$

This dimensionless group invariably occurs in the mathematical solutions of diffusion problems (Crank, 1956).

The relative importance of mass transfer by convection and diffusion is determined by the ratio of the two dimensionless groups in Eqn (14.30). This ratio is the *Peclet number* Pe_M for mass transfer

$$Pe_M = \left(\frac{u_0\tau}{L}\right)\bigg/\left(\frac{D\tau}{L^2}\right) = \frac{u_0 L}{D} \quad (14.32)$$

When the Peclet number is very high, mass transfer by convection predominates in the fluid and the diffusional boundary layer is very thin. When the Peclet number is small the diffusional boundary layer is much thicker and the concentration gradients may extend well into the liquid.

The Peclet number is influenced both by the flow regime and the properties of the liquid, i.e.

$$Pe_M = \frac{u_0 L}{D} = \left(\frac{u_0 L}{\nu}\right)\left(\frac{\nu}{D}\right) = Re \cdot Sc. \quad (14.33)$$

A similar analysis may be applied to the Navier Stokes equation, in component form, if we introduce a reference pressure p_0 and make the simplifying assumption of steady flow

$$\bar{u}_x \frac{\partial \bar{u}_x}{\partial \bar{x}} + \bar{u}_y \frac{\partial \bar{u}_x}{\partial \bar{y}} + \bar{u}_z \frac{\partial \bar{u}_x}{\partial \bar{z}} = -\left(\frac{p_0}{\rho(u_0)^2}\right)\frac{\partial \bar{p}}{\partial \bar{x}} + \left(\frac{\nu}{Lu_0}\right)\nabla^2 \bar{u}_x + \left(\frac{g_x L}{(u_0)^2}\right) \quad (14.34)$$

The dimensionless groups which determine the relative effects of the three terms on the right-hand side of Eqn (14.34) are the *Froude number*, *Fr* (gravitational effects)

$$Fr \equiv (u_0{}^2/Lg_x) \quad (14.35)$$

the *Reynolds Number Re* (viscous effects) and the *Euler Number*, *Eu* (inertial effects)

$$Eu \equiv p_0/\rho u_0{}^2 \quad (14.36)$$

If the inertial and gravitational effects are negligible the steady fluid flow regime is characterised by the Reynolds Number *Re*, for the specific geometry and dimensions of the system. Generally it is necessary that $Re \ll 1$, which is the region of so-called "creeping flow." The dimensions and the geometry of the system influence the problem through the formulation of the boundary conditions, which themselves may be written in dimensionless form. An extension of these ideas to systems in turbulent flow is possible (Levich, 1962).

We may conclude from the "inspectional analysis" of the differential equations for the present problem that the mathematical solutions of convective diffusion problems in the laminar flow regime will involve the dimensionless groups *Re*, *Nu* and *Sc*, i.e.

$$f(Nu, Re, Sc) = 0 \quad (14.37)$$

This knowledge can be made use of in situations in which an exact mathematical solution of the problem is impossible, and it can be used to ensure that systems of similar geometry but of different dimensions will behave in a similar fashion.

If the surface of a solid is not uniformly accessible to the solute it is necessary to introduce local dimensionless groups.

C. The Dimensional Analysis of Convective Diffusion Processes

In some situations even the differential equations and boundary conditions for a problem can not be written down. Often however the important variables are known.

If the important variables are known the methods of *dimensional analysis* are available to resolve them into sets of independent dimensionless groups in terms of which the behaviour can be described. The methods are generally based on *Buckingham's π Theorem* (Langhaar, 1951) but the principles of Group Theory can also be used (Fleischmann, 1951). Explicit examples are given by Langhaar (1951), Palacios (1964), and by Fulford and Pei (1969).

A problem related to dyeing has been examined by Milicevic and McGregor (1966), who considered the sorption of solute by an "infinite cylinder" of length L and radius a ($L \gg a$) immersed in a dye solution.

1. Sorption from a Well-stirred "Infinite Dyebath"

The "infinite cylinder" is immersed in a very efficiently stirred solution of dye of constant concentration. Since $L \gg a$ we do not consider sorption through the ends of the cylinder and the radius a is sufficient to characterise the cylinder. We expect the sorption process to involve the diffusion of dye into the cylinder with a diffusion coefficient D^ϕ, and the final equilibrium concentration of dye in the cylinder is C_∞^ϕ. We are interested in the form of dependence of C_t^ϕ, the dye sorption at time t, on the other variables. We suppose that these variables can be related by a *dimensionally homogeneous* equation which we shall write formally as

$$f(C_t^\phi, C_\infty^\phi, D^\phi, a, t) = 0 \tag{14.38}$$

A dimensionally homogeneous equation is independent of the choice of a particular system of units for measuring the variables.

Buckingham's π-Theorem (Langhaar, 1951) states that any dimensionally homogeneous equation can be transformed into a dimensionless form

$$F(\pi_1, \pi_2, \pi_3, \ldots \pi_p) = 0 \tag{14.39}$$

where $\pi_1, \pi_2, \ldots \pi_p$ are independent dimensionless products of the variables.

We do this by using the fundamental dimensions of mass $[M]$, length $[L]$ and time $[T]$ to construct a *dimensional matrix* for the variables of the problem.

	C_t^ϕ	D^ϕ	C_∞^ϕ	a	t
$[M]$	1	0	1	0	0
$[L]$	−3	2	−3	1	0
$[T]$	0	−1	0	0	1

(14.40)

The components of the matrix are the exponents or powers to which the fundamental dimensions must be raised when writing the dimensions of the variables. For example, the components in the vertical column under C_t^ϕ simply state that the dimensions of C_t^ϕ are $[M][L]^{-3}$. The algebraic theory of dimensional analysis states that the number (p) of independent dimensionless products $\pi_1, \pi_2, \ldots \pi_p$ which can be obtained from a dimensionally-homogeneous equation relating n variables is given by $(n - r)$, where r is the *rank* of the dimensional matrix (Langhaar, 1951). In the present example we have $n = 5$ and the rank of the matrix (14.40) is $r = 3$. We therefore expect to be able to replace Eqn (14.38) by a dimensionless equation of the type

$$F(\pi_1; \pi_2) = 0 \tag{14.41}$$

Each of the products can be written in the general form

$$\pi_i = (C_t^{\phi})^{a_i}(D^{\phi})^{b_i}(C_{\infty}^{\phi})^{c_i}(a)^{d_i}(t)^{e_i} \tag{14.42}$$

where the exponents a_i, b_i ... are to be chosen in such a way that π_i is dimensionless.

The dimensional matrix is now used to construct a set of equations relating these exponents in the desired manner.

The necessary condition for π_i to be dimensionless in mass units is written by using the first row of the matrix to multiply the corresponding exponents, and equating the result to zero, i.e.

$$(a_i \times 1) + (b_i \times 0) + (c_i \times 1) + (d_i \times 0) + (e_i \times 0) = 0$$

so that

$$a_i + c_i = 0 \tag{14.43}$$

For π_i to be dimensionless in units of length

$$(a_i \times -3) + (b_i \times 2) + (c_i \times -3) + (d_i \times 1) + (e_i \times 0) = 0$$

or

$$-3a_i + 2b_i - 3c_i + d_i = 0 \tag{14.44}$$

For π_i to be dimensionless in units of time we find

$$-b_i + e_i = 0 \tag{14.45}$$

The set of equations (14.43), (14.44) and (14.45) has more than one solution. Each solution gives rise to a particular set of dimensionless products. Standard matrix methods have been developed for the solution of this type of problem in dimensional analysis (Langhaar, 1951), but there is an arbitrariness in the procedures since the particular set of dimensionless products obtained is influenced by the detailed arrangement of the matrices when the problem is set up in matrix form for solution. The matrices can generally be so arranged that the similarity variables to be expected from the physical nature of the problem are obtained, in preference to other equally valid but less convenient sets of dimensionless products.

For the present problem the solution can be obtained in the form (Milicevic and McGregor, 1966)

	a_i	b_i	c_i	d_i	e_i
π_1	1	0	−1	0	0
π_2	0	1	0	−2	1

(14.46)

The dimensional analysis leads to the result

$$F(C_t^\phi/C_\infty^\phi;\ D^\phi t/a^2) = 0 \tag{14.47}$$

in which we recognise the Fourier number $\mathcal{F}o_M$ for diffusion. The mathematical solution of this problem can in fact be written in terms of these two variables (Crank, 1956) and the behaviour is shown graphically in Fig. 17.

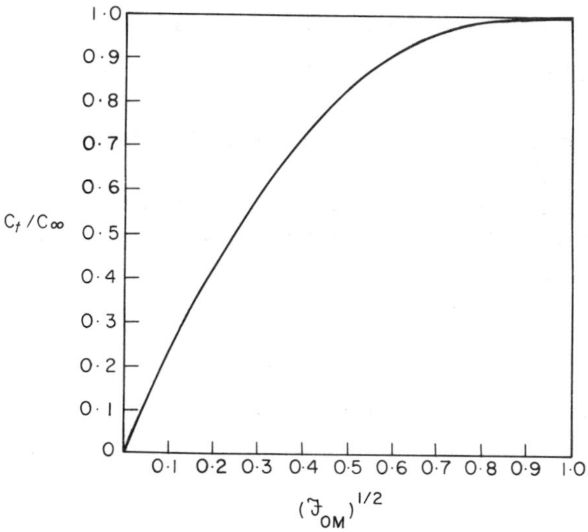

Fig. 17. *Sorption from a Constant Surface Concentration* ("*Infinite Cylinder*"). (Reproduced with permission from Crank, 1956). The relative sorption (C_t/C_∞) is a single-valued function of the Fourier number $\mathcal{F}_{OM}$ and approaches unity asymptotically as $\mathcal{F}_{OM} \to \infty$.

The mathematical solution gives more information. The dimensional analysis isolates the important dimensionless products but it does not say anything about the form of the relationship between these variables, nor does it give any information on the relative importance of the groups or products for the experimental behaviour. The parameter (C_t^ϕ/C_∞^ϕ) for example, is very sensitive to changes in $\mathcal{F}o_M$ when $\mathcal{F}o_M$ is small, but is comparatively insensitive to $\mathcal{F}o_M$ when $\mathcal{F}o_M$ is large.

The mathematical solution is more informative, but its information may be misleading if the boundary conditions have been incorrectly stated. The dimensional analysis is not affected by this difficulty except insofar as its completeness is concerned.

2. A Simple Convective Diffusion Process

Suppose that the cylinder sorbs solute so rapidly that it behaves as an instantaneously adsorbing surface. We can now neglect diffusion in the cylinder and consider only the convective diffusion in the solution. The convective diffusion process is in the laminar flow regime and we suppose the solution to be flowing with a steady velocity u_0 and to have a constant concentration c_0. The dye diffusion in the liquid is described by a constant diffusion coefficient D^σ. We are interested in the steady flux J_D of dye to the cylinder and we expect that

$$f(J_D, u_0, \nu, D^\sigma, c_0, a) = 0 \tag{14.48}$$

Dimensional analysis leads to the result

$$F\left(\frac{J_D a}{D^\sigma c_0}, \frac{u_0 a}{D^\sigma}, \frac{\nu}{D^\sigma}\right) = 0 \tag{14.49}$$

in which we recognise the Nusselt number

$$Nu = \left(\frac{J_D a}{D^\sigma c_0}\right) = \frac{a}{\delta_D} \tag{14.50}$$

as well as the Schmidt number (ν/D^σ) and the Peclet number $(u_0 a/D^\sigma)$, i.e. dimensional analysis leads to the result

$$Nu = Nu(Pe, Sc) = Nu(Re, Sc) \tag{14.51}$$

3. Intermediate Sorption Kinetics

If we have a sorption process influenced by diffusion in the cylinder and by convective diffusion in the dyebath the analysis is more complex. A steady state will not generally be found and so the flux J_D is not a suitable variable. It is better to link the processes through the parameter δ_D for the apparent thickness of the diffusional boundary layer.

The cylinder is initially free from dye. The initial dyebath concentration is C_0^σ and at equilibrium it is C_∞^σ. Since the cylinder is initially free of dye it is possible to calculate the concentration C_t^σ in the solution at time t from the quantities $C_0{}^\sigma$, C_∞^σ, C_t^ϕ, $C_\infty{}^\phi$ and the principle of conservation of mass. $C_t{}^\sigma$ is therefore not an independent variable.

We have

$$f(C_t{}^\phi, C_\infty^\phi, C_0^\sigma, C_\infty^\sigma, a, \delta_D, D^\sigma, D^\phi, t) = 0 \tag{14.52}$$

Dimensional analysis leads to the result (Milicevic and McGregor, 1966)

$$F\left(\frac{C_t{}^\phi}{C_\infty^\phi}, \frac{C_0{}^\sigma}{C_\infty^\sigma}, \frac{C_\infty{}^\sigma}{C_\infty{}^\phi}, \frac{a}{\sqrt{D^\phi t}}, \frac{\delta_D}{\sqrt{D^\phi t}}, \frac{D^\sigma}{D^\phi}\right) = 0 \tag{14.53}$$

For convenience in later chapters alternative variables can be used.

The *equilibrium distribution coefficient* K is

$$K = C_\infty^\phi / C_\infty^\sigma \tag{14.54}$$

A *rate parameter* Rp may be defined by

$$Rp = \frac{D^\sigma}{KD^\phi} \tag{14.55}$$

and an *exhaustion parameter* Ep can be introduced in the form

$$Ep = \frac{C_\infty{}^\phi}{C_0{}^\sigma} \tag{14.56}$$

We have

$$Ep = \alpha \cdot (\text{exh})_\infty \tag{14.57}$$

where the *liquor ratio* is

$$\alpha = V^\sigma / V^\phi \tag{14.58}$$

and the *exhaustion* of the solution at equilibrium is

$$(\text{exh})_\infty = \left(\frac{C_0^\sigma - C_\infty^\sigma}{C_0{}^\sigma} \right) \tag{14.59}$$

The new variables may be introduced into Eqn (14.53) if the absolute value of the determinant derived from the transformation matrix is unity, a restriction which arises from the application of Group Theory to these problems (Fleischmann, 1951; Milicevic and McGregor, 1966).

The final result is

$$F(C_t{}^\phi / C_\infty^\phi, K, Ep, Rp, \sqrt{\mathscr{F}o_M^\phi}, Nu) = 0 \tag{14.60}$$

and so the relative sorption $C_t{}^\phi / C_\infty^\phi$ even in this simple system is dependent on five independent dimensionless groups.

Only if all five of these similarity parameters have the same values in each system will two systems show similar behaviour.

In this analysis, all the parameters are average values for the cylinder or solution. In a more detailed analysis the non-uniform accessibility of the cylinder surface would have to be taken into account and local similarity parameters would have to be introduced (Levich, 1962).

IV. A SIMPLE MATHEMATICAL MODEL FOR INTERMEDIATE SORPTION KINETICS

The mathematical models of Chapter 12 can readily be adapted to include convective diffusion processes at the surfaces of a solid. For high values of the Peclet number we expect a thin, diffusional boundary layer of apparent thickness δ_D adjacent to the solid surface. A formal representation of the effects of this layer can be based on the Nernst model, and combined with the analysis of boundary resistances to diffusion in Chapter 12.

The concentration c^σ in the solution at the membrane surfaces is lower than the bulk concentration $c^{0\sigma}$ by virtue of the concentration gradients in the boundary layer, i.e.

$$(\mathscr{J})_{x=-l} = -\frac{D^\sigma(c^\sigma - c^{0\sigma})}{\delta_D} \tag{14.61}$$

in which D^σ is assumed constant. When Eqn (14.61) is combined with Eqns (12.27) to (12.31) we obtain the following boundary condition at $x = -l$

$$\left(\frac{\partial C^\phi}{\partial x}\right)_{x=-l} - h^0(C^\phi - C^\phi_\infty) = 0 \tag{14.62}$$

which has been obtained for a solution of constant concentration $c^{0\sigma} = c^\sigma_\infty$.

The boundary parameter h^0 is

$$h^0 = \frac{k_2^0 D^\sigma}{D^\phi(D^\sigma + k_1^0\delta_D)} \tag{14.63}$$

and the mathematical solutions involve the resistance parameter $L = h^0 l$ (Fig. 12).

Two limiting forms of behaviour are now apparent

(a) $k_1^0\delta_D \gg D^\sigma$

The boundary effects are now characterised by the parameter L

$$L = h^0 l = \frac{k_2^0 D^\sigma l}{D^\phi k_1^0 \delta_D} = \left(\frac{D^\sigma}{KD^\phi}\right)\left(\frac{l}{\delta_D}\right) \tag{14.64}$$

in which we recognise the rate parameter Rp and the Nusselt number Nu.

The situation $k_1^0\delta_D \gg D^\sigma$ corresponds to a sorption process in which the diffusional boundary layer resistance is the main contributor to the parameter L.

(b) $k_1^0\delta_D \ll D^\sigma$

Now we have

$$L = h^0 l = k_2^0 l / D^\phi \tag{14.65}$$

and it is the interfacial rate processes which dominate the parameter L as in Chapter 12.

In general we can expect the type of sorption behaviour shown in Fig. 12, with the boundary parameter L

$$L = \frac{k_2^0 D^\sigma l}{D^\phi(D^\sigma + k_1^0\delta_D)} \tag{14.66}$$

V. CONVECTIVE DIFFUSION AND MEMBRANE PROCESSES

The effects which surface resistances to mass transfer may have on permeation through a membrane have long been recognised (Barrer, 1939; Carslaw and Jaeger, 1947; Crank, 1956).

However, it is not often that the potentially serious effects that this type of phenomenon may have on orthodox measurements of diffusion coefficients using membranes are taken into account.

Consider a simple membrane system of the following type. For simplicity the concentrations in the solutions will be represented by lower case characters, in the membrane by upper case characters. A membrane of thickness l in the flow direction (x-coordinate) separates an ideally dilute solution of a single nonionic solute at concentration C_1 from a similar solution at concentration C_2 as in Fig. 18.

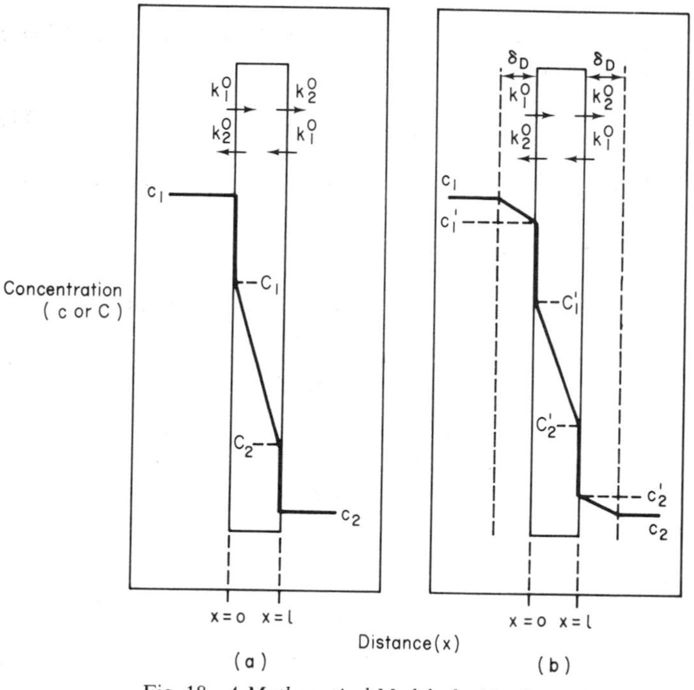

Fig. 18. *A Mathematical Model of a Membrane Process.* (Reproduced with permission from McGregor and Mahajan, 1962). Interfacial resistances to mass transfer modify the boundary relationships between the solution concentrations (c_1; c_2) and the membrane concentrations (C_1; C_2) as in Fig. (a). The presence of diffusional boundary layers introduces an additional modification Fig. (b).

The membrane is initially free from solute

$$C = 0 \quad \text{in} \quad 0 < x < l \quad \text{for } t \leqslant 0 \tag{14.67}$$

Diffusion of solute in the membrane is described by Fick's laws with a constant diffusion coefficient.

$$\frac{\partial C}{\partial t} = D^{\phi} \frac{\partial^2 C}{\partial x^2} \quad \text{in} \quad 0 < x < l \tag{14.68}$$

There are surface resistances to mass transfer at each interface and the radiation boundary conditions are

$$\left(\frac{\partial C}{\partial x}\right)_{x=0} - h_1(C_1 - C_{1\infty}) = 0 \quad \text{at } x = 0 \tag{14.69}$$

$$-\left(\frac{\partial C}{\partial x}\right)_{x=l} - h_2(C_2 - C_{2\infty}) = 0 \quad \text{at } x = l \tag{14.70}$$

$C_{1\infty}$ is the equilibrium concentration in the membrane at interface 1 ($x = 0$) for the solute concentration c_1 in solution 1. We assume that $c_1 = C_{1\infty}$ and remains constant.

$C_{2\infty}$ is the corresponding equilibrium concentration at interface 2 ($x = l$) for $c_2 = c_{2\infty} =$ const.

h_1 and h_2 may be different, but will be treated here as constants having the same values $h_1 = h_2 = h^0$.

Mathematical solutions of this problem have been given by Barrer (1939), Carslaw and Jaeger (1947), Crank (1956), and McGregor and Mahajan (1962).

The distribution of solute in the membrane in the steady state is

$$C = Ax + B \tag{14.71}$$

If $c_2 \to 0$ and therefore $c_1 \gg c_2$, a common experimental situation, then

$$A = -k_1^0 c_1/(2D^\phi + k_2^0 l) \tag{14.72}$$

and

$$B = k_1^0 c_1(D + k_2 l)/k_2^0(2D + k_2^0 l) \tag{14.73}$$

and the steady-state flux of solute is

$$J = -D^\phi \frac{\partial C}{\partial x} = -D^\phi A = \frac{D^\phi k_1^0 c_1}{(2D + k_2^0 l)} \tag{14.74}$$

In equations (14.72) to (14.74) we consider for simplicity only the interfacial resistances k_1^0 and k_2^0 (i.e. $k_1^0 \delta_D \ll D^\sigma$).

Experimentally, a steady state diffusion coefficient D_f would have been measured from the equation

$$J = D_f \frac{C_{1\infty}}{l} \tag{14.75}$$

in which there is the assumption of "*instantaneous equilibrium*" at interface 1 between the solution ($c_{1\infty}$) and the membrane ($c_{1\infty}$), i.e. since the solute behaves ideally in the membrane and in the solution

$$C_{1\infty} = K^0 c_{1\infty} = \frac{k_1^0}{k_2^0} c_{1\infty} \tag{14.76}$$

It follows from Eqns (14.74), (14.75), and (14.76) that

$$\left(\frac{D_f}{D^\phi}\right) = \frac{k_2^0 l}{2D + k_2^0 l} = \frac{hl}{(2 + hl)} \tag{14.77}$$

and

$$\lim_{hl \to \infty} D_f = D^\phi \tag{14.78}$$

The experimental coefficient D_f is equal to D^ϕ only *in the limit* as $hl \to \infty$. This limit may not be so readily attained as is usually supposed.

The steady state is often recognised by measuring the total quantity Q_t of solute which has passed through the membrane at time t, and by plotting Q_t against t as in Fig. 19.

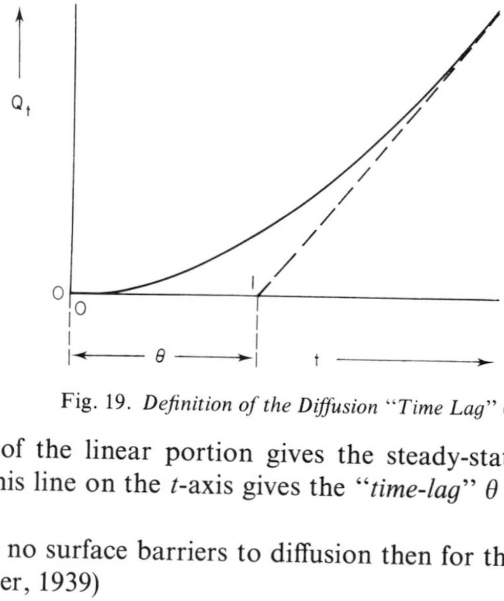

Fig. 19. *Definition of the Diffusion "Time Lag"* θ.

The slope of the linear portion gives the steady-state flux J, and the intercept of this line on the t-axis gives the "*time-lag*" θ in establishing the steady state.

If there are no surface barriers to diffusion then for the present problem we have (Barrer, 1939)

$$D = l^2/6\theta \tag{14.79}$$

This relationship no longer holds if surface barriers are present, and the application of Eqn (14.79) will define an experimental "time-lag" diffusion coefficient D_l, i.e.

$$D_l = l^2/6\theta \tag{14.80}$$

When symmetrical surface barriers are present and the situation is as assumed previously for the membrane in this discussion, then we find that (McGregor and Mahajan, 1962)

$$\left(\frac{D_l}{D^\phi}\right) = \frac{l^2}{6S(2 + hl)} \tag{14.81}$$

where

$$S = 2\sum_{1}^{\infty} \frac{(\alpha_n \sin \alpha_n l - h^0 \cos \alpha_n l)}{\alpha_n^2[(\alpha_n^2 + (h^0)^2)l + 2h^0]} \tag{14.82}$$

and α_n is the nth, non zero, positive root of

$$\tan \alpha_n l = \frac{2\alpha_n h^0}{(\alpha_n^2 - (h^0)^2)} \tag{14.83}$$

We also find

$$\left(\frac{D_f}{D_l}\right) = \left(\frac{6h^0}{l}\right) S \tag{14.84}$$

and for the sum S

$$\lim_{h^0 l \to \infty} S = \frac{l}{6h^0} \tag{14.85}$$

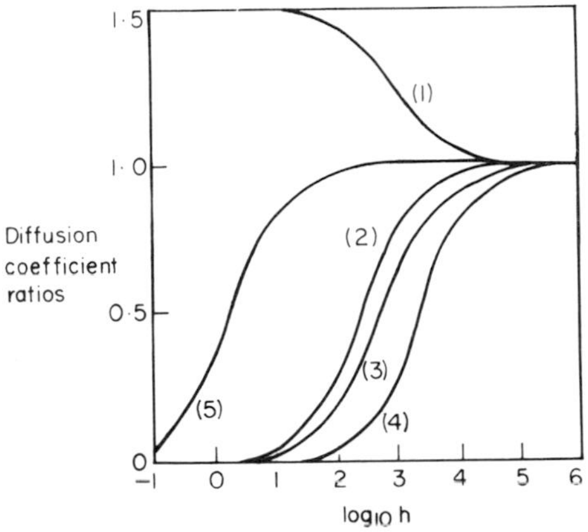

Fig. 20. *The Effect of Surface Barriers on Orthodox Diffusion Measurements Using Membranes.* (Reproduced with permission from McGregor and Mahajan, 1962). Curve 1 is the ratio $D_f(Dl$, curve 2 is D_f/D and curve 3 is D_f/D for a membrane of thickness $l = 8.6 \times 10^{-3}$ cm. The effect of membrane thickness is revealed by curves 4 and 5 which are for $l = 1.0 \times 10^{-3}$ cm and $l = 1.0$ cm, respectively, and represent D_f/D.

Consequently the experimental diffusion coefficients D_f and D_l will have the same values only *in the limit* as $h^0 l \to \infty$. When surface barriers are present we can expect

$$D_l < D_f < D^\phi \tag{14.86}$$

and the "time-lag" diffusion coefficient D_l will deviate more from the expected value D^ϕ than does the steady state diffusion coefficient Df.

Examples of the types of deviation to be expected are shown in Fig. 20. Although the analysis was made for $k_1^0 \delta_D \ll D^\sigma$, it also holds for the effects of symmetrical diffusional boundary layers ($k_1^0 \delta_D \gg D^\sigma$) if the parameter h^0 is interpreted appropriately.

These effects have been shown to be important in practical applications (McGregor *et al.*, 1965; Scattergood and Lightfoot, 1968) but it should be emphasised that additional factors such as the diffusion potentials complicate the problem in ionic systems (Helfferich and Schlögl, 1957). The approach used here is well known in ion exchange studies (Helfferich, 1962) and, crude though it may be by comparison with the analysis of diffusion in liquids in Chapter 11, it does at least indicate the types of effects to be anticipated.

REFERENCES

Ames, W. F. (1965). *Ind. Engng. Chem. Fund.*, **4,** 72.
Barrer, R. M. (1939). *Phil. Mag.*, **28,** 148.
Birkhoff, G. (1955). "Hydrodynamics." Dover Publications, New York.
Carslaw, H. S. and Jaeger, J. C. (1947). "Conduction of Heat in Solids." Oxford University Press, Oxford.
Catchpole, J. P. and Fulford, G. (1966). *Ind. Engng. Chem.*, **58,** 46.
Crank, J. (1956). "The Mathematics of Diffusion." Clarendon Press, Oxford.
Fleischmann, R. (1951). *Z. Physik.*, **129,** 377.
Fulford, G. D. and Pei, D. C. T. (1969). *Ind. Engng. Chem.*, **61,** 47.
Helfferich, F. (1962). "Ion Exchange." McGraw Hill, New York.
Helfferich, F. and Schlögl, R. (1957). *J. Chem. Phys.*, **26,** 5.
Langhaar, H. L. (1951). "Dimensional Analysis and Theory of Models." J. Wiley and Sons, New York.
Levich, V. G. (1962). "Physicochemical Hydrodynamics," Prentice-Hall, New Jersey.
McGregor, R. and Mahajan, I. Y. (1962). *Trans. Faraday Soc.*, **58,** 2484.
McGregor, R., Jadhav, J. S., and Mahajan, I. Y. (1965). *Trans. Faraday Soc.*, **61,** 2569.
Milicevic, B. and McGregor, R. (1966). *Helv. Chim. Acta.*, **49,** 2098.
Nernst, W. (1904). *Z. physik. Chem.*, **47,** 52.
Palacios, J. (1964). "Dimensional Analysis", Engl. Transl., Macmillan, London.
Scattergood, E. M. and Lightfoot, E. N. (1968). *Trans. Faraday Soc.*, **64,** 1135.

Chapter 15 Some Mechanistic Considerations

When diffusion processes are related to three-dimensional molecular motions as in Chapter 2 it is found that the diffusion coefficient D may be related to an *average distance* λ and to an *average frequency* ν for the diffusional "jumps" of the molecules.

$$D = \frac{\lambda^2 \nu}{6} \tag{15.1}$$

If diffusion occurs in some kind of regular space lattice then λ is related to the lattice dimensions. The experimental diffusion coefficients often show an exponential temperature dependence of the Arrhenius type, over sufficiently restricted temperatures ranges, i.e. (Barrer, 1937)

$$D = D^1 \exp(-E_D/RT) \tag{15.2}$$

D^1 is a pre-exponential factor, independent of temperature over the given temperature range. E_D is known as the experimental *activation energy* (per mole) for the diffusion process though, as we shall see, the term *apparent activation energy* is more correct.

I. EYRING'S THEORY OF REACTION RATES

The term activation energy implies a particular type of *activated process* in which a molecule may not execute a diffusion jump unless and until it has acquired energy in excess of the activation energy for the process. The normal fluctuations in the thermal energies of the molecules ensure that on average some finite fraction of the total number of molecules has the required energy and is able to diffuse.

Eyring's rate theory (Glasstone *et al.*, 1941) takes the viewpoint that only the molecule which diffuses requires activation energy, i.e. cooperative diffusive motions are not considered. A local equilibrium is assumed to exist between activated and normal molecules and the following expression is obtained for an ideally dilute solute exercising diffusion "jumps" in one dimension

$$D = \lambda^2 \cdot \frac{kT}{h} \cdot \frac{F^\ddagger}{F} \cdot \exp(-e_0/kT) \tag{15.3}$$

k is Boltzmann's constant, h is Planck's constant, e_0 is the activation energy per molecule and $F^\ddagger$ and F are partition functions for the activated and normal molecules, respectively. The quantity $(F^\ddagger\ F)\exp(-e_0/kT)$ is the equilibrium constant relating the concentrations of activated and normal molecules so that an alternative expression to (15.3) is

$$D = \lambda^2 \frac{kT}{h} \exp(-\Delta G^\ddagger/RT) = \lambda^2 \frac{kT}{h} \exp(\Delta S^\ddagger/R) \exp(-\Delta H^\ddagger/RT) \quad (15.4)$$

in which $\Delta G^\ddagger$, $\Delta H^\ddagger$, and $\Delta S^\ddagger$ are the activation "free energy," enthalpy and entropy (per mole) respectively.

If diffusion is accompanied by a negligible volume change it follows that (Glasstone *et al.*, 1941)

$$D = e\lambda^2 \frac{kT}{h} \exp(\Delta S^\ddagger/R) \exp(-E_D/RT) \quad (15.5)$$

so that the pre-exponential factor D^1 in Eqn (15.1) is related to the entropy changes on activation and to the jump dimensions by

$$D^1 = e\lambda^2 \left(\frac{kT}{h}\right) \exp(\Delta S^\ddagger/R) \quad (15.6)$$

If the activation step is viewed as the opening up of a "hole" in the fluid then the activation energy E_D should be some fraction of the energy of vaporization ΔE_{vap}, i.e.

$$E_D = \Delta E_{vap}/n \quad (15.7)$$

where the factor n may be very different from unity.

In non-ideal systems the assumption that only the diffusing species is involved in the rate determining step leads to the result (Glasstone *et al.*, 1941)

$$D = (\lambda_1^2 v_1)^0 \left(1 + \frac{\partial \ln f_1}{\partial \ln x_1}\right) \quad (15.8)$$

in which x_1 is the mole fraction and f_1 is the activity coefficient. The quantity $(\lambda_1^2 v_1)^0$ is as given in Eqns (15.4) and (15.5) for self diffusion in an ideally dilute system.

A. Applications to Fluid Systems

Since there is at least some short-range molecular order in a fluid (Pryde, 1966) and since Eyring's theory has the advantage of simplicity it is often used to describe diffusion in fluids.

For the limiting case of mutual diffusion in a binary nonionic fluid

(McLaughlin, 1960)

$$D_{11} = \frac{a_1^{\,2}}{v_f^{\frac{1}{3}}} \cdot \left(\frac{kT}{2\pi m}\right)^{\frac{1}{2}} \exp\left(-e_D/kT\right) \tag{15.9}$$

where a_1 is a characteristic jump distance, m is the molecular mass, e_D is the activation energy per molecule and v_f is the "*free volume*" in the fluid. v_f is a measure of the unoccupied free space in the fluid and is given approximately by (Glasstone *et al.*, 1941)

$$v_f^{\frac{1}{3}} \approx \frac{\alpha RTV^{\frac{1}{3}}}{N^{\frac{1}{3}}\,\Delta E_{\text{vap}}} \tag{15.10}$$

in which α is a geometrical constant which describes the molecular packing in the fluid, V is the molar volume and N is Avogadro's number. For regular arrays of hard spheres $\alpha = 2$. Alternatively v_f may be related as follows to the velocity (u_l) of sound in the liquid (Glasstone *et al.*, 1941) and in its gaseous vapour (u_v)

$$\frac{u_l}{u_v} \approx \left(\frac{v}{v_f}\right)^{\frac{1}{3}} \tag{15.11}$$

where v is the molecular volume.

The description of viscous flow on the basis of Eyring's theory is more complex. The shear viscosity η is found to depend on the applied shear stress so that the behaviour is in general predicted to be non-Newtonian. For sufficiently small shear stresses (McLaughlin, 1960; Glasstone *et al.*, 1941)

$$\eta = \frac{a_2}{a_1^{\,2} a_3 a_4}\left(2\pi mkT\right)^{\frac{1}{2}} v_f^{\frac{1}{3}} \exp\left(e_v/kT\right) \tag{15.12}$$

in which e_v is the activation energy per molecule for viscous flow. a_1, a_2, a_3, a_4 are characteristic distances within and between the different planes of molecules which may be identified in the fluid.

Calculations of η and D_{11} require specific assumptions about the parameters v_f, e_D, e_v, a_i and are not often in good agreement with experiment. However η can be estimated from Eqn (15.12) within about 100% for simple fluids (McLaughlin, 1960).

From Eqns (15.9) and (15.12)

$$\eta D_{11} = \frac{a_2}{a_3 a_4} \cdot kT \cdot \exp\left[(e_v - e_D)/kT\right] \tag{15.13}$$

whereas the *Stokes–Einstein equation* (Chapter 2) requires that

$$\eta D_{11} = \frac{kT}{6\pi a} \tag{15.14}$$

where a is the radius of the equivalent sphere. Equation (15.14) refers to the diffusion of large molecules, in a continuum which by implication consists of much smaller molecules. If Eqn (15.14) is to be used for the diffusion of molecules comparable in size with those of the surrounding medium, then the numerical constant is nearer to 4 than to 6, its actual value depending on temperature and concentration, though insensitive to pressure (McLaughlin, 1960).

There is as yet no completely satisfactory statistical mechanical theory of the transport properties of pure liquids, and the theories which do exist are very complex. Bearman (1961) and Himmelblau (1964) have reviewed some of the existing molecular approaches, which have also been considered by Kumins and Kwei (1968) and by Rice and Gray (1965).

Although the transport of mass in fluids involves both molecular convection and diffusion, the transfer of heat and momentum can involve convective, vibrational and rotational mechanisms. It appears that heat is conducted mainly by vibrational mechanisms but that momentum can be transferred by a variety of processes depending on the molecular type (McLaughlin, 1960).

The theory of reaction rates suggests that the pre-exponential factor D^1 in Eqn (15.2) should depend on temperature. Where this is not observed then either the temperature dependencies of the lattice parameters have cancelled out with the factor $(kT/h)\exp(\Delta S^{\ddagger}/R)$ in Eqn (15.6) or the temperature dependence of D^1 in Eqn (15.6) has become included in E_D. In this case E_D would not be a pure activation energy but some kind of composite factor (McLaughlin, 1960).

B. Diffusion in an Adsorbing Medium

Eyring's theory is considered here in some detail because it has been applied to dyeing studies and will be needed in Part IV. At this stage it may be useful to note that the diffusion of dyes in fibers is often considered to be associated with internal adsorption processes. If the adsorption processes are considered to immobilise the diffusing molecules, and if a state of "*instantaneous internal equilibrium*" is supposed to exist between the concentrations of the "free" and the "adsorbed" molecules, then the conservation of mass requires that the apparent diffusion coefficient be *reduced* in proportion to the equilibrium distribution coefficient K_p for this internal partition. For a linear "internal isotherm" such as might be obtained in an ideally dilute system (Willis *et al.*, 1945; Crank, 1956)

$$\mathrm{D}_{\mathrm{app}} = D/(K_p + 1) \tag{15.15}$$

so that for systems in which $K_p \gg 1$

$$\mathrm{D}_{\mathrm{app}} \approx D/K_p = D \cdot \exp(\Delta\mu^0{}_p/RT) \tag{15.16}$$

in which $\Delta\mu^0{}_p$ is the standard chemical potential difference for the internal partition.

$$\Delta\mu^0{}_p = \Delta\bar{H}_p^0 - T\Delta\bar{S}_p^0 \tag{15.17}$$

where $\Delta\bar{H}_p^0$ and $\Delta\bar{S}_p^0$ are the standard differences in partial molar enthalpy and entropy, respectively. We find that Eqn (15.4) becomes

$$D_{\text{app}} = \lambda^2 \frac{kT}{h} \exp\left(\frac{\Delta S^{\ddagger} - \Delta\bar{S}_p^0}{R}\right) \exp\left(\frac{\Delta\bar{H}_p^0 - \Delta H^{\ddagger}}{RT}\right) \tag{15.18}$$

These internal adsorption processes, if of the type suggested, must have a significant effect on the parameters D^1 and E_D of Eqn (15.2) and must be taken into account when interpreting experimental data. Diffusion in an adsorbing medium tends to be slower than in the absence of these effects.

Additional complications arise if these internal adsorption processes are non-linear or if they occur at a rate comparable with that of the diffusion itself. The general problem of diffusion with chemical reaction is extremely complex. The behaviour of simple model systems has been analysed in detail by Crank (1956) both for reversible and irreversible chemical reactions. The chemical engineering literature in particular abounds with papers on this topic, and attention has been paid to the existence of multiple mathematical solutions for problems of combined mass transfer and chemical reaction (Hatfield and Aris, 1969). The topic is too extensive to consider in detail here. See Rys (1973) and Weisz (1973).

II. DIFFUSION IN AN ATOMIC LATTICE

Eyring's theory can be applied to diffusion in atomic lattices, though it is necessary to consider the relative roles of "volume diffusion" homogeneously throughout the atomic lattice and "interface diffusion" or "grain boundary diffusion" which may occur at internal interfaces, and at a very different rate. The detailed expressions obtained for D depend on whether the activated jumps are considered to involve vibrational or translational degrees of freedom (Glasstone *et al.*, 1941).

The statistical mechanical theories are very complex. Allnatt and Cohen (1964a, b) have discussed diffusion in defect-containing solids and Reiss (1964) has examined the nature of the thermodynamic driving force for diffusion along a one-dimensional point lattice. He concludes that the rate of diffusion is proportional to the gradient of the thermodynamic *activity*, with constant coefficient. This is in contrast to nonequilibrium thermodynamic approaches which consider the chemical potential gradients as the driving forces for diffusion, but as Coleman and Truesdell (1960) have pointed out there is still considerable uncertainty about the correct identification of the thermodynamic forces in nonequilibrium thermodynamics.

A *stochastic approach* to molecular diffusion in crystal lattices (Manning, 1965) gives the following result for the diffusion of a tracer atom along an x-coordinate in the $\langle 100 \rangle$ direction of a face centred cubic crystal, in the absence of a driving force and in the absence of a diffusion coefficient gradient

$$J_x = -D\frac{\partial C}{\partial x} \tag{15.19}$$

where

$$D = \langle x^2 \rangle / 2\tau = f \cdot \frac{\lambda^2 \nu}{6} \tag{15.20}$$

J_x is defined with respect to the local diffusion plane, D is closely related to the tracer diffusion coefficient as measured in a homogeneous system, $\langle x^2 \rangle$ is the mean square displacement in time τ, λ is the jump distance between lattice planes, ν is the jump frequency and f is a *correlation factor*.

The correlation factor f takes account of any tendency of an atom to return preferentially to its previous position after a diffusion jump, rather than to proceed down the x-axis i.e.

$$D_{\text{actual}} = f \cdot D_{\text{random}} \tag{15.21}$$

The *Nernst-Einstein* relation between the diffusion coefficient D and the drift mobility $\mathscr{V}^0$ of an ion carrying an ionic charge q is now (Moelwyn–Hughes 1965; Manning, 1965)

$$D_{\text{actual}} = f \cdot \frac{\mathscr{V}^0 kT}{q} \tag{15.22}$$

so that correlations of this type lead to departures from the conventional Nernst–Einstein equation in which $f = 1$.

As we have seen in Chapter 2 the concentration gradients produce a purely statistical bias which leads to a directional diffusion flux and are *not* to be regarded as driving-forces for diffusion.

From the atomic viewpoint of the stochastic approaches, a *driving-force* is any influence which makes the *probability* of an individual atomic jump in one direction between two given sites *differ* from the probability of a jump in the opposite direction.

Such a force often behaves as if it superimposes an average *drift velocity* $\langle u \rangle$ on the otherwise random diffusive motions, i.e. (Manning, 1965)

$$J_x = -D\frac{\partial C}{\partial x} + \langle u \rangle C \tag{15.23}$$

so that for D and $\langle u \rangle$ independent of x we have a form of convective diffusion equation

$$\frac{\partial C}{\partial t} = D\left(\frac{\partial^2 C}{\partial x^2}\right) - \langle u \rangle \frac{\partial C}{\partial x} \tag{15.24}$$

For the driving force associated with a single chemical concentration gradient, Manning (1965) derives the result

$$J_x = -D\left\{1 + \frac{\partial \ln y}{\partial \ln c}\right\}\frac{\partial C}{\partial x} + 2C\frac{D}{\lambda}B \qquad (15.25)$$

in which the second term is a contribution from the drift of the lattice vacancies, B being a small quantity.

If the vacancy diffusion term is ignored, and the system is very dilute, Eqn (15.25) is consistent with Eqn (15.8) but the analysis here emphasises that it is in this instance the *activity coefficient gradient* which is responsible for the existence of a thermodynamic driving force.

If the system is thermodynamically "ideal" (e.g. ideally dilute or chemically homogeneous) then diffusion is not to be attributed to the action of specific driving-forces. In this respect the stochastic theories differ significantly from the macroscopic nonequilibrium thermodynamic theories.

III. COOPERATIVE MOLECULAR MOTIONS

Computer simulations of molecular motions in a hard sphere fluid have suggested that cooperative molecular motions are important even for diffusion in simple fluids (Emeis and Fehder, 1970).

If diffusion is regarded as an activated process then the activation energy must be shared by several molecules, i.e. distributed over several degrees of freedom f (Barrer, 1941, 1957).

Barrer's *zone theory* (Barrer, 1957) is based on the idea that the activation energy E (per mole) is distributed over an *activated zone* of molecules. The size of the activated zone is described by the parameter f, which represents the number of degrees of freedom involved in the diffusion movement. The expression obtained for D is complex (Barrer, 1957), i.e.

$$D = \frac{\lambda^2 v}{2}\sum_{f=1}^{f_{\max}} P_f\left\{\left(\frac{E}{RT}\right)^{f-1}\left[\frac{1}{(f-1)!}\right]^{-1}\right\}\exp\left(-\frac{E}{RT}\right) \qquad (15.10)$$

in which v is now the frequency of thermal vibration of the diffusing molecule. P_f is the probability that the f degrees of freedom will cooperate in a diffusion step. The expression within the outer square brackets is the probability that the energy E is distributed over the f degrees of freedom. $f_{\max}$ is the number of degrees of freedom for which this probability is at a maximum. If only one degree of freedom $f = 1$ is involved then

$$D = \frac{\lambda^2 v}{2} \cdot P_1 \cdot \exp(-E/RT) \qquad (15.11)$$

which is consistent with Eyring's approach.

If it is assumed for simplicity that only the term in f_{max} need be considered then (Barrer, 1943)

$$D = \frac{\lambda^2 v}{2} \cdot P_{f_{max}} \left(\frac{E}{RT}\right)^{f_{max}-1} \left[\frac{1}{(f_{max}-1)!}\right]^{-1} \exp(-E/RT) \quad (15.12)$$

If plausible values of D, v, and E are used to calculate the apparent average jump distance $\langle\lambda\rangle$

$$\langle\lambda\rangle = \sqrt{\lambda^2 P f_{max} \left(\frac{E}{RT}\right)^{f_{max}-1} \left[\frac{1}{(f_{max}-1)!}\right]^{-1}} \quad (15.13)$$

then for the diffusion of gases in polymers the values of $\langle\lambda\rangle$ are in excess of 100 Å, and to reduce $\langle\lambda\rangle$ to molecular dimensions values of f_{max} of the order of 10 have been found necessary.

This important result has drawn attention to the importance of cooperative molecular motions, especially in polymers (Kumins and Kwei, 1968).

The zone theory leads to the result that the activation energy E_D for diffusion is temperature dependent if more than one degree of freedom is involved (Barrer and Skirrow, 1948).

$$\frac{dE_D}{dT} = -(f_{max} - 1)R \quad (15.14)$$

A variation of E_D with temperature can therefore be related to the size of the activated zone, as described by f_{max}.

In many instances, good correlations have been found between the pre-exponential factors D^1 and the experimental activation energies E_D for diffusion (Barrer and Skirrow, 1948), or between activation entropies and activation enthalpies for diffusion (Barrer, 1957). Lawson (1957, 1960) has offered an explanation in which the volume change $\Delta V^\ddagger$ in forming the "activated complex" for diffusion is considered to be related as follows to the activation enthalpy $\Delta H^\ddagger$.

$$\Delta V^\ddagger \approx K\alpha \, \Delta H^\ddagger \quad (15.15)$$

where K is a dimensionless constant and α is the isothermal compressibility.

The apparent activation entropy $\Delta S^\ddagger$ for diffusion would be expected to depend on the size of the activated zone in Barrer's theory (1957). Lawson proposes the relationship (1960)

$$\Delta S^\ddagger = \beta/\alpha \, \Delta V^\ddagger \quad (15.16)$$

in which β is the isobaric coefficient of volume expansion. Taken together, Eqns (15.15) and (15.16) lead to Keyes's result (Keyes, 1958)

$$\Delta S^\ddagger = K\beta \, \Delta H^\ddagger \quad (15.17)$$

in which $\Delta S^\ddagger$ and $\Delta H^\ddagger$ are implicitly related through a common dependence on the volume relationships during diffusion.

In studying entropy-enthalpy correlations of this type due attention must be paid to the possible existence of spurious correlations (Barrer and Skirrow, 1948; Barrer, 1957; Exner, 1964; McGregor and Milicevic, 1966).

The importance of the activation volume $\Delta V^\ddagger$ for diffusion provides a link with the "free volume" theories of viscosity and diffusion.

IV. "FREE VOLUME" THEORIES

So far it has been assumed that the effective frequency of the diffusion jumps is determined by a "free energy of activation" which may be resolved into an activation energy E_D and a contribution that is entropic in nature. The entropy factor may include an activation entropy $\Delta S^\ddagger$ or it may be related to the size of an activated zone through the parameter f_{max}, for example.

An alternative viewpoint is that the normal statistical fluctuations in the local density of a fluid periodically open up voids of molecular dimensions into which a diffusing molecule may jump. The process has been thought to require no activation energy and the frequency of the diffusion jumps depends on the probability of the occurrence of a local void greater in volume than some minimum volume $v^\ddagger$.

If we define the "*free volume*" v_f as

$$v_f = v - v_0 \tag{15.18}$$

where v is the average volume per molecule in a fluid and v_0 is the van der Waals volume of the molecule itself then in a hard sphere fluid the probability $P(v^\ddagger)$ of finding a hole of volume exceeding $v^\ddagger$ is (Cohen and Turnbull, 1959)

$$P(v^\ddagger) = \exp\{-\gamma v^\ddagger/v_f\} \tag{15.19}$$

where the factor γ, ($\frac{1}{2} \leqslant \gamma \leqslant 1$), corrects for the overlap of free volume. The critical volume $v^\ddagger$ is expected to be of order $10v_f$. Eqn (15.19) is derived by assuming that no energy change is associated with the redistribution of free volume.

The diffusion coefficient D for self diffusion in the hard-sphere fluid is (Cohen and Turnbull, 1959)

$$D = ga^\ddagger u \exp\{-\gamma v^\ddagger/v_f\} \tag{15.20}$$

where $a^\ddagger$ approximately equals the molecular diameter, g is a geometric factor and u is the natural gas-kinetic velocity of the molecules of the hard-sphere fluid. Eqn (15.20) has the form

$$D = A \exp -\{\gamma v^\ddagger/v_f\} \tag{15.21}$$

and, at constant volume, D should vary at least as $T^{\frac{1}{2}}$ because of the dependence of A on u. The temperature dependence of D is also influenced by the temperature dependence of v_f, which is supposed to be of the form

$$v_f = \beta \bar{v}_m (T - T_0) \qquad (15.22)$$

where β is an average coefficient of thermal expansion and $\bar{v}_m$ is an average molecular volume for the temperature-range T_0 to T, β and $\bar{v}_m$ being assumed independent of pressure for simplicity in the present discussion. At constant pressure then we find

$$D = ga^{\ddagger} u \exp\left\{\frac{-\gamma v^{\ddagger}}{\bar{v}_m \beta (T - T_0)}\right\} \qquad (15.23)$$

Eqn (15.23) gives a satisfactory account of the behaviour of several simple fluids (Cohen and Turnbull, 1959). If D is taken to be inversely proportional to the viscosity of the liquid i.e. proportional to the *fluidity*, then Eqn (15.23) is in agreement with the empirical equation of Doolittle (1951) for the temperature dependence of the fluidity of simple hydrocarbons. For agreement with Doolittle's data the product $\gamma v^{\ddagger}$ must be close to the molecular volume v_0, as might be anticipated (Cohen and Turnbull, 1959).

The Doolittle equation has the form

$$\eta = A^1 \exp\left(\frac{Bv_0}{v_f}\right) \qquad (15.24)$$

in which the constant B is not far from unity.

The variation of the diffusion coefficient with other factors such as concentration and pressure may also be attributed to changes in the free volume v_f, but here we shall concentrate on the temperature dependence.

Eqn (15.23) implies the existence of a temperature T_0 at which diffusion ceases because of the disappearance of free volume.

Turnbull and Cohen (1960) point out that at very low temperatures there will be negligible free volume because the redistribution of free volume will require considerable energy and any volume added in expansion will tend to be uniformly distributed throughout the system. There will be an *excess volume* $\Delta v = v - v_0$ but virtually none of this will be available for localised redistribution: the thermal expansion will be of the order of that for a crystalline solid.

As the temperature increases in the low temperature region the excess volume will increase to a value Δv_g characteristic of the "*glass transition temperature*" T_g at which molecular motions begin to occur with some freedom.

On this basis the appropriate reference temperature in Eqn (15.23) is the glass transition temperature T_g.

The Doolittle equation (15.24) can now be written as

$$\frac{1}{\eta} = A^1 \exp\left(-B\left\{\frac{1}{f} - 1\right\}\right) \quad (15.25)$$

where the *fractional free volume* $f = v_f/v$ is taken to have a definite value $f = f_g$ at T_g

$$f = f_g + \beta_f(T - T_g) \quad (15.26)$$

and β_f is a thermal expansion coefficient for the fractional free volume. If the viscosity η has a finite value η_g at T_g then the assumption that A^1 does not vary significantly with temperature by comparison with the exponential term in Eqn (15.25) leads to the Williams–Landell–Ferry equation (W.L.F. equation; Williams *et al.*, 1955)

$$\text{In}\,\frac{\eta}{\eta_g} = -\frac{(B/f_g)(T - T_g)}{(f_g/\beta_f) + (T - T_g)} \quad (15.27)$$

This equation applies in the range $T_g < T < (T_g + 100°\text{C})$. Data for a variety of pure amorphous polymers and for a variety of other materials can be described with the same "universal" parameters $(B/2.303\ f_g) = 17.44$ and $(f_g/\beta_f) = 51.6$. For $B = 1$ we then have $f_g = 0.025$ and $\beta_f = 4.8 \times 10^{-4}$ (Kumins and Kwei, 1968).

Alternative "free volume" theories have been developed and are discussed in detail by Kumins and Kwei (1968). The Cohen–Turnbull theory suffices to bring out the essential features of these approaches, which offer explanations for the temperature dependence of the fluidity or diffusion coefficient, and suggest that the diffusion of an impurity (or solute) in a solvent will be determined by its molecular size. A solute molecule which is large compared with v_f, but small by comparison with the solvent, will diffuse at the same rate as the solvent, because solvent motions are necessary to complete the diffusion jumps. If the solute is much larger than the solvent molecules the critical void for diffusion will be larger and diffusion should be slower (Cohen and Turnbull, 1959).

V. DIFFUSION IN AMORPHOUS POLYMERS

The phenomenon of slow *volume relaxation* (Kovaks, 1966; Struik, 1966) shows that the molecular motions in polymers do not entirely cease below T_g and that limited segmental mobility is still possible there. The free volume v_f is extremely small but not quite zero below T_g so that glassy polymers tend to be in a "frozen-in" nonequilibrium state. A thermodynamic description of the properties of such a system can not be made without the introduction of additional parameters to describe this state of internal order (Breuer and Rehage, 1966; Staverman, 1966) or the slow relaxation of the internal order (Frisch, 1964).

Diffusion processes which occur well above T_g for a polymer–penetrant system show very different features from those which are found in the vicinity of T_g. In the vicinity of T_g slow relaxation processes take place at rates comparable with those of the diffusion processes themselves and the behaviour becomes extremely complex (Frisch, 1964; Park, 1968; Wang *et al.*, 1969; Hopfenberg and Frisch, 1969).

It has been suggested that the relationship between the average free volume $\bar{V}$ in a polymer–penetrant system and the minimum void volume b for dispersal of a penetrant is crucial for the type of behaviour observed in polymer systems which are well above T_g (Frisch, 1965).

For very large penetrant molecules ($b \gg \bar{V}$) a large number of polymer segments must cooperate in any diffusive motions and the temperature-dependence of diffusion at zero penetrant concentration correlates with the temperature-dependence of the viscosity of the pure polymer. The polymer segmental mobility controls the diffusion process.

For very small penetrant molecules ($b \ll \bar{V}$) diffusion is postulated to occur via localised, activated jumps from one pre-existing cavity in the polymer to another, only a few chain segments being involved in the diffusion jumps. This mechanism is believed responsible for "*Type A Fickian diffusion*" of small molecules such as hydrogen in polymers, which is characterised by ideally dilute sorption behaviour, concentration-independent diffusion coefficients, and an apparent activation energy E_D independent of temperature and concentration.

"*Type B Fickian diffusion*," often observed with larger organic molecules, is generally characterised by concentration dependent diffusion coefficients, temperature dependent activation energies and strong polymer-penetrant interactions, as evinced by high penetrant solubility, for example. In these instances the pre-existing voids are not large enough for a void diffusion mechanism and the diffusion involves large numbers of polymer segments. This is the situation ($b \gg \bar{V}$) in which the polymer segmental mobility controls diffusion. Frisch believes that type B diffusion predominates above a certain penetrant size and that this is often revealed by a large shift in the characteristic relations between log D^1 and E_d (Frisch, 1965; Barrer, 1957).

We shall see in Part IV that the diffusion of the large, nonionic disperse dye molecules in polymers shows little or no concentration dependence of the diffusion coefficient and that the dyes appear to form ideally dilute solutions in the polymers. Nevertheless this is not Type A diffusion because the polymer segmental mobility apparently determines the rate of penetration and not the pre-existence of a void system.

A. Diffusion in Highly Swollen Gels

A highly swollen polymer gel above its glass transition temperature T_g can perhaps be regarded as a randomly cross-linked molecular network permeated by a fluid in which diffusion may occur. As the degree of swelling increases, more and more of this internal fluid will have essentially the same properties as the bulk fluid itself.

If the molecules which diffuse in the gel do not interact significantly with the polymer chains, or with the ionisable groupings on these chains, then the effect of the polymer matrix on the diffusion processes may simply be one of geometrical obstruction. The average cross sectional area open to diffusion will be less than in the bulk fluid, and the average "paths" of the diffusing molecules will also be more tortuous but they should generally be interconnected, at least in very highly swollen gels.

The problem of describing fluid flow or diffusion in such a system are similar to those met in applying macroscopic mass transfer equations to porous media in general. The flows and the concentration gradients are defined in terms of the external dimensions and configuration of the whole solid, so that some kind of averaging of the local properties is implied. Whitaker (1969) has examined this "volume averaging" process for the case of diffusion in a porous medium. If l is a characteristic length for the dimensions of the "averaging volume" V, if d is of molecular dimensions and if L is a characteristic dimension of the macroscopic system, then for a valid averaging process we require the apparently obvious conditions

$$d \ll l \ll L \tag{15.28}$$

Except in a "highly structured medium" the conditions (15.28) ensure that the volume averages and the area averages for flow or diffusion through the medium are essentially equivalent. This is the justification for using the volume porosity ε to calculate the cross-sectional area open to flow in a porous solid (Chapter 13).

A simple viewpoint might be to relate the obstruction effect directly to the average cross-sectional area open to diffusion or fluid flow and to expect an expression of the type

$$D_{\mathrm{exp}} = \varepsilon \cdot D \tag{15.29}$$

where D refers to diffusion in the fluid in the gel and ε is the "porosity" or volume fraction Φ_v of fluid. D_{exp} is the observed diffusion coefficient for the gel. However Eqn (15.29) neglects the tortuosity of the diffusion pathways and one might introduce an empirical tortuosity factor τ_D, i.e.

$$D_{\mathrm{exp}} = \left(\frac{\Phi_v}{\tau_D{}^2}\right) \cdot D \tag{15.30}$$

Such an empirical approach is common and we shall see to what extent it may be justified.

Cremers *et al*. (1966) have examined the diffusion of simple inorganic ions in highly swollen Agar gels. The measured diffusion coefficients for those ions which do not interact with the gel matrix decrease linearly with an increase in the weight fraction of Agar in the gel. The "*obstruction effect*" of the gel matrix is essentially the same for all these ions and it is implied that the ion diffusion is a function of the volume fraction Φ_v of the permeating liquid in the gel, i.e.

$$D_{\mathrm{exp}} = f(\Phi_v) \tag{15.31}$$

The diffusion coefficient of benzene in highly swollen rubber increases linearly with the volume fraction of benzene in the rubber, and as the volume fraction of benzene increases above 0.5, the self diffusion coefficient of benzene in the rubber approaches that of pure benzene (Kuhn, 1966).

On the basis of simple models it is possible to calculate the effect which an ordered array of particles may have on the average diffusion coefficient for a species which diffuses only in the liquid between the particles, when this average diffusion coefficient D_{exp} is based on the external dimensions of the array of particles (Barrer, 1968a).

There is very little dependence on the particle geometry and on the nature of the array of particles if the system is very dilute in the particles, i.e. "highly swollen." For values of $\Phi_v \to 1$, we have

$$D_{\mathrm{exp}} = D\left(\frac{2}{3 - \Phi_v}\right) \tag{15.32}$$

in which Φ_v is the void volume fraction and D is the diffusion coefficient in the liquid filling the voids.

If the particles are more densely packed the detailed dimensions and geometry become more important and the void volume fraction Φ_v alone is not sufficient to describe the behaviour.

The statistical approach of Prager (1960) leads to expressions in terms of the volume fraction of the suspension medium, or of the void volume, to the exclusion of geometrical factors and so must be limited in its application.

Rayleigh's analysis of the properties of a cubic array of cylinders leads to the following approximate expression for the average diffusion coefficient for diffusion normal to the cylinder axes (Barrer, 1968a)

$$\langle D_{\mathrm{exp}} \rangle = \frac{D}{\Phi_v}\left(1 - \frac{3\Phi_d}{2 + \Phi_d - 0.30\Phi_d^4 - 0.0134\Phi_d^8}\right) \tag{15.33}$$

where Φ_d is the volume fraction of the dispersed phase (impermeable cylinders) and Φ_v is the volume fraction of the permeating fluid ($\Phi_d + \Phi_v = 1$) in which diffusion occurs with the diffusion coefficient D.

Analogue experiments using Teledeltos paper suggest that Eqn (15.33) should be appropriate for values of $\Phi_d \leqslant 0.4$ and that the behaviour in this range of volume fractions is not yet very sensitive to the detailed geometry and dimensions of the array (Barrer, 1968a).

A generalisation of Eqn (15.32) to include the effects of particle geometry has been proposed by Fricke (1931), i.e.

$$D_{\text{exp}} = D \frac{k}{(k + 1) - \Phi_v} \tag{15.34}$$

where the *shape factor* k ranges from 2 for random spheres to 1.1 for oblate spheroids with axial ratio 4:1, but the expression is applicable only to dilute assemblies or suspensions of particles.

In conclusion, for diffusion in highly swollen gels or in very dilute suspensions of impermeable particles we can expect a simple dependence of the experimental diffusion coefficients on the volume fraction Φ_v of the permeating medium. As the gel becomes more dense, or as the assembly becomes more compact, specific geometrical effects will become increasingly important and other parameters must enter the analysis. In general it will not be possible to do more than construct semi-empirical relationships between the experimental diffusion coefficient D_{exp}, the diffusion coefficient D in the permeating matrix, the volume fraction Φ_v of void or of permeating fluid, and certain shape factors.

The empirical tortuosity factor τ_D of Eqn (15.30) would from Eqn (15.34) have the form

$$\tau_D = \sqrt{\frac{\Phi_v[(k + 1) - \Phi_v]}{k}} \tag{15.35}$$

and therefore be a function of Φ_v and k.

The expression

$$D_{\text{exp}} = D(\Phi_v)^n \tag{15.36}$$

has also been used to take account of porosity and tortuosity effects. The exponent n reflects the particular geometry and dimensions of the system in a purely empirical manner.

If a system is of the type assumed, and if there are no specific interactions to consider, then the temperature dependence of D_{exp} should be the same as for diffusion in the permeating fluid and D_{exp} should be related to the viscosity of this fluid. There is experimental evidence for good correlations between the diffusion coefficients of liquids in cross-linked rubbers and the viscosities of these liquids (Southern and Thomas, 1967).

B. Diffusion in Amorphous Polymers above T_g

At low penetrant concentrations the preceding model breaks down because the penetrant does not have the properties of the pure liquid penetrant, for example. The structure of an amorphous polymer may change in the presence of the penetrant, either by induced crystallisation or by induced swelling. Some penetrants may "cluster" within the polymer (Zimm and Lundberg, 1956) and where pronounced swelling occurs stresses may develop and frame of reference effects may become serious. Time-dependent relaxation processes associated with slow swelling may further complicate the picture. The penetrant may influence the polymer segmental mobility by its effect on the local free volume v_f or on the polymer chain interactions. These "plasticisation effects" are complicated. A review of this topic has been given by Fujita (1968) and we shall restrict attention here to the diffusion of a penetrant in a polymer-penetrant system which is in *equilibrium swelling* at all times and which has a *time-independent structure*, i.e. it does not crystallise or change in volume during diffusion. Such a system could be studied by equilibrating a polymer with a certain vapor concentration of penetrant and then carrying out sorption experiments with labelled "tracer molecules" of the penetrant. This could be repeated at different concentration levels of penetrant.

The concentration dependence of the penetrant diffusion coefficient $(D_1)_R$ in an arbitrary reference frame R, (for a single nonionic penetrant) is

$$(D_1)_R = (D_1)_0 F_R(\Phi_1) \tag{15.37}$$

where $(D_1)_0$ is the limiting diffusion coefficient obtained as $\Phi_1 \rightarrow 0$ and is the same for all reference frames. The apparent concentration dependence is revealed by $F_R(\Phi_1)$ which is different for different reference frames if swelling or bulk flow are appreciable. (Szekeley *et al.*, 1967; Szekeley, 1965, 1964.) We have (Fujita, 1961, 1968)

$$(D_1)_p = \frac{(D_1)_V}{1 - \Phi_1} \tag{15.38}$$

where p is the polymer-fixed diffusion coefficient and V is the volume-fixed reference frame. If there are no "plasticisation effects" to consider and if

$$(D_1)_V = (D_1)_0 \left(\frac{\partial \ln a_1}{\partial \ln \Phi_1}\right) \tag{15.39}$$

then

$$(D_1)_p = \frac{(D_1)_0}{1 - \Phi_1} \left(\frac{\partial \ln a_1}{\partial \ln \Phi_1}\right) \tag{15.40}$$

If however the penetrant causes changes in the free volume of the system then an additional term is needed in Eqn (15.40). Eqn (15.40) does indeed prove inadequate in practice and Fujita (1961) has proposed an equation containing a term of the Doolittle type, i.e.

$$(D_1)_p = \frac{RT \cdot A_D \exp(-B_D/f)}{(1 - \Phi_1)} \cdot \left(\frac{\partial \ln a_1}{\partial \ln \Phi_1}\right) \tag{15.41}$$

f is the average fractional free volume in the polymer-penetrant system. B_D is a measure of the minimum "hole" required for a diffusion jump of the penetrant and A_D is a constant. The fractional free volume at a given temperature T is assumed to depend both on T and on Φ_1, i.e.

$$f(\Phi_1, T) = f(0, T) + \beta(T)\Phi_1 \tag{15.42}$$

where $f(0, T)$ is a property of the pure polymer and $\beta(T)$ is a temperature dependent coefficient which describes the effectiveness of component 1 in increasing the free volume in the system.

We have now

$$(D_1)_0 = RT\, A_D \exp(-B_D/f(0, T)) \tag{15.43}$$

in which the parameter A_D is independent of concentration and may be related to the molecular shape and size of the penetrant molecules. Also

$$(D_1)_p = RT \cdot A_D \exp\left(-\frac{B_D}{f(0, T) + \beta(T)\Phi_1}\right)\frac{1}{1 - \Phi_1}\left(\frac{\partial \ln a_1}{\partial \ln c_1}\right) \tag{15.44}$$

If we have an ideally dilute solution in which frame of reference effects are negligible (the sample is in near-equilibrium swelling) we can use the equation

$$\ln\left(\frac{(D_1)_0}{RT}\right) = \ln A_D - \frac{B_D}{f(0, T)} \tag{15.45}$$

to obtain the result (Fujita, 1961, 1968)

$$\frac{1}{\ln\left(\dfrac{(D_1)_p}{(D_1)_0}\right)} = \frac{f(0, T)}{B_D} + \frac{[f(0, T)]^2}{[B_D\, \beta(T)]\Phi_1} \tag{15.46}$$

Although interactions strong enough to induce marked changes in free volume may be somewhat incompatible with the concept of an ideally dilute solution, Eqn (15.46) expresses the concentration dependence of $(D_1)_p$ in terms of the "free volume" mechanism.

Since the free volume has a similarly pronounced effect on viscous phenomena in a polymer-penetrant system it is useful to relate the behaviour of $(D_1)_0$ to that of the viscosity η_0 of the pure polymer, for example.

We expect to find

$$f(0, T) = f(0, T_s) + \beta_f(T - T_s) \tag{15.47}$$

where the reference temperature T_s is usually equated to the glass transition temperature T_g. The viscosity η_0 should be described by an equation of the Doolittle type

$$\eta_0 = A_p \exp\left(\frac{B_p}{f(0, T)}\right) \tag{15.48}$$

where the constants A_p and B_p have similar significance to A_D and B_D but may not have the same values: in viscous phenomena it is the *polymer segments* which are involved. In diffusion it is possible that the diffusion jumps will be determined or limited by the polymer segmental motions, but only when this is entirely so can we expect to find $A_D = A_p$ and $B_D = B_p$.

Eqn (15.45) can now be written as

$$\ln\left(\frac{(D_1)_0}{RT}\right) = C - B \log \eta_0 \tag{15.49}$$

with

$$C = \ln A_D + \frac{B_D}{B_p} \ln A_p \tag{15.50}$$

and

$$B = \frac{B_D}{B_p} \tag{15.51}$$

The temperature independent parameter C can not be predicted in advance, but B should be near to unity for the diffusion of molecules greater than or equal to a polymer segment in size.

The relationship between $(D_1)_0$ and η_0 in Eqn (15.49) is a consequence of the assumption that the polymer segmental motions dominate both the diffusion of penetrant and the viscous processes in the polymer-penetrant system. This relationship will prove important for dye diffusion in fibres and in polymer films.

VI. FICKIAN DIFFUSION, SORPTION, AND PERMEATION

The term "*Fickian diffusion*" no longer carries the connotation of diffusion according to Fick's first and second laws, with a constant diffusion coefficient independent of the concentration gradients, of concentration, position and time.

The term currently describes processes in which the diffusion coefficient is independent of the concentration gradients, of position and of time but it includes concentration-dependent diffusion coefficients.

Barrer (1968b) distinguished between "*Ideal Fickian Diffusion*" in which the diffusion coefficient is a constant, and "*Non-Ideal Fickian Diffusion*" in which it may vary with concentration.

We shall define "*Fickian sorption*" as a sorption process controlled by the Fickian diffusion of a solute into the sorbing medium from a constant surface concentration: the boundary condition is time-invariant. We shall distinguish between ideal Fickian sorption (or desorption) and non-ideal Fickian sorption (or desorption) on the basis of the constancy of the diffusion coefficient.

In a similar fashion, "*Fickian permeation*" may be defined as a membrane permeation process involving Fickian diffusion within the membrane and time-independent concentrations at the membrane boundaries. The dependence of the diffusion coefficient on concentration determines whether we have ideal or nonideal Fickian permeation.

These distinctions have been made so that the classification of the behaviour of an experimental *process* (sorption, desorption or permeation) will not be confused with a classification of the local diffusion behaviour itself. For example we can not have Fickian sorption or permeation unless we also have Fickian diffusion. But we can have non-Fickian sorption and permeation when we do have Fickian diffusion. This distinction is necessary to emphasise that non-Fickian sorption or permeation can arise from *time-dependent boundary conditions* and need not necessarily imply that the diffusion itself is locally non-Fickian.

Some of the principal characteristics of Fickian sorption and desorption, and of Fickian permeation, will now be summarised for representative model systems.

A. Fickian Sorption

An example of ideal Fickian sorption is provided by the mathematical model of Eqns (12.23) to (12.25), the behaviour of which is shown in Figs. 10 and 17. The relative sorption ($C_t^{\phi}/C_{\infty}^{\phi}$) is a single-valued function of the Fourier number $\mathscr{F}o_M = D^{\phi}t/a^2$ *and the same curve describes both sorption and desorption*. In the case of desorption the initial condition is

$$C^{\phi} = C_{\infty}^{\phi} \quad \text{in} \quad -l < x < +l \quad \text{at} \quad t = 0 \tag{15.52}$$

and the boundary conditions are

$$C^{\phi} = 0 \quad \text{at} \quad x = \pm l \quad \text{for all} \quad t \geqslant 0 \tag{15.53}$$

($1 - C_t^{\phi}/C_{\infty}^{\phi}$) is then the fraction desorption at time t.

For short times t the mass M_t^{ϕ} of solute which has passed through unit area of the surface of the solid is given by (Crank, 1956)

$$M_t^\phi = 2C_\infty^\phi \sqrt{\frac{D^\phi t}{\pi}} \tag{15.54}$$

Eqn (15.54) applies to a solid of arbitrary shape, so long as the sorption process is in its initial stages. The concentration C_t^ϕ sorbed at time t is

$$C_t^\phi = \frac{M_t^\phi A^\phi}{V^\phi} = M_t^\phi S_0^\phi \tag{15.55}$$

where $S_0^\phi = (A^\phi/V^\phi)$ is the *specific surface area* of the solid. Consequently,

$$\left(\frac{C_t^\phi}{C_\infty^\phi}\right) = 2S_0^\phi \sqrt{\frac{D^\phi t}{\pi}}. \tag{15.56}$$

In non-ideal Fickian sorption the sorption and desorption curves may no longer coincide. At short times t Eqn (15.56) still applies but D^ϕ is then some average $\langle D^\phi \rangle$ of the values of D^ϕ for the concentration range of the experiment, and $\langle D^\phi \rangle$ is generally different for sorption and desorption. The general shapes of the curves of C_t^ϕ/C_∞^ϕ against time are insensitive to the concentration dependence of D^ϕ, which *cannot* be deduced from the shape of a single sorption or desorption curve of (C_t^ϕ/C_∞^ϕ) against time t. When D^ϕ increases with C^ϕ Eqn (15.56) may be valid in sorption even up to $C_t^\phi/C_\infty c$ values well in excess of 0.5; when D^ϕ decreases with C^ϕ the linear region is much less extensive in sorption.

Crank (1956) presents many computed results showing the type of behaviour to be expected in non-ideal Fickian sorption and desorption.

B. Fickian Permeation

The most common experimental arrangement is one in which one of the solutions bounding the membrane is maintained at a constant concentration c_1, say, while the other solution is kept at zero solute concentration. The behaviour of the membrane specified by Eqns (14.72) to (14.79) corresponds to ideal Fickian sorption in the limit as $h^0 l \to \infty$.

In this limit we have

$$J = D^\phi \frac{C_{1\infty}^\phi}{l} \tag{15.57}$$

where $C_{1\infty}^\sigma$ is the equilibrium concentration corresponding to c_1. The concentration gradient in the membrane is linear

$$C^\phi = C_{1\infty}^\phi \left(1 - \frac{x}{l}\right) \tag{15.58}$$

and the average concentration of solute in the membrane in the steady state is therefore $C_{1\infty}^{\phi}/2$. The time lag θ is given by

$$\theta = \frac{l^2}{6D^{\phi}} \tag{15.59}$$

because the same diffusion coefficient is obtained from both the steady-state flux and the time lag.

In *non-ideal Fickian permeation* the concentration gradients in the membrane are not linear in the steady state (Barrer, 1946; Crank, 1956) and the average concentration of solute in the membrane exceeds $C_{1\infty}{}^{\phi}/2$ if D^{ϕ} increases with C^{ϕ}, and is less than $C_{1\infty}{}^{\phi}/2$ if D^{ϕ} decreases with C^{ϕ}. The experimental diffusion coefficient D_f from the steady state flux is the average value

$$\langle D_f \rangle = \frac{1}{C_{1\infty}{}^{\phi}} \int_0^{C_{1\infty}{}^{\phi}} D^{\phi}(C^{\phi})\, dC^{\phi} \tag{15.60}$$

and differs from $\langle D_l \rangle$ which is related to $C_{1\infty}{}^{\phi}$ in a complex fashion (Frisch, 1957, 1958, 1959).

More extensive information on the possible sources of deviations from the models of Fickian Sorption and Fickian Permeation are to be found in Crank's monograph (Crank, 1956) and in the monograph edited by Crank and Park (1968). A recent review by Stannett *et al.* (1972) is also useful.

VII. DIFFUSION IN CRYSTALLINE POLYMERS

There is no very firm basis on which to discuss diffusion in crystalline polymers because the details of their structures are still imperfectly understood (Hosemann, 1966).

The structure of a polymeric solid, such as a fiber, is very dependent on its history and on the immediate conditions of experiment. The structure is often unstable and may change during the course of a diffusion experiment. Appropriate pre-treatments can be used to stabilise the structure for diffusion studies, but of course one is then studying diffusion in a modified substrate.

The simplest model for diffusion in a crystalline polymer is based on the "two-phase" concept. Diffusion is assumed to occur in an "amorphous" matrix of polymer molecules in which the crystalline regions are dispersed rather like particles of inert filler in a rubber. The crystalline regions have an *obstruction effect* which is purely geometrical but they may also modify the *state* of the "amorphous" matrix in respect of average packing density and orientation. The crystalline regions may exercise stresses or constraints on the "amorphous" matrix and so modify the polymer segmental mobility in these regions. We then have diffusion in "amorphous" regions of variable viscosity, modified by the geometrical effects of the crystalline regions, which can be assumed to be impermeable to molecules of the size of most dye molecules.

This picture is obviously too simple. There will be some distribution of order in a polymer rather than a discrete separation into regions with two distinct levels of accessibility or permeability. Prevorsek and Butler (1971) have stated that the diffusion of a dye in nylon 6 fibers can be explained only by taking into account the existence of a third phase of intermediate order. Even this must be an over-simplification.

Nevertheless, the "two-phase" model is the only simple model which has been widely used, and it has been shown by Barrer (1968a) to be capable of explaining some of the features of diffusion in crystalline polymers.

We shall adopt this model in Part IV because it makes it possible to relate not only fiber structure to dye diffusion, but also dye diffusion to the anelastic behaviour of fibers (Prevorsek, 1969; McCrum *et al.*, 1968; Takayanagi, 1963).

If a crystalline polymer is regarded as a special type of heterogeneous solid (Barrer, 1968a), then we can use the information available on diffusion in heterogeneous media to establish the importance of "blind pores," for example, and to interpret diffusion coefficients obtained by different methods. For example, heterogeneity has in some instances different effects on the *steady state* diffusion parameters for membranes from those which it has on the *time-lag* quantities (Barrer, 1968a; Petropoulos and Roussis, 1969; Ash *et al.*, 1969; Goodknight *et al.*, 1960; Goodknight and Fatt, 1961; Fatt, 1962). The presence of "blind pores" can have an effect which is formally similar to that in diffusion accompanied by chemical reaction (Crank, 1956; McGregor and Peters, 1964).

VIII. DIFFUSION IN ANISOTROPIC MEDIA

When simple diffusion occurs in an isotropic system, the diffusion coefficient D in the equation

$$\boldsymbol{j} = -D \operatorname{grad} C \tag{15.61}$$

is the same for all orientations of $\boldsymbol{j}$ and grad C. The diffusion flux vector $\boldsymbol{j}$ is oriented normal to the surface of constant concentration which passes through the point of interest, and, therefore, points in the same direction as the gradient vector $-\operatorname{grad} C$.

These observations no longer hold in anisotropic systems, where the diffusion flux vector $\boldsymbol{j}$ may point in a different direction from the gradient vector $-\operatorname{grad} C$.

Let j_x, j_y, j_z, be the components of the diffusion flux vector $\boldsymbol{j}$ in a system of Cartesian coordinates x, y, z. The component j_x represents the diffusion flux in the x-direction, through a reference plane oriented normal to the x-axis, for example.

In general, we have

$$\left.\begin{aligned} -j_x &= D_{xx}\frac{\partial C}{\partial x} + D_{xy}\frac{\partial C}{\partial y} + D_{xz}\frac{\partial C}{\partial z} \\ -j_y &= D_{yx}\frac{\partial C}{\partial x} + D_{yy}\frac{\partial C}{\partial y} + D_{yz}\frac{\partial C}{\partial z} \\ -j_z &= D_{zx}\frac{\partial C}{\partial x} + D_{zy}\frac{\partial C}{\partial y} + D_{zz}\frac{\partial C}{\partial z} \end{aligned}\right\} \tag{15.62}$$

or, in matrix notation:

$$\begin{pmatrix} -j_x \\ -j_y \\ -j_z \end{pmatrix} = \begin{pmatrix} D_{xx} & D_{xy} & D_{xz} \\ D_{yx} & D_{yy} & D_{yz} \\ D_{zx} & D_{zy} & D_{zz} \end{pmatrix} \begin{pmatrix} \dfrac{\partial C}{\partial x} \\ \dfrac{\partial C}{\partial y} \\ \dfrac{\partial C}{\partial z} \end{pmatrix} \tag{15.63}$$

In vector-tensor notation Eqn (15.63) is

$$-\boldsymbol{j} = \mathbf{D} \text{ grad } C \tag{15.64}$$

where D is the second order *diffusivity tensor*

$$\mathbf{D} = (D_{ij}) \qquad i, j = x, y, z \tag{15.65}$$

The tensor $\mathbf{D}$ may be considered to "rotate" the gradient vector $-$grad C into the diffusion flux vector $\boldsymbol{j}$ for an anisotropic system.

The magnitudes of the scalar elements D_{ij} $(i, j = x, y, z)$ will depend on the orientation of the coordinate axes x, y, z with respect to the axes or planes of crystallographic symmetry of the medium in which diffusion occurs.

When the principles expressed in Eqns (1.10–1.12) are used to obtain an equation of conservation of mass for the diffusion process described by Eqns (15.62), one finds that (Carslaw and Jaeger, 1947; Crank, 1956)

$$\begin{aligned} \frac{\partial C}{\partial t} &= D_{xx}\frac{\partial^2 C}{\partial x^2} + D_{yy}\frac{\partial^2 C}{\partial y^2} + D_{zz}\frac{\partial^2 C}{\partial z^2} \\ &\quad + (D_{yz} + D_{zy})\frac{\partial^2 C}{\partial y\,\partial z} + (D_{zx} + D_{xz})\frac{\partial^2 C}{\partial z\,\partial x} \\ &\quad + (D_{xy} + D_{yx})\frac{\partial^2 C}{\partial x\,\partial y} = \text{Constant} \end{aligned} \tag{15.66}$$

in deriving which, the D_{ij} have been treated as constants.

Equation (15.66) has the form of the equation for an *ellipsoid:*

$$D_{xx}x^2 + D_{yy}y^2 + D_{zz}z^2 + (D_{yz} + D_{zy})yz + (D_{zx} + D_{xz})zx + (D_{xy} + D_{yx})xy = \text{Constant} \quad (15.67)$$

When the equation for an ellipsoid is written in relation to the *principal axes* ξ, η, ζ of the ellipsoid, it takes the form

$$D_\xi \xi^2 + D_\eta \eta^2 + D_\zeta \zeta^2 = \text{Constant}. \quad (15.68)$$

and, similarly, it is possible to transform the diffusion equation (15.66) in terms of the *principal axes of diffusion* ξ, η, ζ and the *principal diffusion coefficients* D_ξ, D_η, D_ζ (Carslaw and Jaeger, 1947; Crank, 1956)

$$\frac{\partial C}{\partial t} = D_\xi \frac{\partial^2 C}{\partial \xi^2} + D_\eta \frac{\partial^2 C}{\partial \eta^2} + D_\zeta \frac{\partial^2 C}{\partial \zeta^2} \quad (15.69)$$

The *diffusivity ellipsoid* associated with Eqn (15.69) is characterized by the three constants D_ξ, D_η, D_ζ. This ellipsoid has the property that the square (r^2) of the magnitude (r) of its radius vector $\boldsymbol{r}$ is inversely proportional to a diffusion coefficient D. The diffusion coefficient D describes diffusion normal to surfaces of constant concentration, at points where the normals to these surfaces point in the direction of the radius vector $\boldsymbol{r}$. Let α, β, γ be the direction cosines of the radius vector r with respect to the principal axes of diffusion ξ, η, ζ, respectively. Then

$$D = \alpha^2 D_\xi + \beta^2 D_\eta + \gamma^2 D_\zeta \quad (15.70)$$

Suppose that r lies along the principal axis ξ. Then $\beta = \gamma = 0$ and $\alpha = 1$ so that

$$D = D_\xi \quad (15.71)$$

Diffusion along a principal axis of diffusion, under the influence of a concentration gradient vector directed along that axis only, is described by the appropriate principal diffusion coefficient.

Consider a highly oriented cylindrical fiber. One of the principal axes of diffusion will be directed parallel to the long axis of the fiber. If the fiber structure has angular symmetry, then diffusion radially into the fiber will correspond to diffusion along a principal axis of diffusion. If the concentration gradients are exclusively normal to the fiber radius at all points in the fiber, then the diffusion process may be described by the diffusion equations for an *isotropic* medium of cylindrical geometry, and the diffusion coefficient $D_\perp$ so obtained will be the diffusion coefficient for diffusion along a radial principal axis in the fiber. Measurements of the diffusion coefficient $D_\parallel$ along the fiber axis will in general give a different numerical value because a different principal axis is involved.

Polymer films will often be anisotropic. The polymer molecules can be expected to lie with their long axes parallel, in general, to one another and to the plane surfaces of the film, and to point in some preferred direction in the plane of the film. The principal axes of diffusion will be normal to the plane of the film; parallel to the plane of the film but in the direction of orientation in this plane; and orthogonal to these two directions. If diffusion occurs through the plane surfaces of the film, and the concentration gradients are everywhere normal to these surfaces, the diffusion processes can be described by the diffusion equations for an *isotropic* medium in the form of a plane slab, and the diffusion coefficient $D_{\perp}$ so obtained will be the principal diffusion coefficient for the principal axis oriented normal to the plane of the film. Measurements of diffusion through the edges of the film, in the plane of the film, can be made to yield the two remaining principal diffusion coefficients, which will not in general have the same numerical value as $D_{\perp}$.

Carslaw and Jaeger (1947) and Crank (1956) have shown how some problems of diffusion in anisotropic media can be reduced to the same form as problems of diffusion in isotropic media, and have pointed out the importance of the crystallographic symmetry of the anisotropic medium which, in some instances, may itself lead to a simpler description of the diffusion processes.

The problems of multicomponent diffusion in anisotropic systems are clearly formidable, the more so in view of the complex nature of the expected thermodynamic coupling of the different flows in anisotropic systems (Chapter 10).

IX. SOME GENERAL COMMENTS

The methods available for measuring diffusion coefficients have been reviewed by Crank and Park (1968). These methods are generally based on applications of simple mathematical models (Crank, 1956) such as the mathematical models of *Fickian Sorption* and of *Fickian Permeation*.

When the experimental behaviour is different from that of the simple models then the experimental diffusion coefficients may need careful interpretation, and diffusion measurements should be made by as many independent methods as are available, to establish the nature of the deviations from the simple models.

The difficulty does not lie so much in the selection of a mathematical model which can *describe* the observed deviations from ideal behaviour, as it does in establishing the physical relevance of the chosen model and the significance of the parameters which enter it. For this reason Parts I–III of this book have concentrated on the physical aspects of mass transfer processes, rather than on the mathematics of diffusion. Excellent summaries of the mathematical aspects can be found in the standard texts by Barrer (1941), Jost (1960), Crank (1956) and Carslaw and Jaeger (1947). The physical aspects have also been discussed in some detail by Barrer (1941), Jost (1960), Rogers (1965) and by several authors in the monograph edited by Crank and Park (1968).

In Volume 2 we shall attempt to apply the physical ideas developed in Parts I–III of this monograph to an interpretation of selected experimental data from the alarmingly extensive literature on dye diffusion in fibers and films. A useful recent review has been given by Peters (1968).

REFERENCES

Allnatt, A. R. and Cohen, M. H. (1964a). *J. Chem. Phys.* **40,** 1860.

Allnatt, A. R. and Cohen, M. H. (1964b). *J. Chem. Phys.* **40,** 1871.

Ash, R., Barrer, R. M., and Palmer, D. G. (1969). *Trans. Faraday Soc.*, **65,** 121.

Barrer, R. M. (1937). *Nature, Lond.* **140,** 106.

Barrer, R. M. (1941). "Diffusion in and througn Solids." Cambridge University Press.

Barrer, R. M. (1943). *Trans. Faraday Soc.* **39,** 237.

Barrer, R. M. (1946). *Proc. Phys. Soc.* **58,** 321.

Barrer, R. M. (1957). *J. Phys. Chem.*, **61,** 178.

Barrer, R. M. (1968a). "Diffusion and Permeation in Heterogeneous Media." *In* "Diffusion in Polymers" (Eds., Crank, J. and Park, G. S.) Academic Press, London and New York.

Barrer, R. M. (1968b). "Molecular Aspects of Diffusion." A lecture presented at the symposium on "Diffusion of Large Molecules in Polymers," U.M.I.S.T., Manchester.

Barrer, R. M. and Skirrow, G. (1948). *J. Polym. Sci.* **3,** 549.

Bearman, R. J. (1961). *J. Phys. Chem.* **65,** 1961.

Breuer, H. and Rehage, G. (1966). *Ber. Bunsengesellschaft phys. Chem.* **70,** 1149.

Carslaw, H. S. and Jaeger, J. C. (1947). "Conduction of Heat in Solids." Oxford University Press.

Cohen, M. H. and Turnbull, D. (1959). *J. Chem. Phys.* **31,** 1164.

Coleman, B. D. and Truesdell, C. (1960). *J. Chem. Phys.* **33,** 28.

Collier, J. R. (1969). *Ind. Engng. Chem.* **61,** 50.

Crank, J. (1956). "The Mathematics of Diffusion." Clarendon Press, Oxford.

Crank, J. and Park, G. S. (1968). "Diffusion in Polymers." Academic Press, London and New York.

Cremers, A. E., Thomas, H. C., anh Slade, A. L. (1966). *J. Phys. Chem.* **70,** 2840.

Doolittle, A. K. (1951). *J. Appl. Phys.* **22,** 1471.

Emeis, C. A. and Fehder, P. L. (1970). *J. Amer. Chem. Soc.* **92,** 2246.

Exner, O. (1964). *Coll. Czech. Chem. Commun.*, **29,** 1094.

Fatt, I. (1962). *J. Phys. Chem.*, **66,** 760.

Fricke, H. (1931). *Physics* **1,** 106.

Frisch, H. L. (1957). *J. Phys. Chem.* **61,** 93.

Frisch, H. L. (1958). *J. Phys. Chem.* **62,** 401.

Frisch, H. L. (1959). *J. Phys. Chem.* **63,** 1249.

Frisch, H. L. (1964). *J. Chem. Phys.* **41,** 3679.

Frisch, H. L. (1965). *J. Polym. Sci. B*, **3,** 13.
Fujita, H. (1961). *Fortschr. Hochpolym.-Forsch.* **3,** 1.
Fujita, H. (1968). "Organic Vapors above the Glass Transition Temperature." *In* "Diffusion in Polymers" (Eds. Crank, J. and Park, G. S.). Academic Press, London and New York.
Glasstone, S., Laidler, K. J., and Eyring, H. (1941). "The Theory of Rate Processes." McGraw-Hill, New York.
Goodknight, R. C., Klikoff, W. A. Jr., and Fatt, I. (1960). *J. Phys. Chem.*, **64,** 1162.
Goodknight, R. C. and Fatt, I. (1961). *J. Phys. Chem.* **65,** 1709.
Hatfield, B. and Aris, R. (1969). *Chem. Engng. Sci.* **24,** 1213.
Himmelblau, D. M. (1964). *Chem. Revs.* **64(5),** 527.
Hopfenberg, H. B. and Frisch, H. L. (1969). *J. Polymer Sci.*, **B7,** 679.
Hosemann, R. (1966). *Pure and Appl. Chem.*, **12,** 311.
Jost, W. (1960). "Diffusion in Solids, Liquids, Gasses." 3rd Edn., Academic Press, London and New York.
Keyes, R. W. (1968). *J. Chem. Phys.* **29,** 467.
Kovacs, A. J. (1966). *Rheologica Acta* **5,** 262.
Kuhn, H. J. (1966). *Kolloid-Z. und Z.-für Polymere* **213,** 124.
Kumins, C. A. and Kwei, T. K. (1968). "Free Volume and Other Theories." *In* "Diffusion in Polymers" (Eds. Crank, J. and Park, G. S.). Academic Press, London and New York.
Lawson, A. W. (1957). *J. Phys. Chem. Solids* **3,** 250.
Lawson, A. W. (1960). *J. Chem. Phys.* **32,** 131.
McCrum, N. G., Read, B. E., and Williams, G. (1968). "Anelastic and Dielectric Effects in Polymeric Solids." John Wiley and Sons, London.
McGregor, R. and Milicevic, B. (1966). *Nature, Lond.* **211,** 523.
McGregor, R. and Peters, R. H. (1964). *Trans. Faraday Soc.*, **60,** 2062.
McLaughlin, E. (1960). *Quart. Rev. Chem. Soc.* **14,** No. 3, 236.
Manning, J. R. (1965). *Phys. Review*, **139,** A126.
Moelwyn-Hughes, E. A. (1965). "Physical Chemistry." Pergamon Press, Oxford.
Park, G. S. (1968). "The Glassy State and Slow Process Anomalies." *In* "Diffusion in Polymers." (Eds. Crank, J. and Park, G. S.). Academic Press, London and New York.
Peters, R. H. (1968). "Kinetics of Dyeing." *In* "Diffusion in Polymers." (Eds. Crank, J. and Park, G. S.). Academic Press, London and New York.
Petropoulos, J. H. and Roussis, P. P. (1969). *J. Chem. Phys.* **51,** 1332.
Prager, S. (1960). *J. Chem. Phys.* **33,** 122.
Prevorsek, D. C. (1969). Private communication.
Prevorsek, D. C. and Butler, R. H. (1971). Lecture to A.A.T.C.C. Golden Jubilee Conference, Boston.
Pryde, J. A. (1966). "The Liquid State." Hutchinson, London.
Reiss, H. (1964). *J. Chem. Phys.* **40,** 1783.
Rice, S. A. and Gray, P. (1965). "The Statistical Mechanics of Simple Liquids." Interscience, New York.
Rogers, C. E. (1965). *In* "Physics and Chemistry of the Organic Solid State." (Eds. D. Fox, M. M. Labes and A. Weissberger) Interscience Pub., New York.
Rys, P. (1973). *Textile Res. J.*, **43,** 24.
Southern, E. and Thomas, A. G. (1967). *Trans. Faraday Soc.* **63,** 1913.
Stannett, V. T., Hopfenberg, H. B., and Petropoulos, J. H. (1972). "Diffusion in Polymers", Chapter 9. *In* "Macromolecular Science" (Bawn, C. E. H. Ed.). M.T.P. International Reviews of Science, Vol. 8, Butterworths, London.

Staverman, A. J. (1966). *Rheologica Acta* **5,** 283.
Struik, L. C. E. (1966). *Rheologica Acta* **5,** 303.
Szekeley, J. (1964). *Chem. Engng. Sci.* **19,** 51.
Szekeley, J. (1965). *Trans. Faraday Soc.* **61,** 2679.
Szekeley, J., Todd, M. R., and Martins, G. P. (1967). *Chem. Engng. Sci.* **22,** 81.
Takayanagi, M. (1963). *Mem. Fac. Eng. Kyushu Univ.*, **23,** No. 1, pl.
Turnbull, D. and Cohen, M. H. (1960). *J. Chem. Phys.* **31,** 1164.
Wang, T. T., Kwei, T. K., and Frisch, H. L. (1969). *J. Polymer Sci. A*, **7,** 2019.
Weisz, P. B. (1973). *Science*, **179,** 433.
Whitaker, S. (1969). *Ind. Engng. Chem.*, **61,** 14.
Williams, M. L., Landel, R. F., and Ferry, J. D. (1955). *J. Amer. Chem. Soc.* **77,** 3701.
Willis, H. F., Warwicker, J. O., Urquhart, A. R., and Standing, H. A. (1945). *Trans. Faraday Soc.* **41,** 506.
Zimm, B. H. and Lundberg, J. L. (1956). *J. Phys. Chem.*, **60,** 425.

author index

A

B

C

D

E

F

G

H

J

K

L

M

N

O

P

R

S

T

subject index

A

B

C

D

E

F

G

H

I

J

K

L

M

N

O

P

R

S

T

U

V

W

Z